IMAGES
of America

GLASGOW

On the Cover: Members and friends of First Presbyterian Church of Glasgow gathered for this photograph while attending a church picnic at Highland Park. Now a residential street, Highland Park was once a popular outdoor gathering spot for Glasgow and Barren County residents. (Courtesy First Presbyterian Church and James M. Nelson.)

IMAGES
of America

GLASGOW

William S. Terry IV

ARCADIA
PUBLISHING

ISBN 978-0-7385-6791-4

Published by Arcadia Publishing
Charleston SC, Chicago IL, Portsmouth NH, San Francisco CA

Printed in the United States of America

Library of Congress Control Number: 2009922505

For all general information contact Arcadia Publishing at:
Telephone 843-853-2070
Fax 843-853-0044
E-mail sales@arcadiapublishing.com
For customer service and orders:
Toll-Free 1-888-313-2665

Visit us on the Internet at www.arcadiapublishing.com

This book is dedicated to the memory of J. Mitchell Ellis and Lyle E. Snavely, two gentlemen who shared a love of photography and Glasgow, Kentucky, and whose hobby contributed greatly to this book.

Contents

Acknowledgments

With appreciation to all who helped make this book possible, especially the South General Kentucky Cultural Center, Gayle B. Berry, B. Kay Harbison, June Jackson, James M. Nelson, Jane S. Coleman, Jane Terry Goodman, and the Kentucky Library.

INTRODUCTION

Glasgow has been the center of the community of people living in Barren County for more than 200 years. What was a literal wilderness has evolved into a small town in which residents of both the city and the county have carved out a life. In days of our earliest existence, there was no such thing as "downtown." Glasgow was simply "town." Glasgow's site was chosen because of the proximity of the Big Spring, a plentiful source of the all-necessary water. In 1799, one hundred acres was divided into 109 square lots, several varied lots of fractional sizes and 17 larger lots containing 3–5 acres. In the early years, businesses in town were those important to the sustenance of a growing community: blacksmith shops, tanyards, tin shops, hatters, tailors, shoemakers, silversmiths, tavern-keepers, and the like. In the central part of the town was the courthouse square, home of our local government for the past 210 years, though in six different courthouses.

From settlement through the Civil War years, Glasgow was a small town inhabited by a variety of citizens, overall fairly well-educated, which helped the town progress but at a moderate pace. Following the war years, Glasgow soon had a downtown thanks to several additions to the community, mostly to the south of the courthouse square. A number of immigrant businessmen had settled in Glasgow, making available products, services, skills, and opportunities not previously enjoyed here. While Glasgow grew, the basis of the local economy remained constant: agriculture was the backbone of both county and town. While much can be said of the progressive leaders who sought improvements, agriculture and the marketing of raw products produced thereon provided the financial power for both the people and the community to grow.

The seat of local government, manifested in the courthouse, has remained a constant emblem of the community and its residents and a particularly unifying symbol of Glasgow. Surrounding the courthouse square, businesses and professional offices of all types evolved throughout the years. A series of catastrophic fires in the early 1900s followed by the Great Depression brought Glasgow's downtown to its knees on more than one occasion.

Glasgow has been more than a home to government and business. Glasgow remains the religious center of the county—from the town's oldest congregation still on its original 1802 lot, to congregations that waxed and waned, to others who chose to move outside the downtown to more spacious environs. The Glasgow Normal Institute, Urania College, the Glasgow Training School, and the celebrated Liberty College all called Glasgow home. With Barren County among the top Kentucky agricultural producers in the state, Glasgow played the all-important role of helping the farmer market his product. Cattle and other farm animals as well as crops could easily be transported to distant areas by rail from Glasgow. Tobacco reigned supreme in Glasgow, with millions of pounds being sold and shipped from the town. The Glasgow Railway Company, created in defiance of Bowling Green having lured the L&N Railroad away from the town, provided the necessary means of transporting products, supplies, and people. Such acts gave Glasgow the reputation of being "the biggest little town in Kentucky." Glasgow has been a social center and has hosted both the famous and the infamous throughout the years. Glasgow has entertained us—and our ancestors—be it a bandstand concert, Ferris wheels, horse shows, street fairs, movie theaters, or even the colorful antics of residents and visitors.

In Glasgow, we can celebrate our progress and our heritage. The town's tentacles have long ago stretched beyond the courthouse square and into tree-lined streets and neighborhoods of Barren County and, ultimately, into the very heart of America. Come and join the celebration as we take a few steps back in time and savor the images of Glasgow's past.

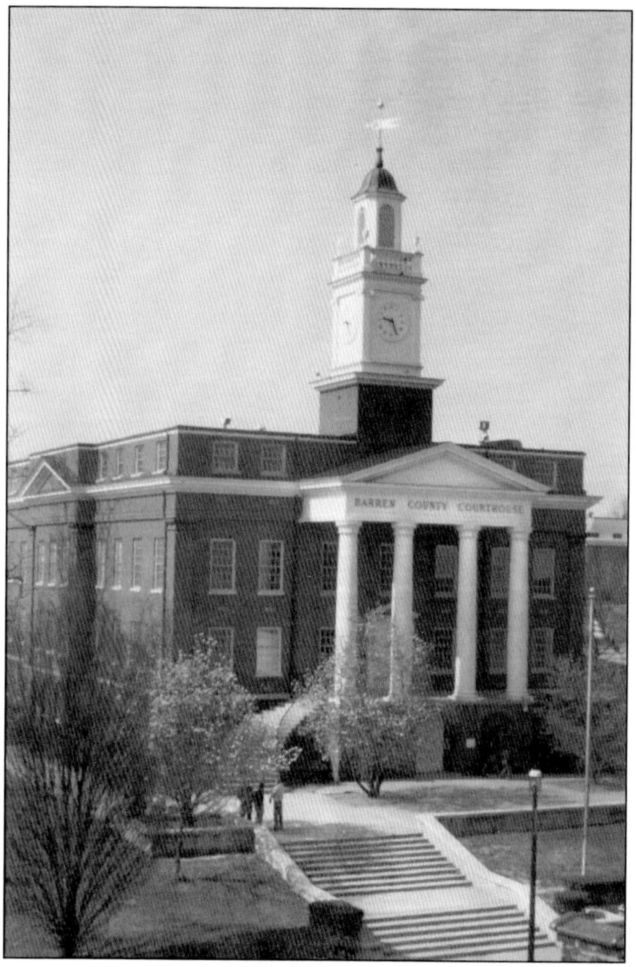

Glasgow, the seat of Barren County, has centered around a courthouse square on land once belonging to Revolutionary War veteran John Gorin. The image at left is the sixth and present courthouse to be erected since the naming of the county seat in 1799. Today the building houses the court system serving Barren County while local government offices are located in a newer building on the north side of the square. (Courtesy South Central Kentucky Cultural Center, Snavely Collection.)

One

FACES AND PLACES IN GLASGOW

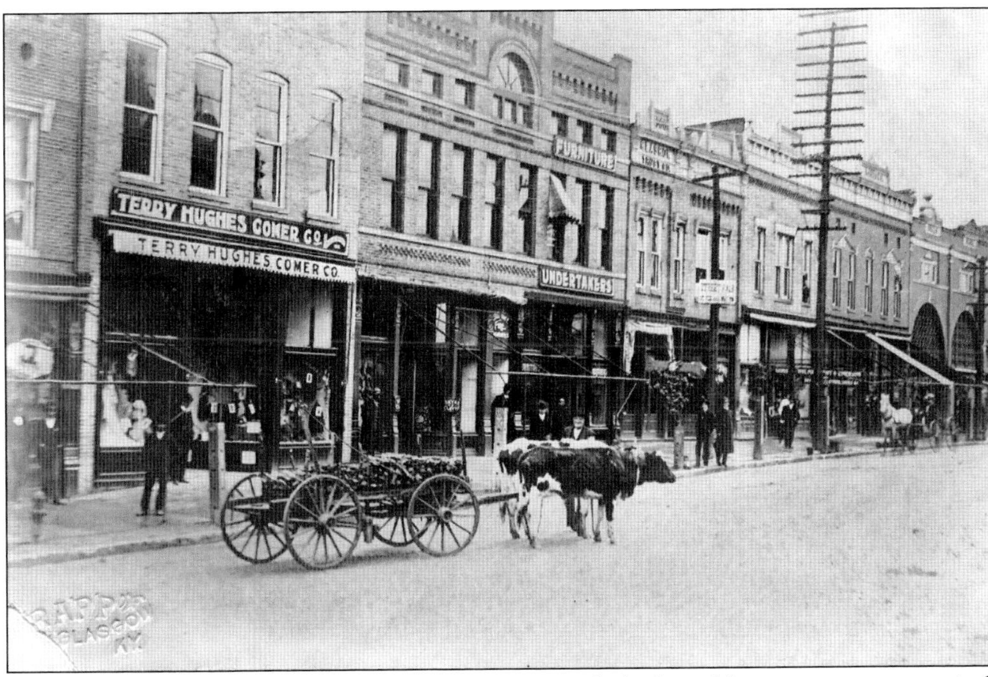

When considering Glasgow, the downtown area, particularly the public square, comes to mind. This early-20th-century image of the East Public Square reminds people that for nearly two centuries the downtown area contained virtually everything a person would need in the course of life. This photograph includes the Terry-Hughes-Comer Dry Goods Company and F. P. Williams Undertaker's establishment, which was housed with his furniture store. The large structure on the right of the image later became National Stores and now houses Glasgow City Hall. (Courtesy author's collection.)

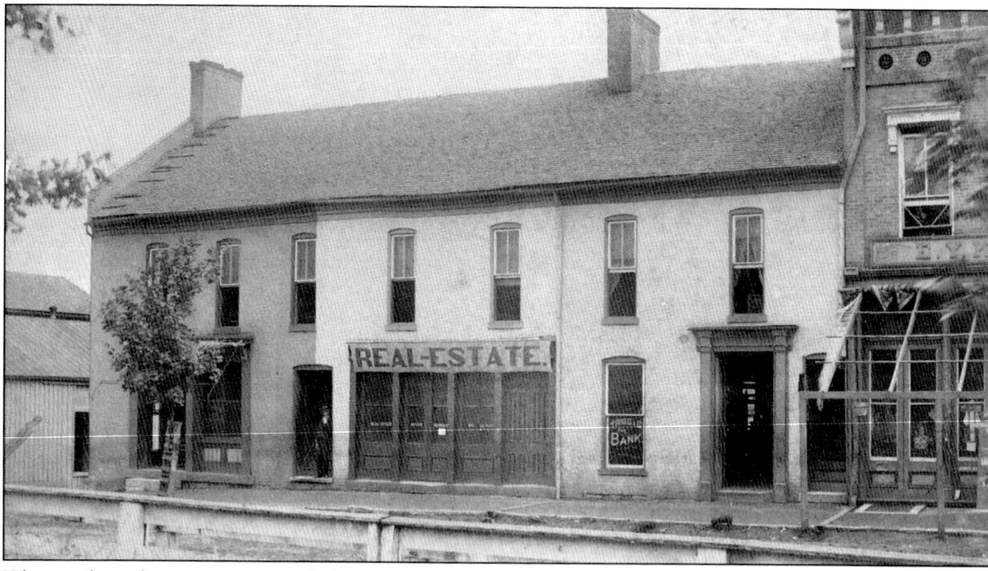

The earliest known image of the North Public Square, this photograph captures the earlier appearance of what is known as the "Lou Ellis corner." The structure on the left received a remodeling to become the First National Bank building (later L. C. Ellis Drugs and later still Lou Ellis Photography Studio); the wall of this building facing North Race Street remains and is one of the original brick walls of the town. The middle building housed the O. H. Pennock Real Estate office, while the third building housed Trigg and Company Bank. (Courtesy South Central Kentucky Cultural Center.)

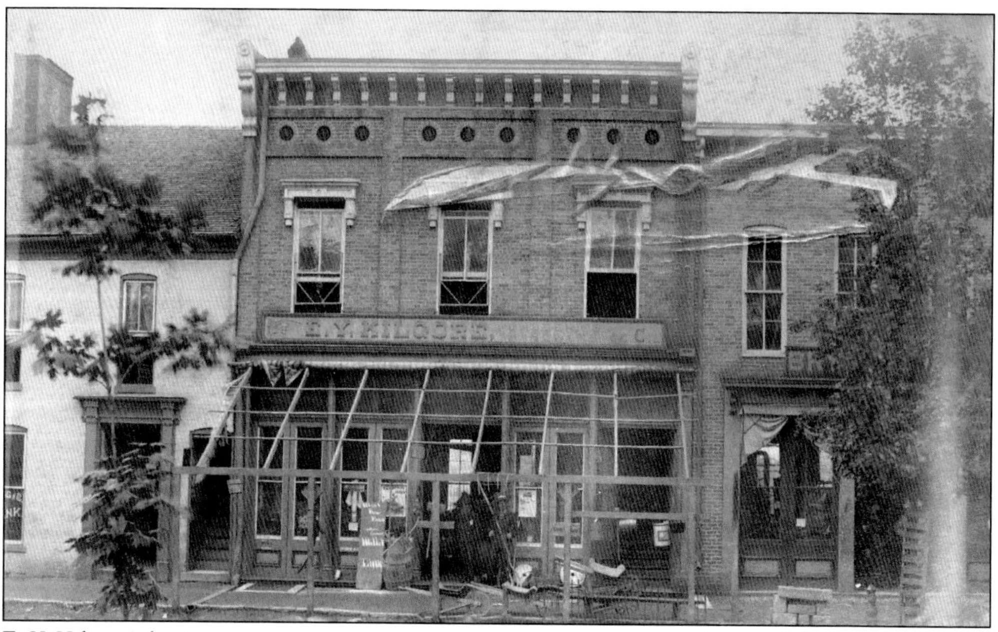

E. Y. Kilgore's business establishment stood just to the right of the Trigg and Company Bank on the North Public Square. This image shows new sidewalks being installed in front of the store. Kilgore sold books, stationery, dry goods, real estate, and much more. The stile block to the right of Kilgore's would aid riders on horseback and in carriages to easily mount and dismount their mode of transportation. (Courtesy South Central Kentucky Cultural Center.)

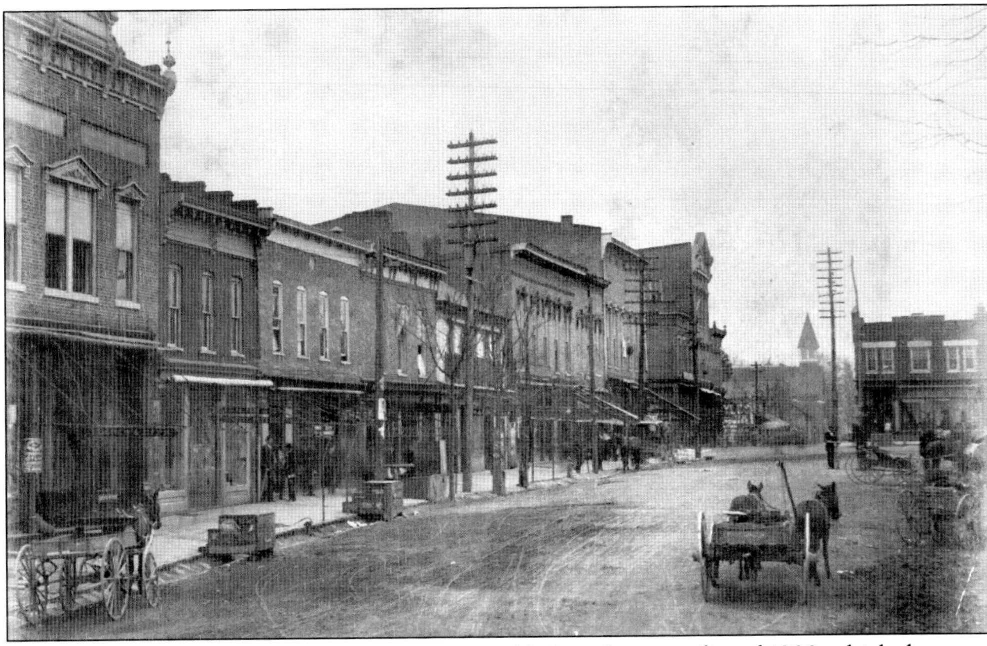

This view of the East Public Square was captured before the great fire of 1900, which destroyed much of this section of downtown. At first glance, the viewer might confuse this for the North Public Square with the structure on the left being similar to the First National Bank building. The building on the far right, the E. Morris building, and the church steeple, the then location of First Christian Church, set the record straight. (Courtesy of the Kentucky Library.)

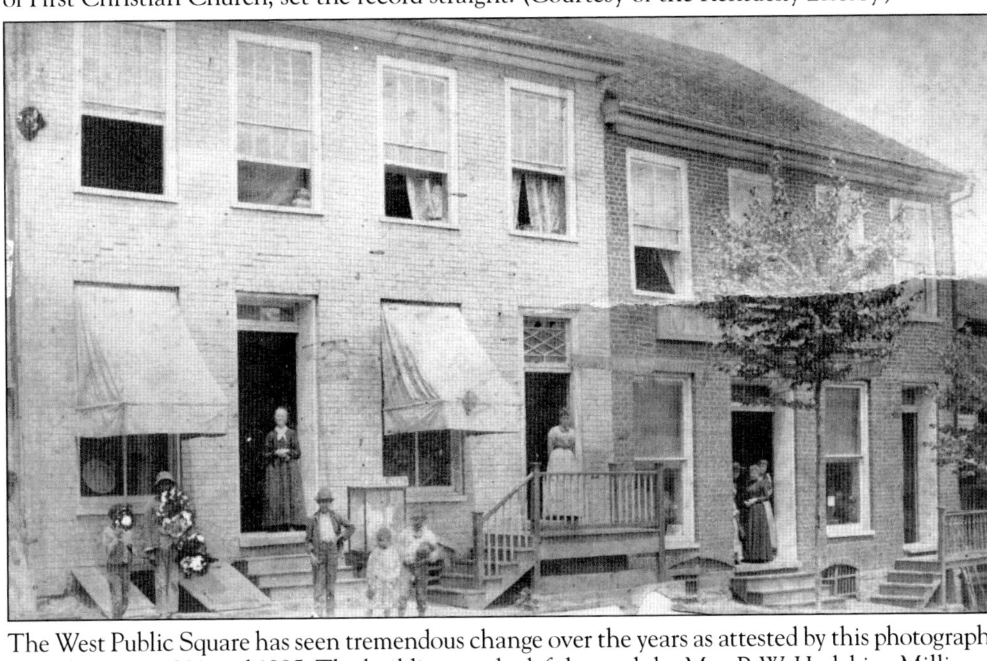

The West Public Square has seen tremendous change over the years as attested by this photograph, made between 1891 and 1895. The building on the left housed the Mrs. P. W. Hodgking Millinery and Fancy Goods shop, and to the right is the A. J. Courtney Boarding House. These structures were located below the Murrell Hotel; in later years, Holmes Restaurant occupied this space. (Courtesy South Central Kentucky Cultural Center.)

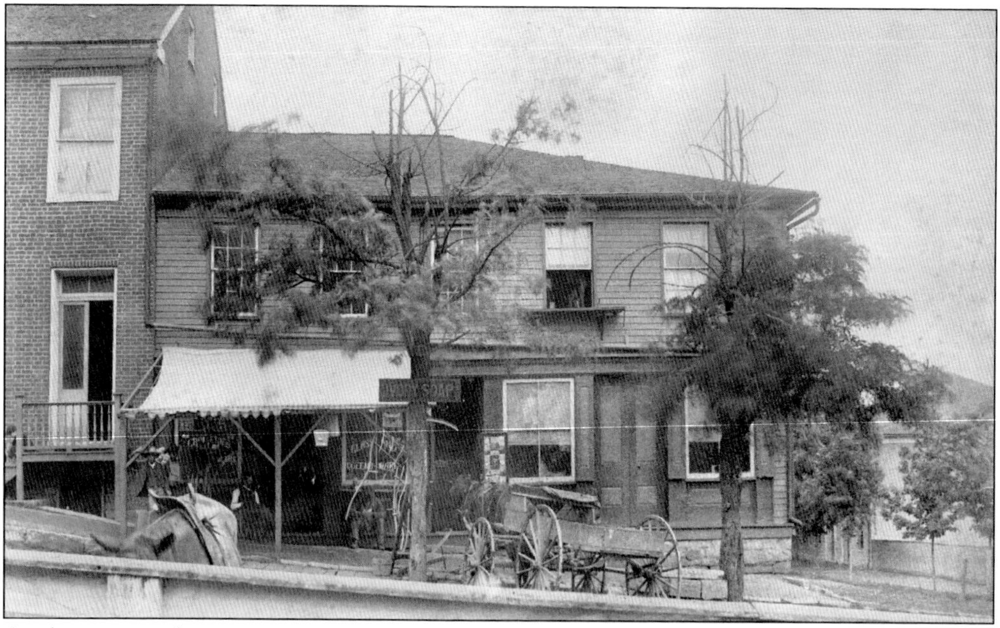

As the sign on the tree prominently announces, Ivory Soap was available for purchase on the West Public Square. Groceries, glassware, and Queen's ware dishes could be had from the business on the left. The building on the corner of South Race Street and West Main Street housed the Misses Depp dressmaker's shop. (Courtesy South Central Kentucky Cultural Center.)

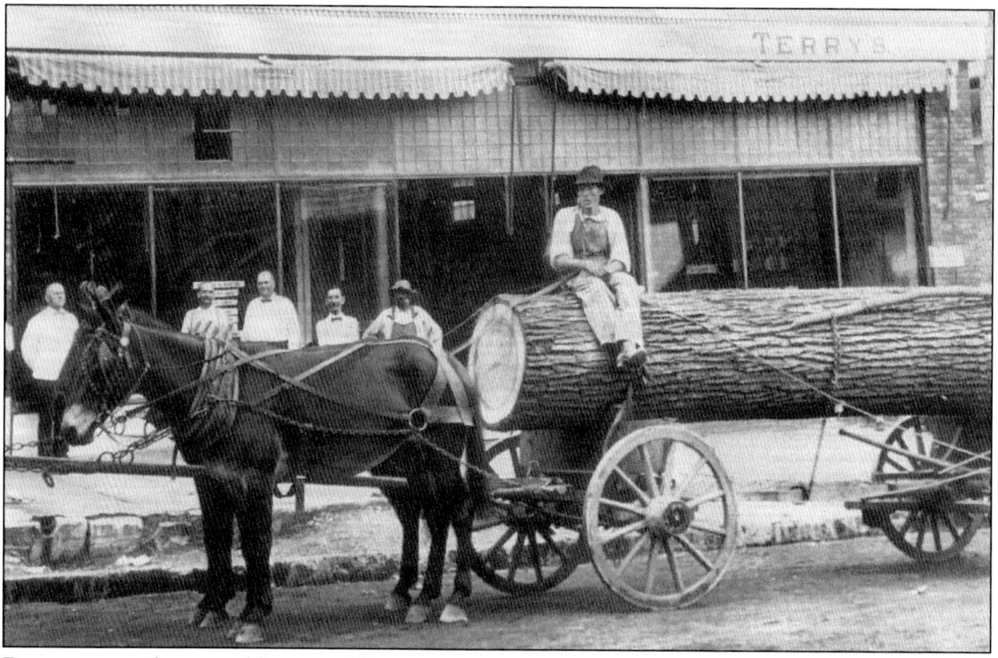

Despite some of its town-like ways, Glasgow's downtown was the scene of much farm and commercial activity, as evidenced by this image showing timber traveling through the business district. This photograph was taken on the North Public Square in front of Terry's Dry Goods (later Bernard's Department Store, present site of Cave Country Communications). (Courtesy South Central Kentucky Cultural Center.)

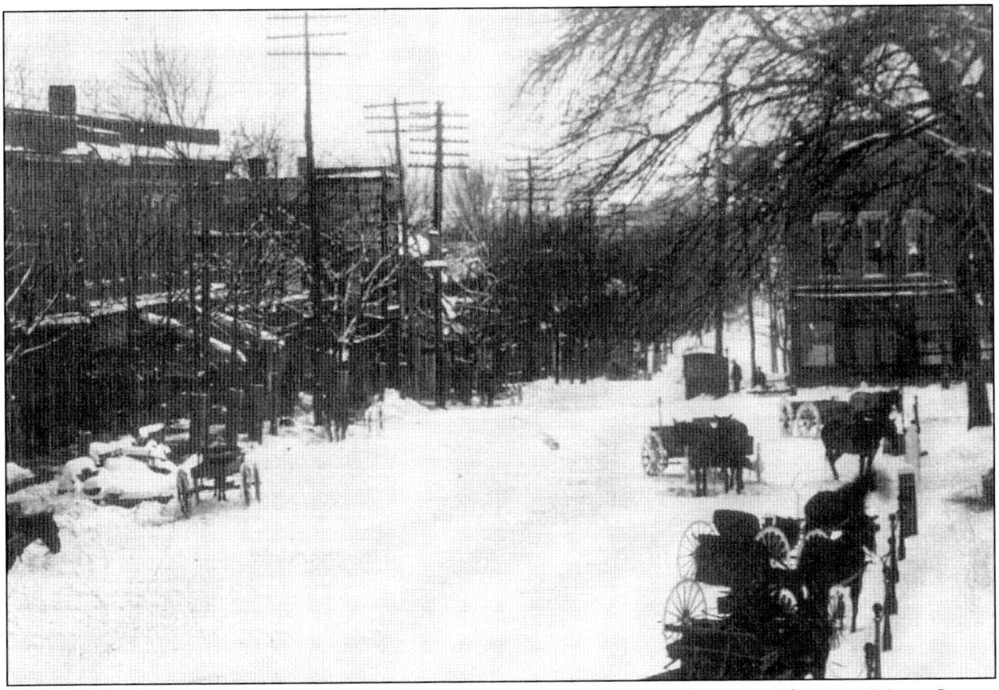

Adolph Rapp captured these chilly snow scenes in downtown Glasgow. Above is Main Street looking east with the North Public Square on the viewer's left. Below is a view of North Race Street looking north. The horse-drawn wagon is in front of Dickinson Brothers Garage, while the bridge in the center of the photograph is above the stone tunnels on Water Street. (Both, courtesy author's collection.)

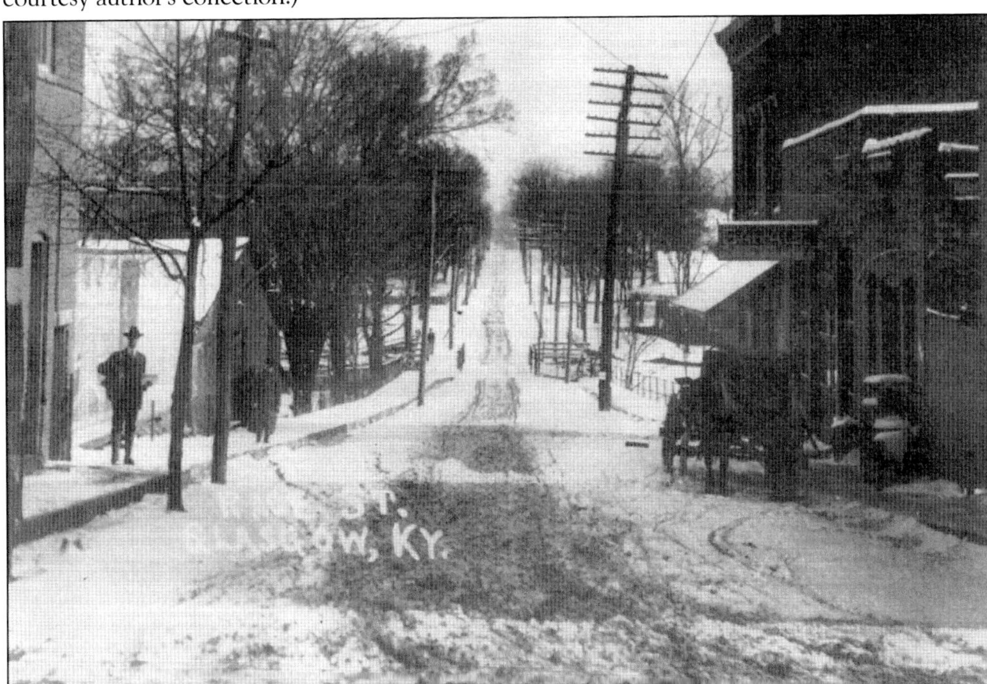

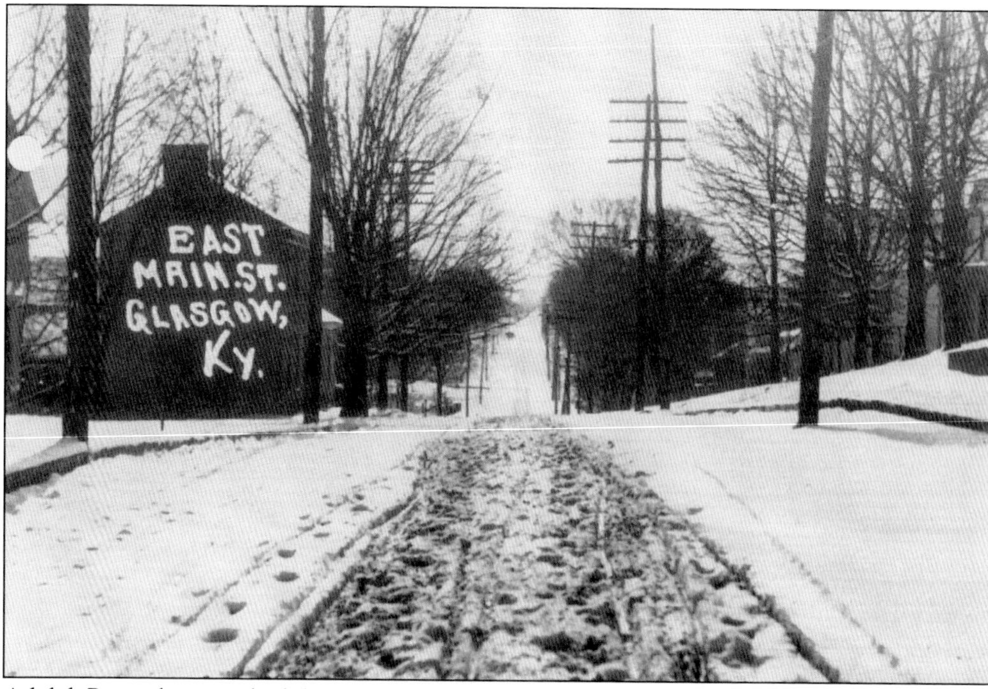

Adolph Rapp photographed this view of a snow-covered East Main Street while standing in front of the Dickinson-Greer house, two blocks from the town square. East Main Street was one of the most traveled routes into Glasgow from locations to the east. (Courtesy author's collection.)

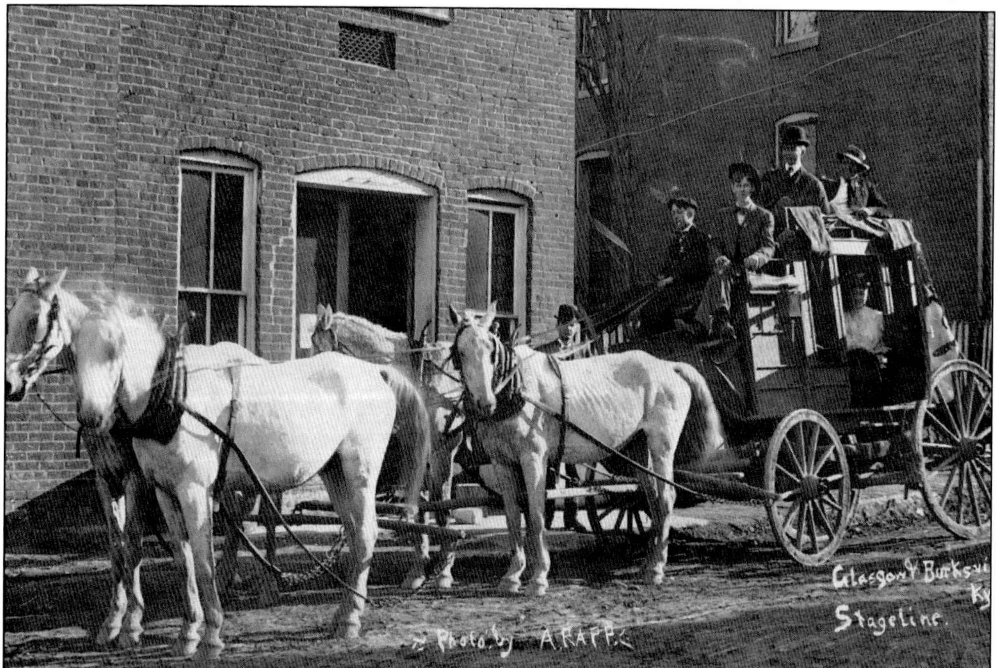

The Glasgow-Burkesville Stage Line in front of Adams Express Company is seen in this image. The stage line used the sometimes treacherous East Main Street–Burkesville Road corridor to make the routine trek between the two towns. (Courtesy South Central Kentucky Cultural Center.)

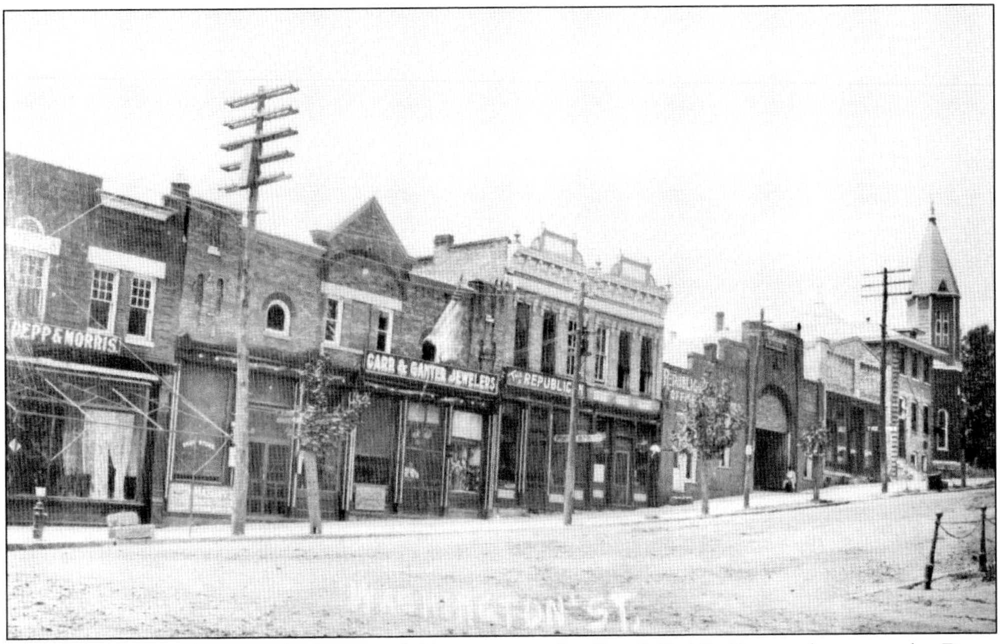

One of the least photographed areas of Glasgow was the South Public Square between the Depp and Morris store and First Christian Church. This image captures Carr and Ganter Jewelers, the *Republican* newspaper offices, the livery stable and feed store, and other business concerns. (Courtesy author's collection.)

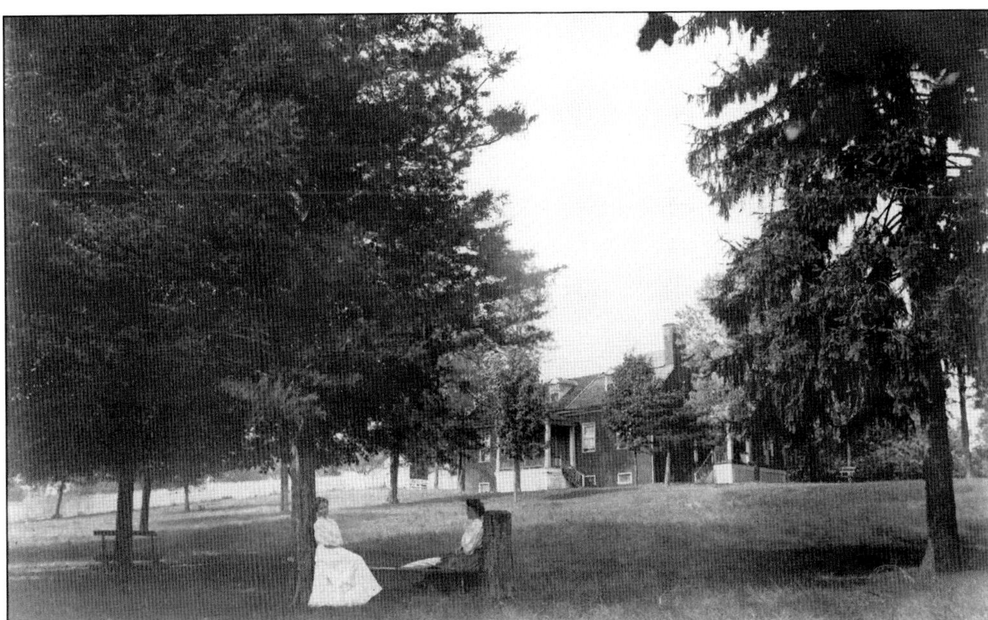

This turn-of-the-20th-century view of the historic Spotswood house recalls a time of slower-paced, quaint lifestyles. This rare image shows the house before various 20th-century alterations were made. (Courtesy author's collection.)

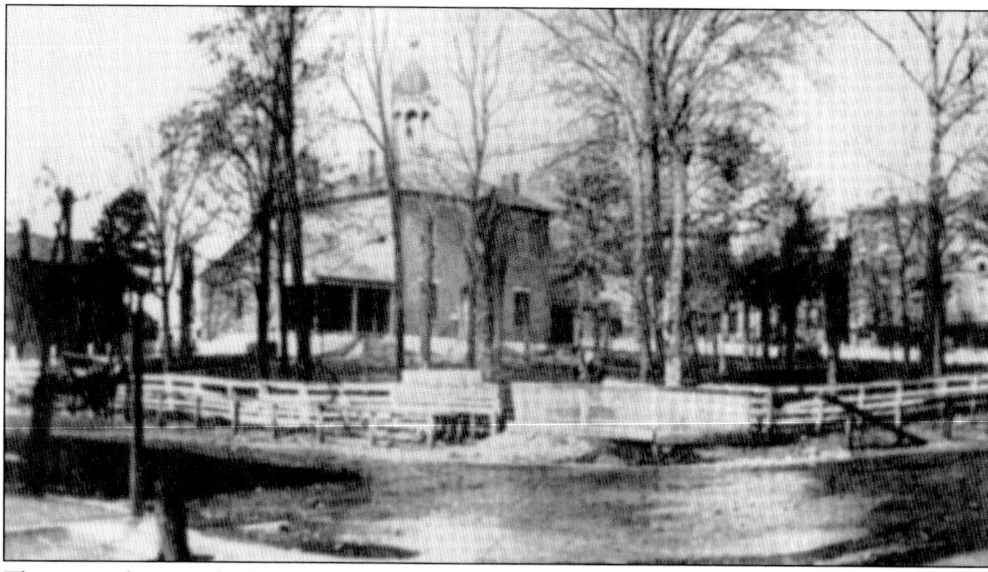

These rare photographs show Barren County's fourth courthouse. Like those before it, the structure was situated on one corner of the town square, rather than in the middle. The entire courtyard was enclosed with a board fence. The simple building was surmounted with a handsome cupola containing the courthouse bell. (Both, courtesy South Central Kentucky Cultural Center.)

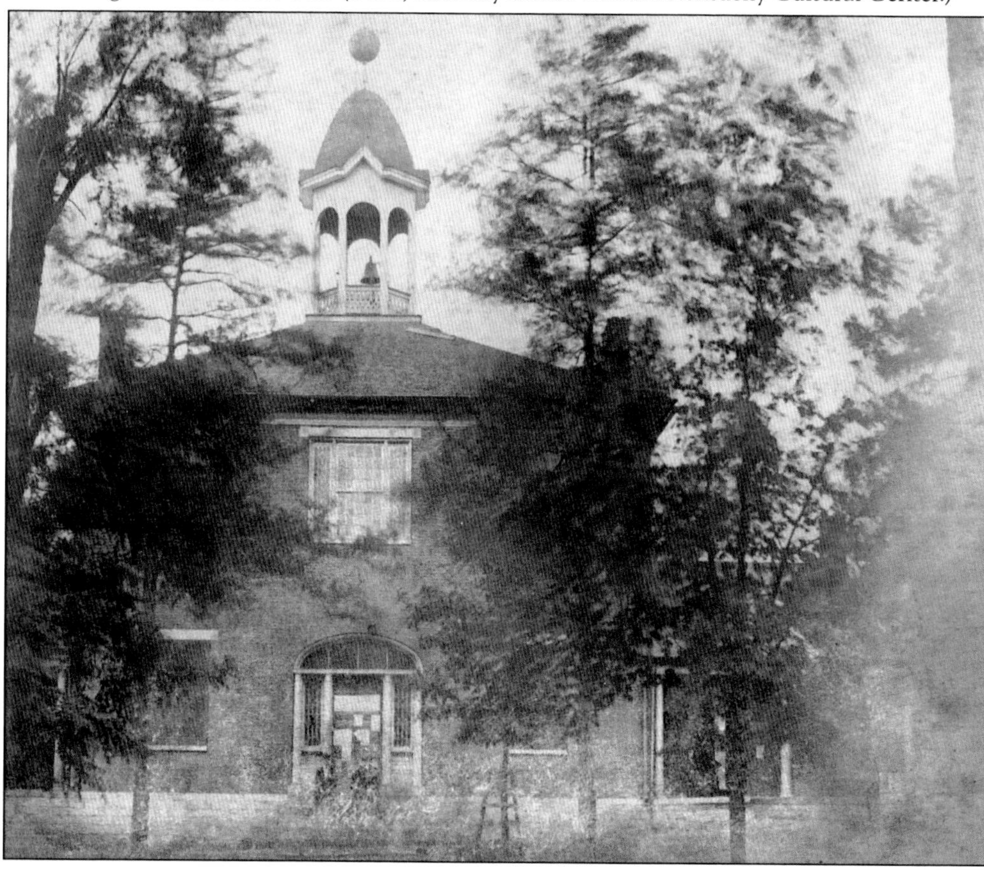

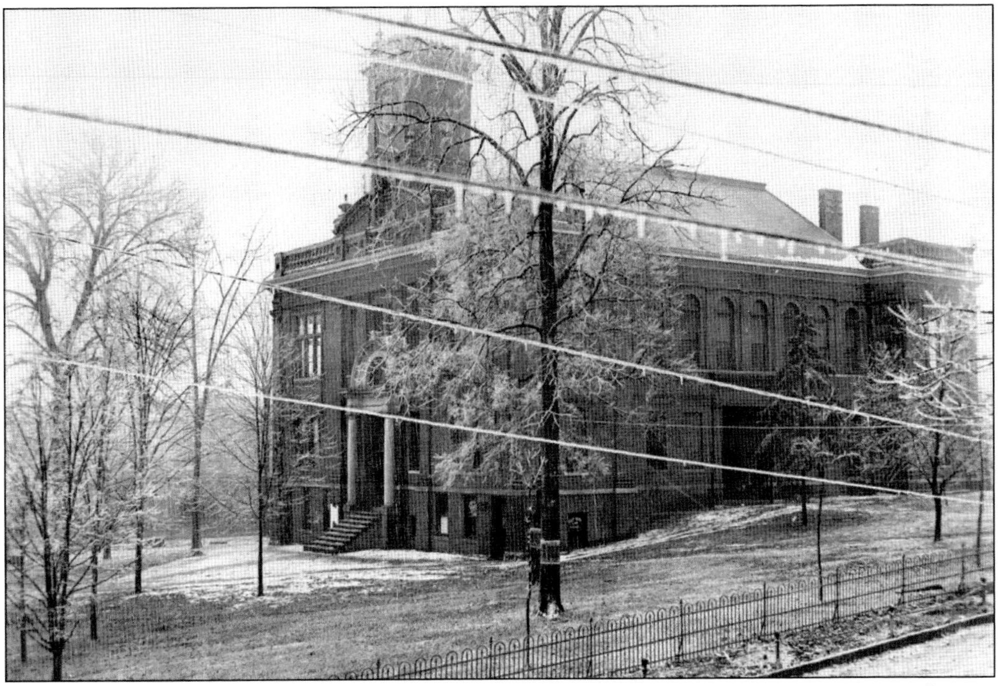

The fifth Barren County Courthouse was an impressive and imposing structure as seen in these c. 1900 photographs. The courthouse and its surrounding environs have traditionally been meeting and gathering places for individuals and groups in addition to persons visiting the structure on official business. The below image shows additional adornments such as the fanciful bandstand, a water tank, and the ubiquitous "courthouse crowd" posed at the street. The white-haired gentleman with hat cocked to one side in the center of the group is John A. "Old Reb" Murray, a popular county court clerk. (Both, courtesy South Central Kentucky Cultural Center.)

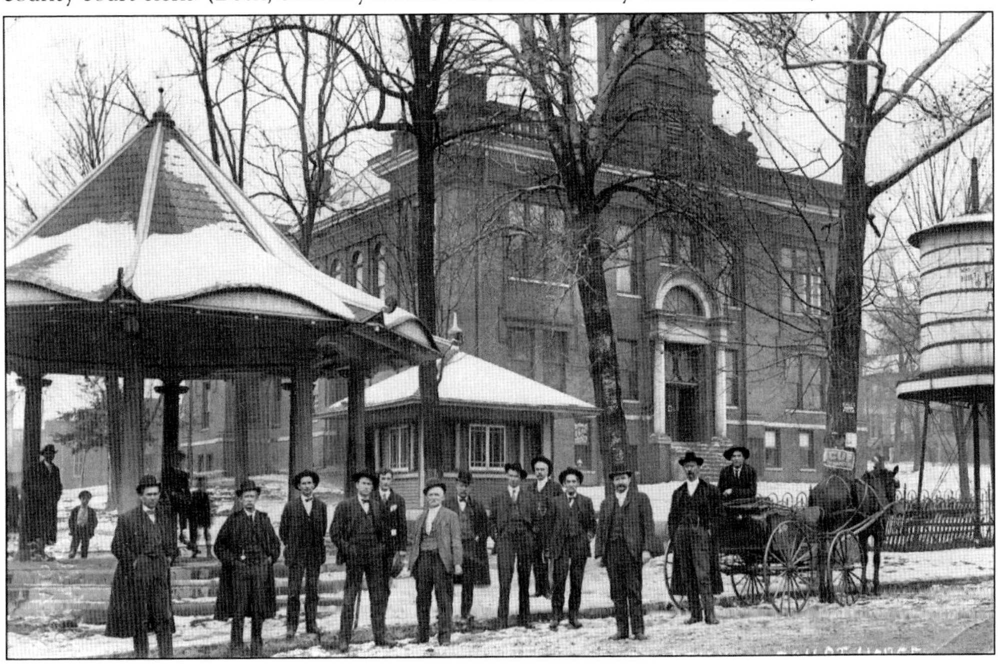

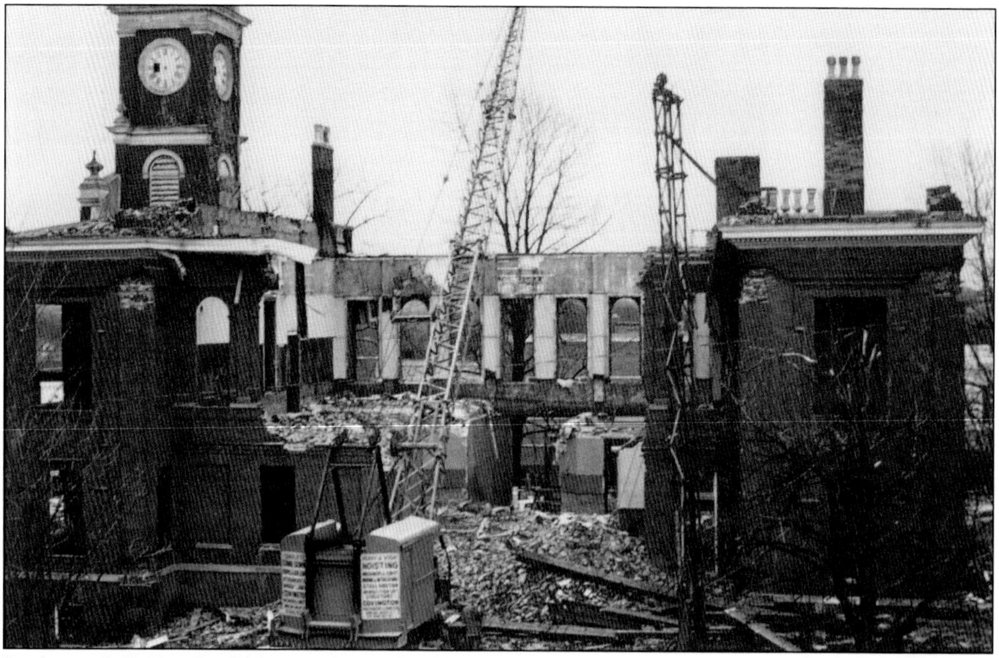

In the mid-1960s, the fifth courthouse had become outdated and crowded and was replaced with the present Georgian-style structure. The old building's clock had been procured by a local fund-raising effort in the form of a play, *The Old Singin' Skule*, performed by townspeople. The effort raised the $1,500 cost of the clock. (Courtesy South Central Kentucky Cultural Center.)

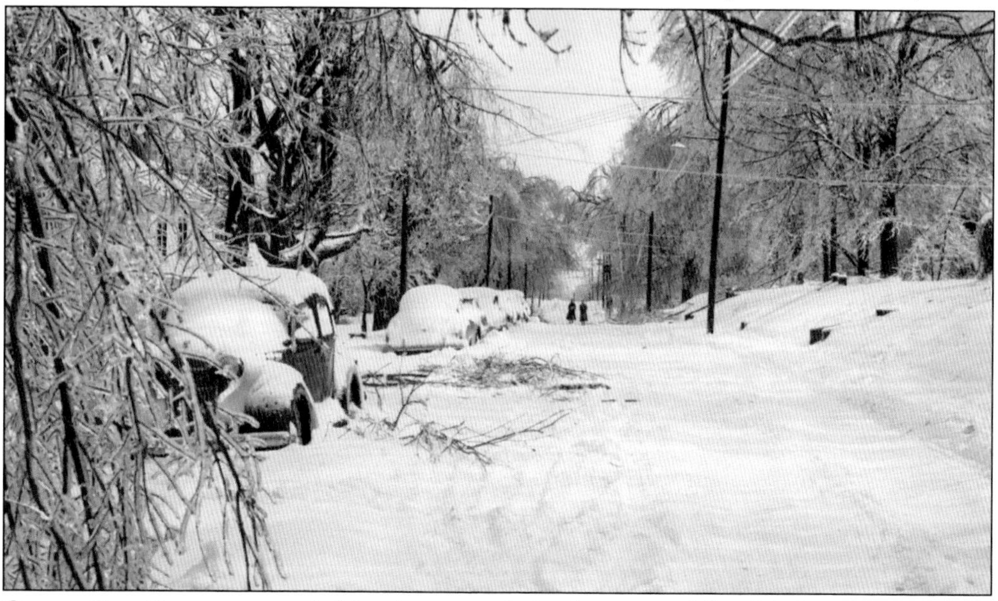

George Carr Ganter captured this winter wonderland scene on West Washington Street on February 1, 1951. Ganter's sister-in-law, Kate Dickinson Ganter, noted that this was known as "the Great Sleet" storm that arrived on January 23, the day her husband, Dr. Fred Ganter, and others in his battalion left for Fort Bragg, North Carolina. The storm cut off all utilities and all forms of communication for more than two weeks. (Courtesy South Central Kentucky Cultural Center.)

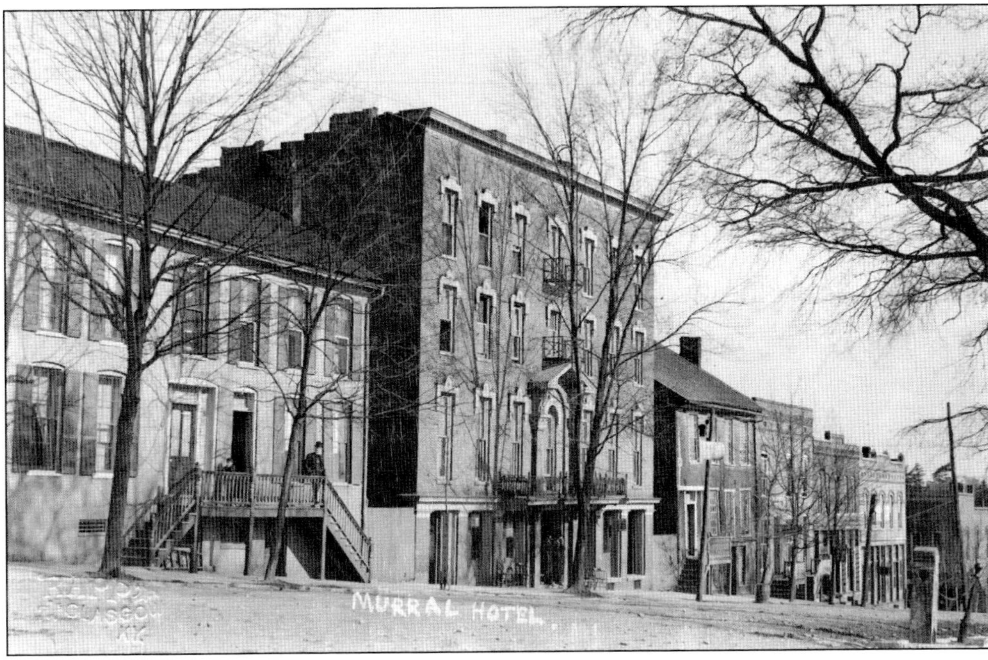

At the time of the above photograph, the large building in the center of the image was known as the Murrell Hotel (note incorrect spelling on the image). The same structure was also known as the Hotel Spotswood for many years. The hostelry was a center for travelers but also much of the social life of Glasgow as it hosted balls, tea dances, banquets, and programs of all types. (Both, courtesy author's collection.)

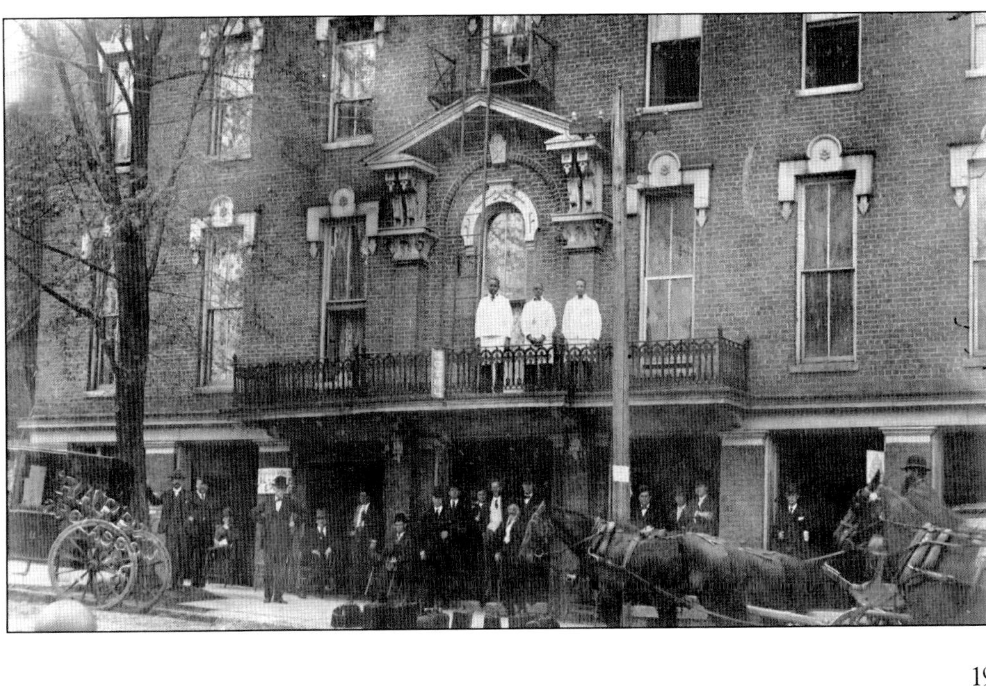

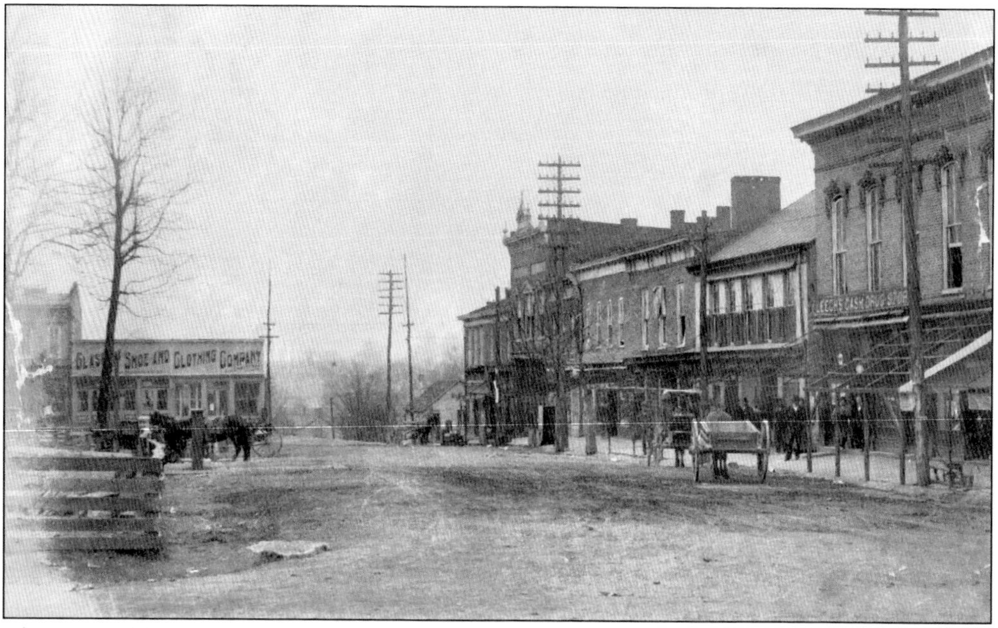

The East Public Square appears here around 1895. The building on the right advertises Leech's Cash Drug Store (operated between 1893 and 1896). Dr. Joseph S. Leech served Glasgow as a leading physician, businessman, and mayor during his lifetime. Over the years, Leech paired with others in a variety of drugstores, the longest running being Leech and Davis Drugs. (Courtesy the Kentucky Library.)

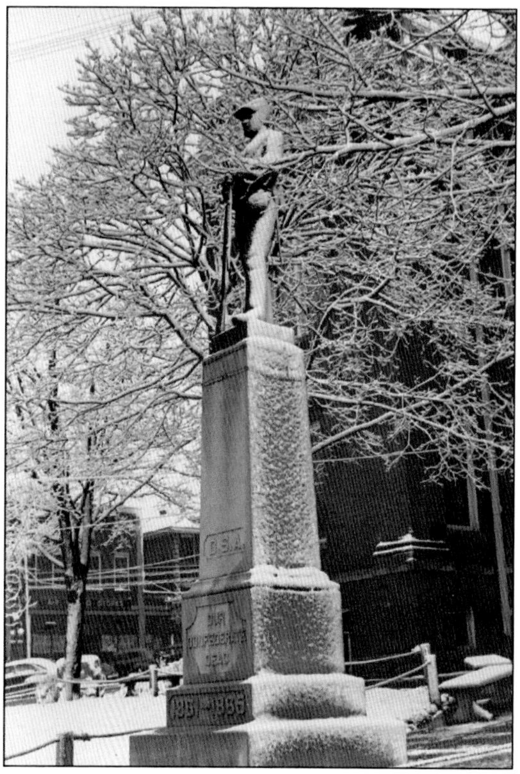

J. Mitchell Ellis snapped this image of the Confederate Monument with a perfect backdrop of snow-laden tree branches in the winter of 1960. The monument was a project initiated by longtime county court clerk John A. "Old Reb" Murray. Murray raised the money for the bronze statue with heart-tugging pleas such as, "You know, that could be your Pappy there." The model for the statue was John Garnett, brother of Murray's wife, Eugenia Garnett Murray. (Courtesy author's collection.)

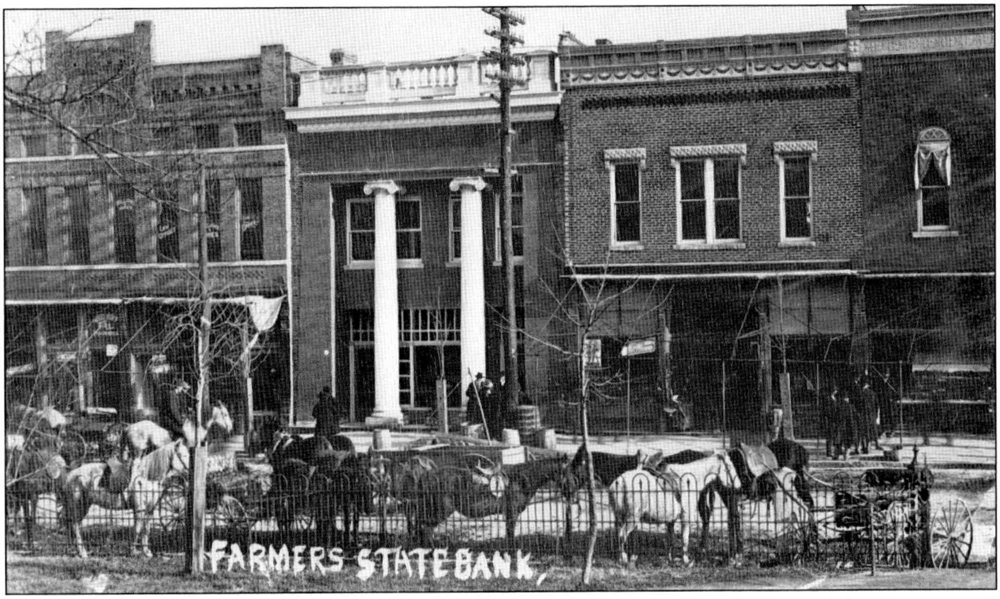

Farmers State Bank long occupied a prominent position in Glasgow's physical landscape and business interests. This early-1900s image shows the bank's East Public Square edifice with twin stone columns. Years later, a more modern facade was created and the columns were removed. Today the columns stand silent sentinel at the veteran's memorial inside Glasgow Municipal Cemetery. The building is the present home of the Glasgow–Barren County Chamber of Commerce. (Courtesy author's collection.)

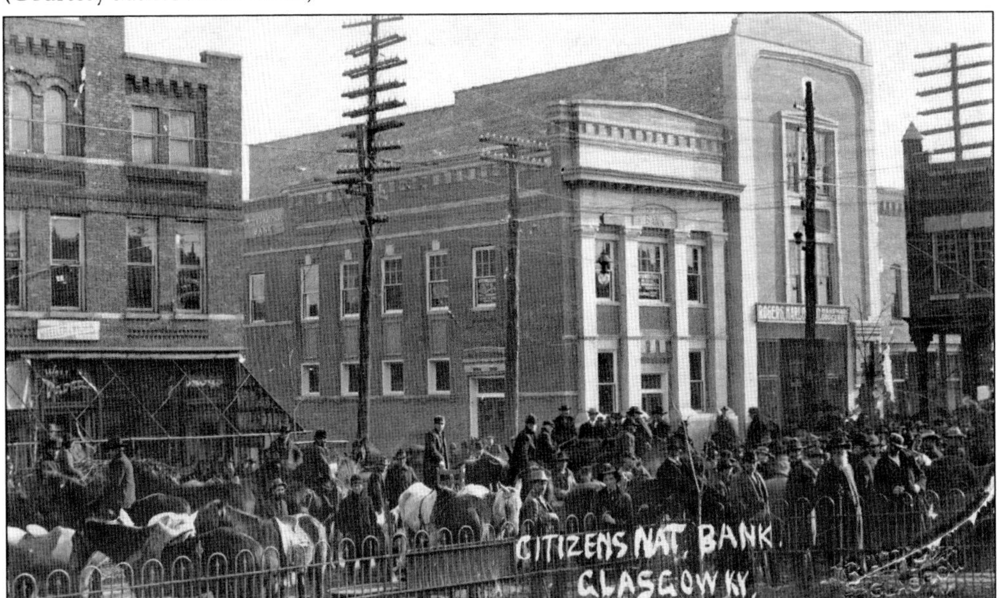

Citizens National Bank has occupied the corner of South Green and East Washington Streets for many decades. Lallah M. Rapp's image of the bank and the Masonic Building, along with Rogers and Harlow Company, shows the corner in the early 20th century. Lallah M. Rapp, wife of Adolph Rapp, was instrumental in capturing many cherished photographs of Glasgow. (Courtesy South Central Kentucky Cultural Center.)

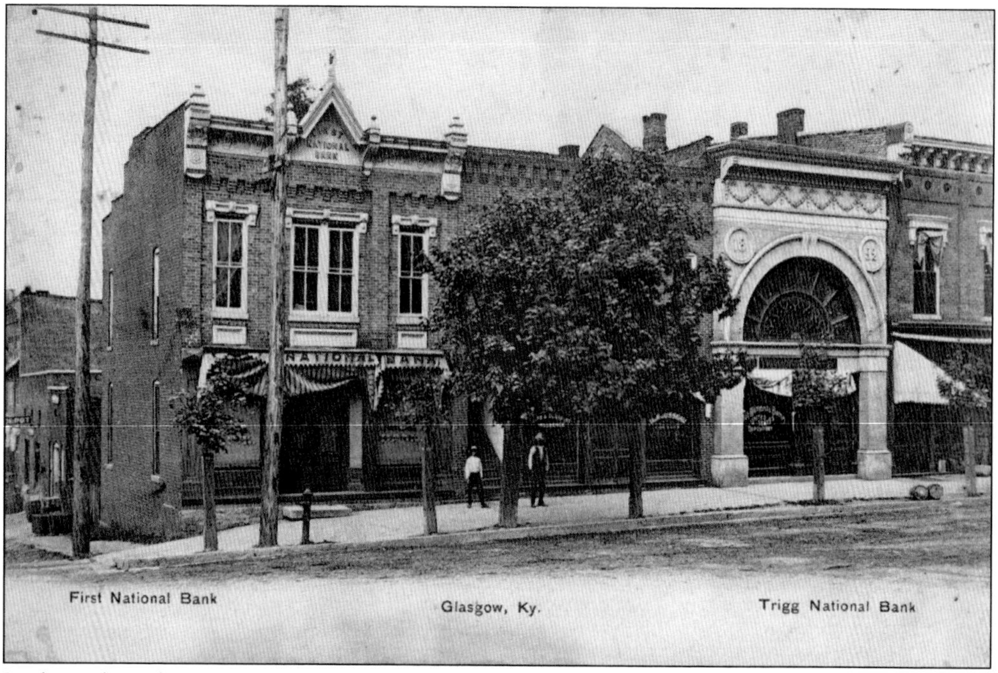

In the early 20th century, First National Bank and the Trigg National Bank were two of the main banking institutions operating in Glasgow. Both were located on the North Public Square and both succumbed during the Great Depression. (Courtesy author's collection.)

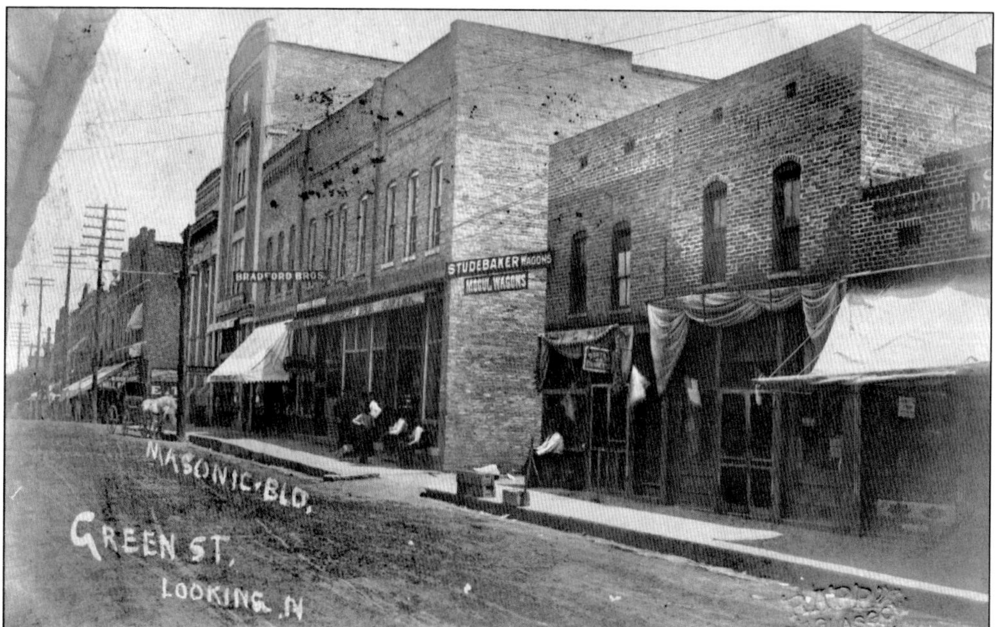

The Allen Lodge No. 24, Free and Accepted Masons erected the imposing structure on South Green Street. The upper portion of the building was occupied by the lodge while Rogers, Harlow, and Company occupied the street level. To the right of the lodge was Bradford Brothers Hardware, and finally Studebaker Wagons and Mogul Wagons were being sold next door. (Courtesy South Central Kentucky Cultural Center.)

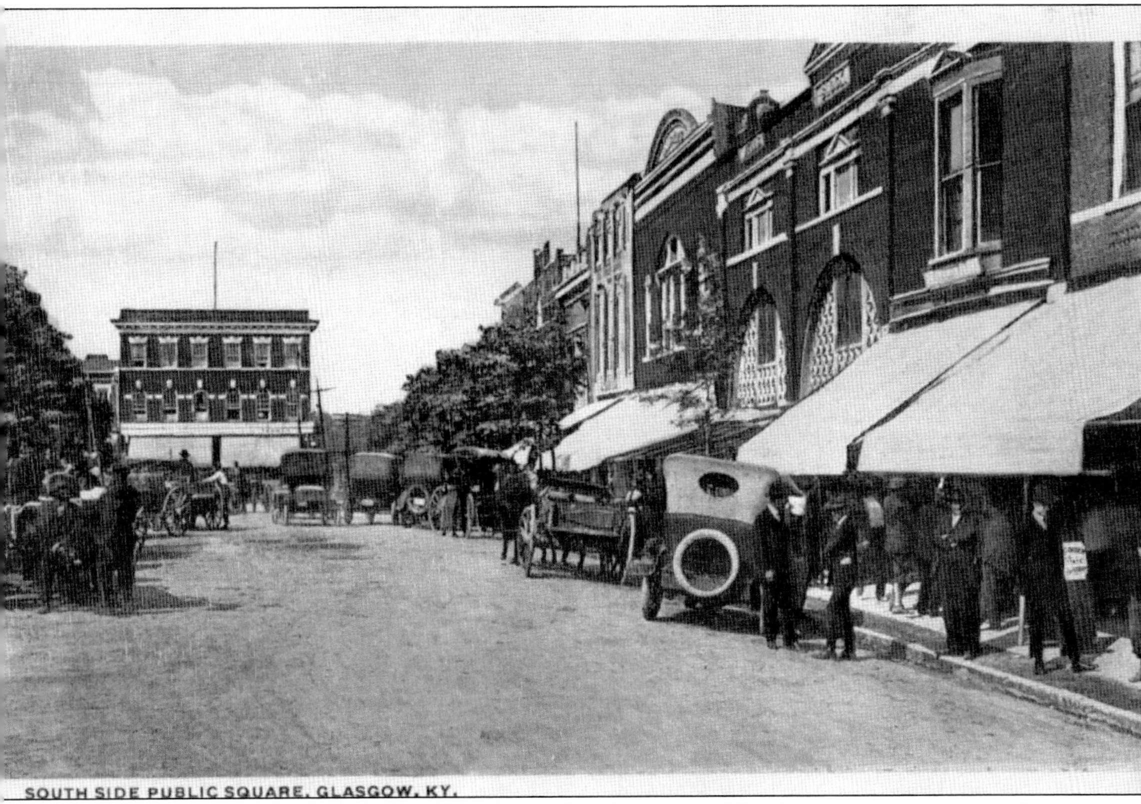

The East Public Square, looking north, is captured in this image. The three-story structure in the distance was occupied for many years by Bernard's Department Store. At the time this photograph was made, Ellis and Ellison Drugs was operating in the building at far right. The structure with the rounded pediment was Henry Raubold's confectioner's shop. (Courtesy author's collection.)

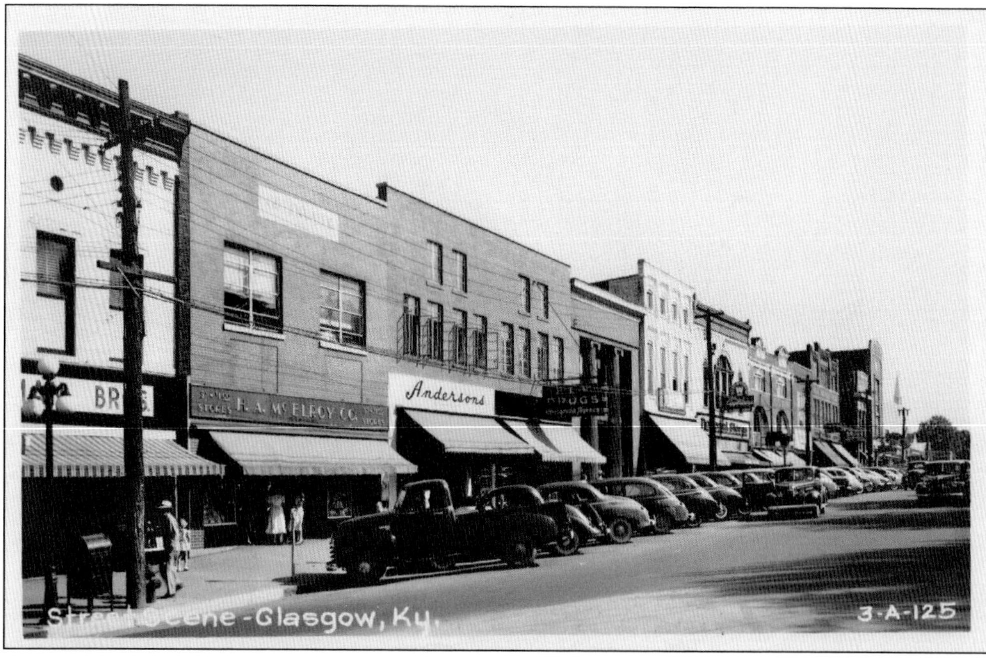

The East Public Square in the 1940s and 1950s saw much of its Victorian-inspired architecture remodeled to a more streamlined appearance. Beginning at left were Lerman Brothers, H. A. McElroy Company, Anderson's Dress Shop, Clayton-Pedigo, New Farmer's National Bank, and National Stores Department Store. (Courtesy South Central Kentucky Cultural Center.)

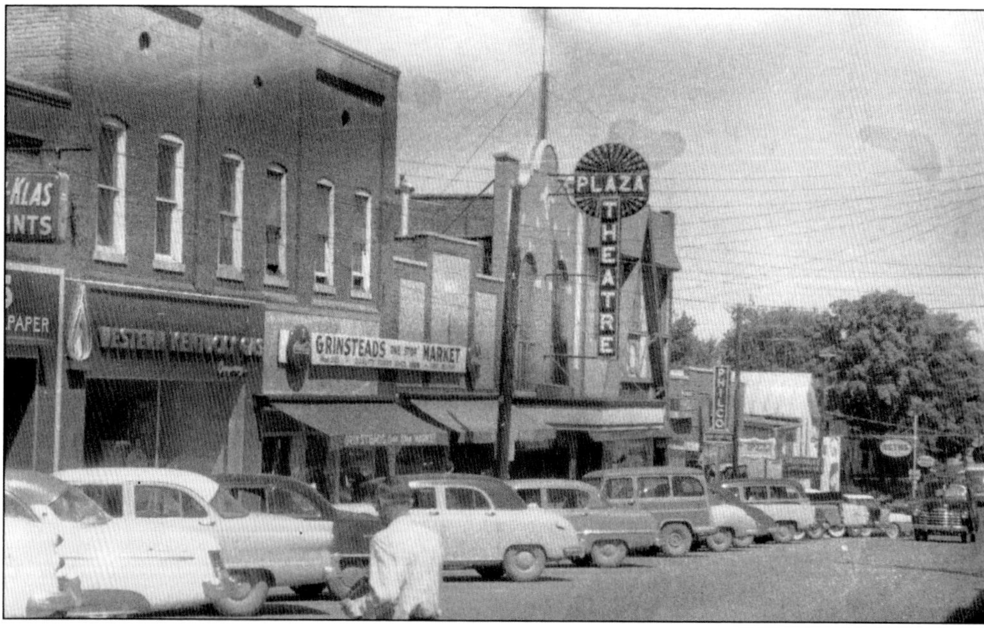

This scene on East Main Street, just off the square, shows Phillips' Paint and Wallpaper Studio, Western Kentucky Gas, Grinstead's One-Stop Market, the famed Plaza Theatre, Lessenberry and Jones, and other businesses in this block. The Plaza Theatre opened in the 1930s with amenities such as air-conditioning and twinkling stars in the ceiling. (Courtesy South Central Kentucky Cultural Center.)

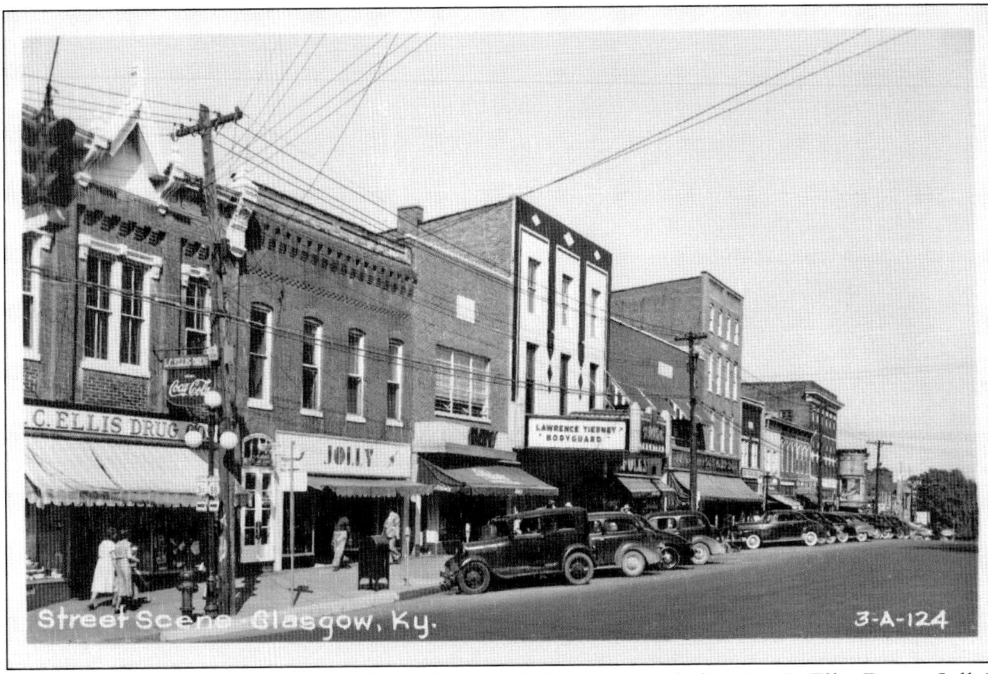

The North Public Square was anchored by establishments, including L. C. Ellis Drugs, Jolly's Men's Store, and the Trigg Theatre. (Courtesy South Central Kentucky Cultural Center.)

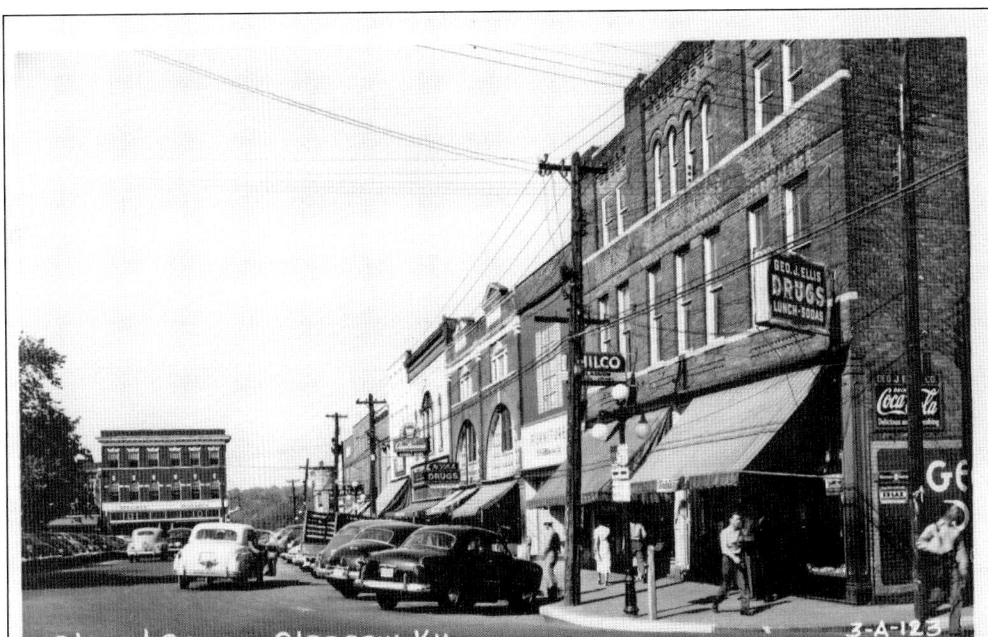

This image captures a view of the East Public Square looking north. The block was anchored by George J. Ellis Drugs on the right, as seen in this 1950s scene. (Courtesy South Central Kentucky Cultural Center.)

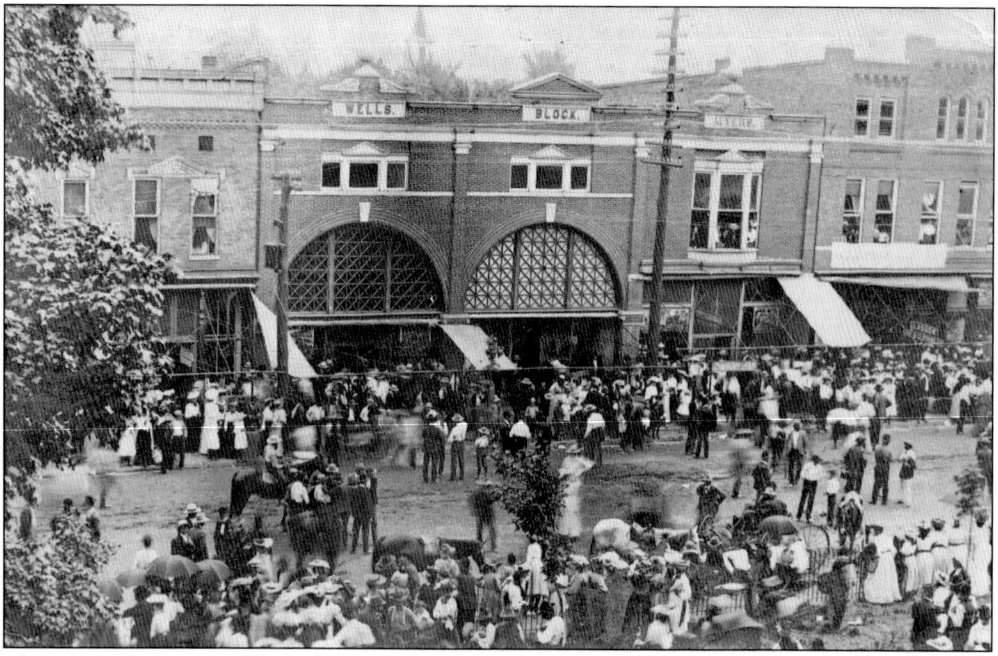

The East Public Square shows a trio of pediments atop early-20th-century buildings. While the Wells and Block structures appear alike, their pediments are unique and the Myers building to the right boasts a bay window and a pediment matching the Wells building. This scene is from the 1910s. (Courtesy author's collection.)

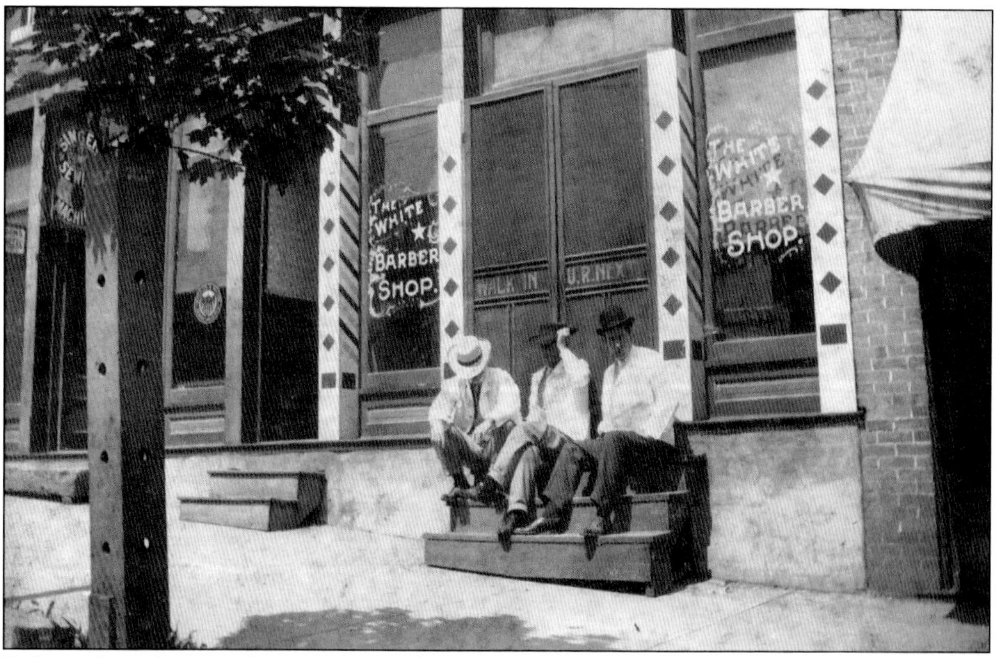

Perhaps these three gentlemen were watching the girls go by while passing time at the White Star Barber Shop. Long before the idea of text-messaging abbreviations, the owner welcomes patrons with screen doors announcing, "WALK IN U R NEXT." (Courtesy South Central Kentucky Cultural Center.)

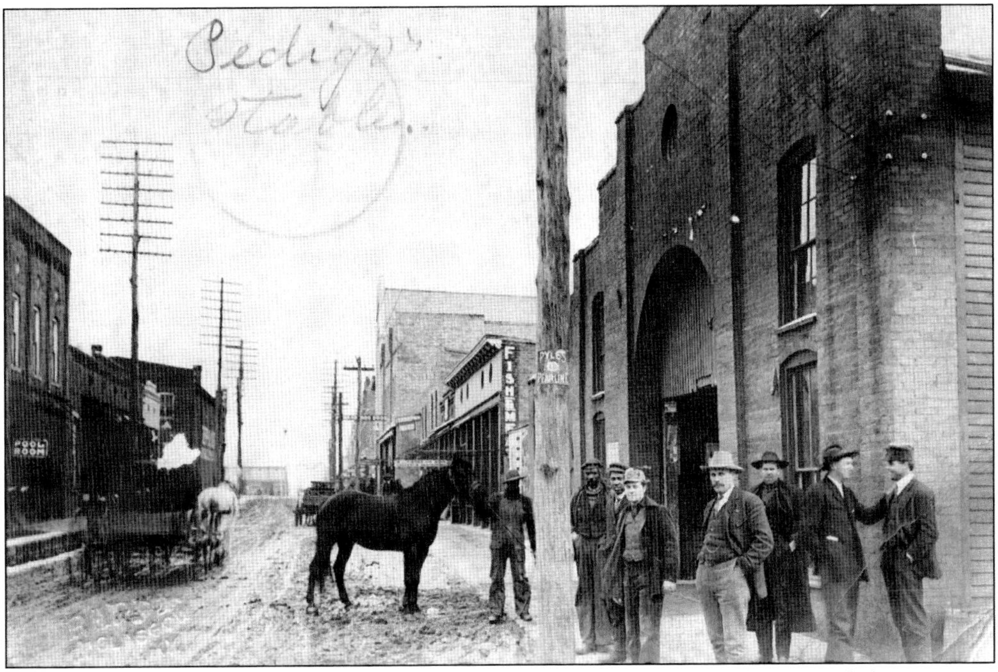

Pedigo Stables on South Green Street below Bradford Brothers Hardware and the Masonic Lodge provided livery services to Glasgow. The business evolved over time from horse-powered conveyances to motorized automobiles. (Courtesy South Central Kentucky Cultural Center.)

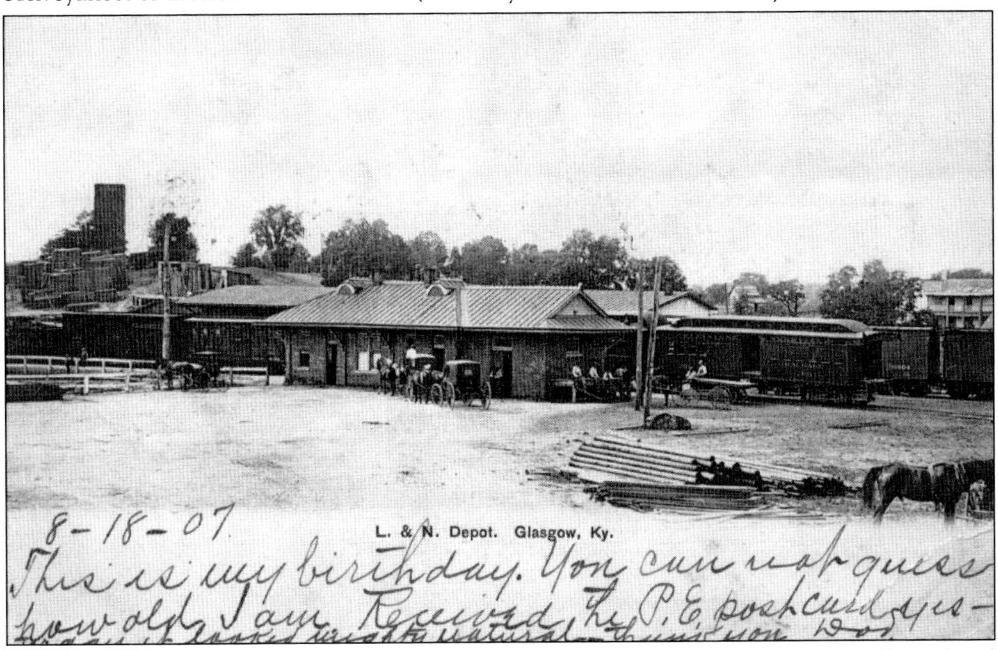

The effort to have railroad service in Glasgow dates to 1856. The Louisville and Nashville Railroad chose a route bypassing Glasgow in favor of Bowling Green, leaving the former without rail service. Though delayed by various issues, the spur from Glasgow Junction (now Park City) to Glasgow came into active service in 1870. This 10-mile run of track gave Glasgow full access to rail service for both goods and passengers. (Courtesy South Central Kentucky Cultural Center.)

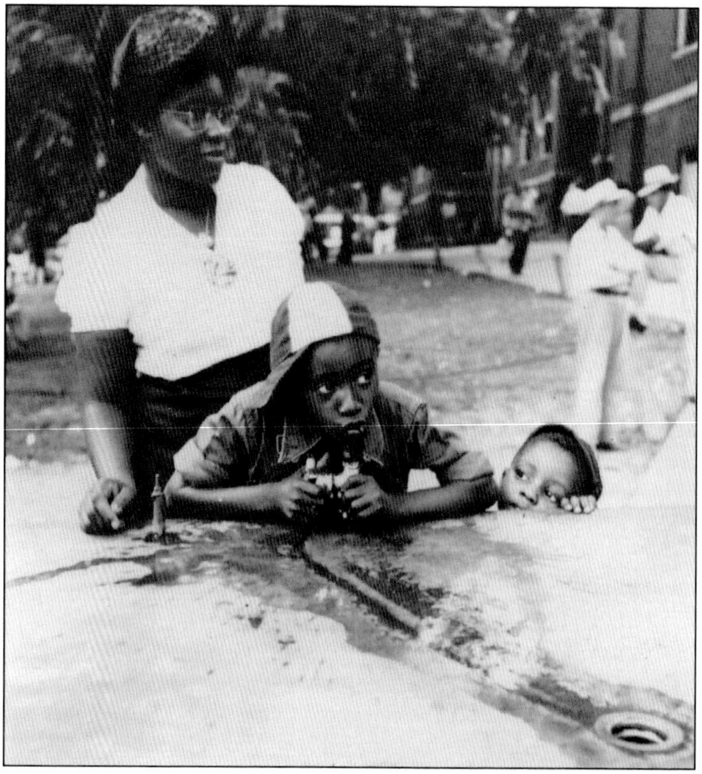

The availability of cool, clean water has been paramount in Glasgow's history. The town location was selected in part because of the nearby Big Spring, which provided water for man and beast. (Courtesy author's collection.)

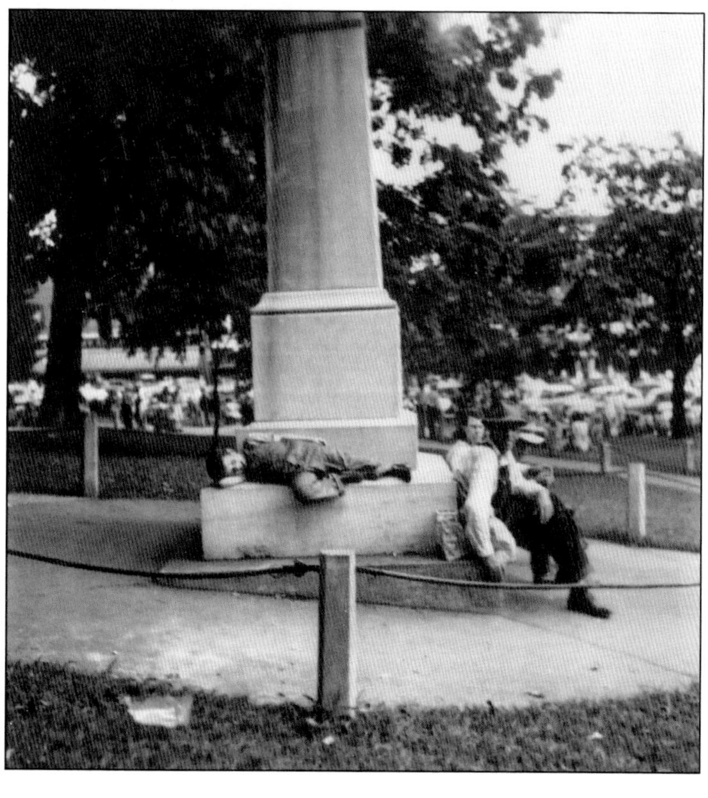

Glasgow's Courthouse Square has been an accepted gathering spot, even for those seeking a little rest. The cool stone and shade overhead has made the monument a popular resting place for generations. J. Mitchell Ellis captured this scene of the base of the Old Reb Monument in the 1930s. (Courtesy author's collection.)

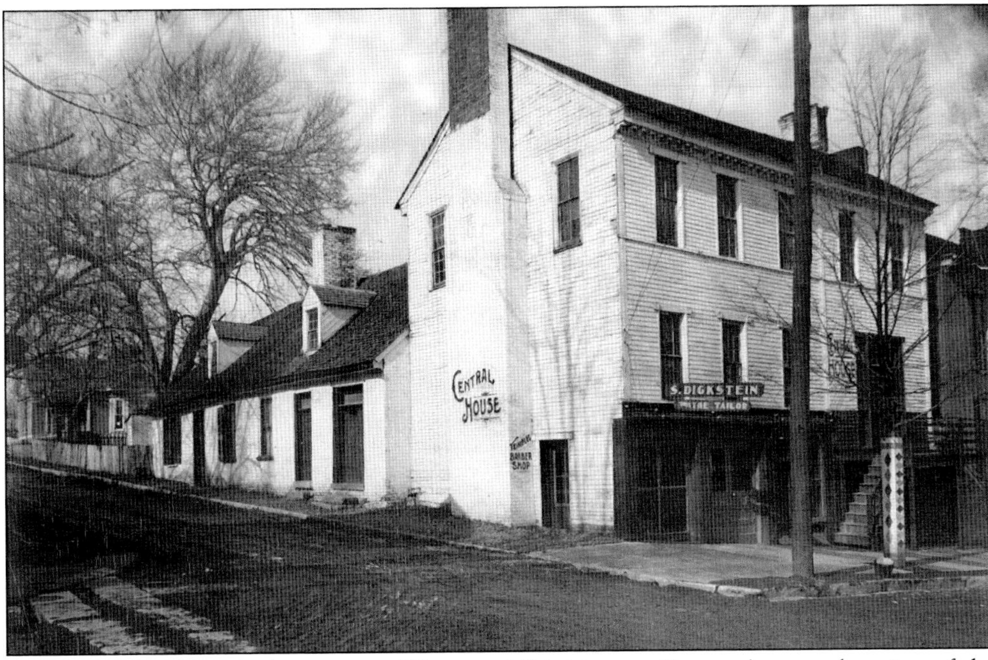

The Central House on the corner of Race and Washington Streets (present location of the Prescription Center) housed a variety of businesses over the decades. In this instance, Trimble's Barber Shop and S. Dickstein the Tailor beckon customers to the location. (Courtesy South Central Kentucky Cultural Center.)

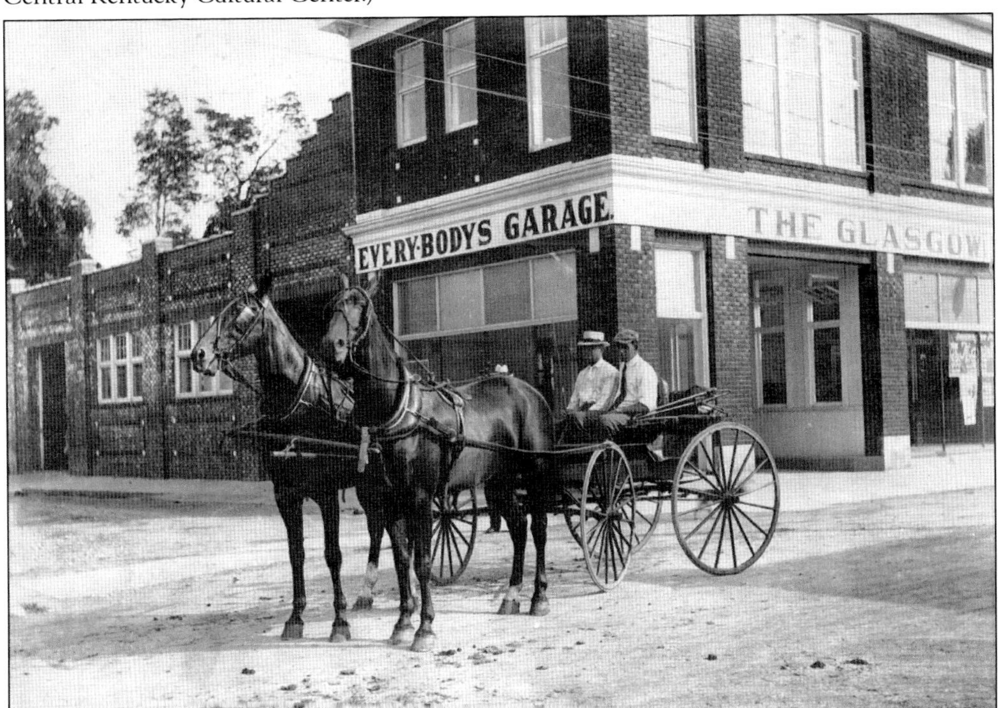

Everybody's Garage and the Glasgow Motor Company seem an ironic backdrop for the horse-drawn carriage captured in this 1916 image. (Courtesy South Central Kentucky Cultural Center.)

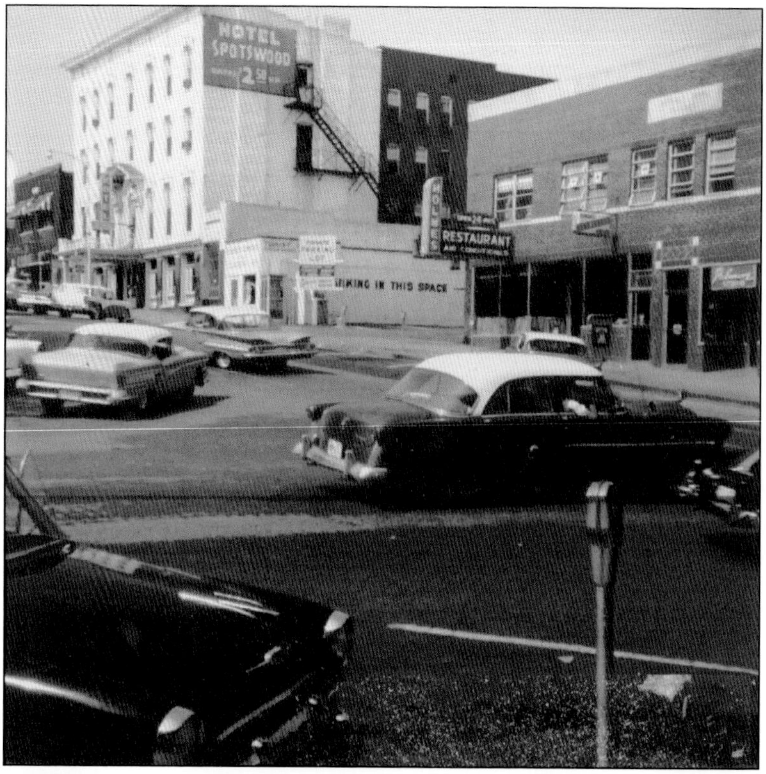

The old four-story Murrell Hotel became Hotel Spotswood in 1929 and continued for some time thereafter. In this late-1950s scene, the hotel is advertising rates of $2.50 and up while nearby Holmes Restaurant was air-conditioned and open 24 hours a day. Next door to the eatery, Palmore Studio captured images of young and old. (Courtesy South Central Kentucky Cultural Center.)

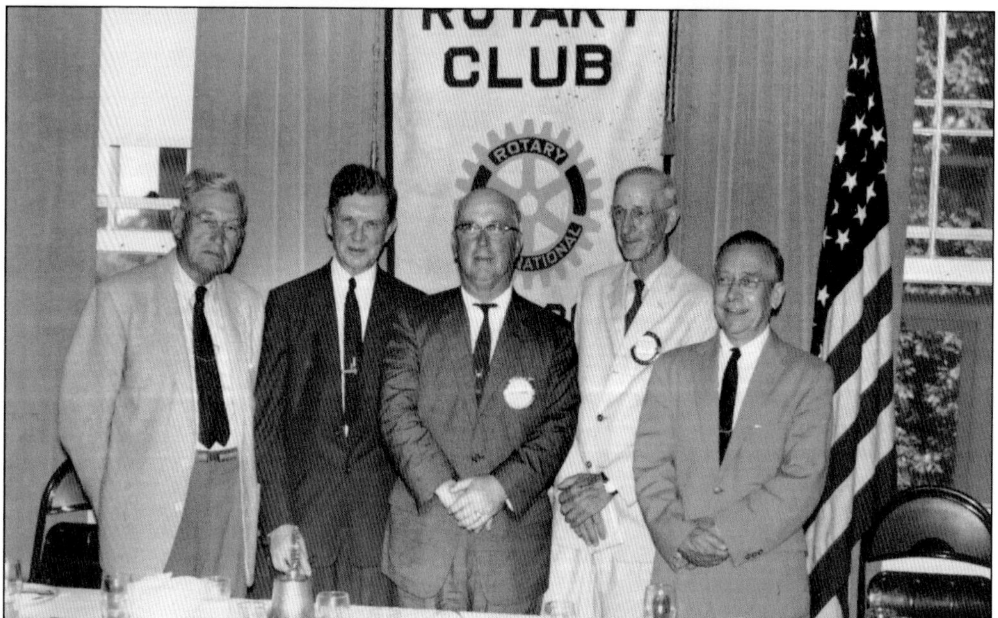

The Glasgow Rotary Club dates to the 1920s and continues as one of Glasgow's most active civic organizations. This 1960s image of Rotarians includes, from left to right, Brice R. Leech, Winn Davis, Sewell C. Harlin, J. O. Horning, and Dr. Gordon Clark. (Courtesy South Central Kentucky Cultural Center.)

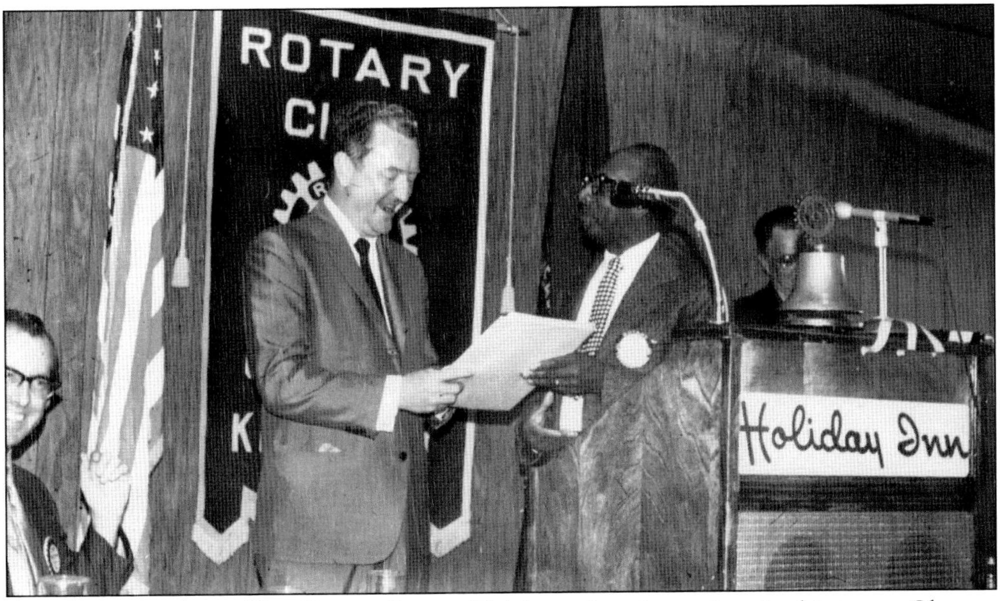

Guests and members of the Glasgow Rotary Club have shared notoriety. In this image, Glasgow native Julian Goodman is receiving a presentation from Mayor Luska J. Twyman. Goodman made his career in broadcast journalism, was the Washington editor of *News for the World*, and in 1966 became president of the National Broadcasting Company. Twyman, an educator, was the first African American mayor in Kentucky and was reelected numerous times. (Courtesy South Central Kentucky Cultural Center.)

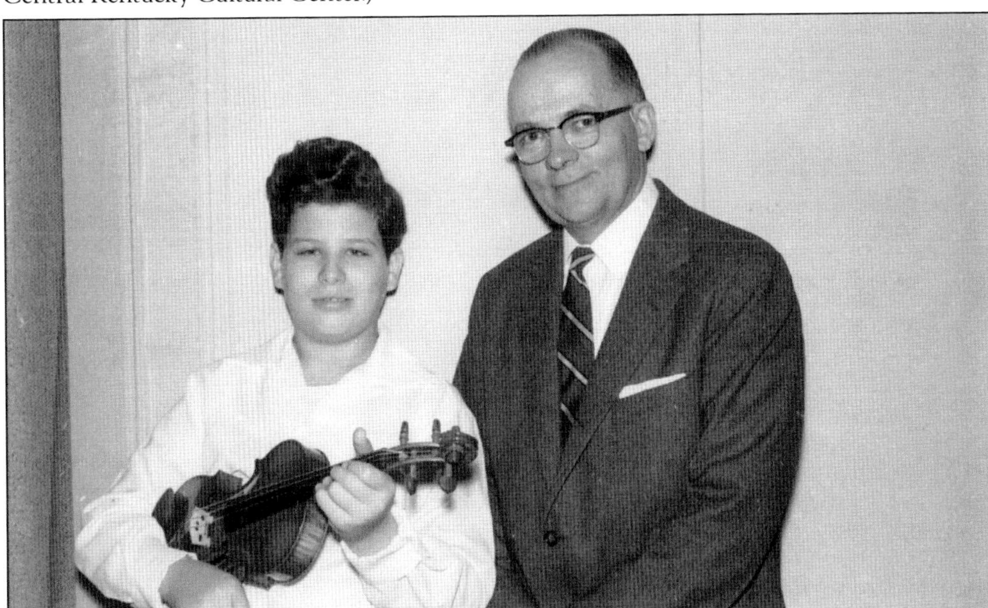

In November 1958, the *Ed Sullivan Show* presented the Israeli tour, which featured a young violinist, Itzhak Pearlman. Glasgow resident J. Mitchell Ellis was so moved by the young boy's spirit and talent that he launched a movement to purchase an artist-quality Fawick violin for Pearlman. Ellis flew to Cleveland to present the violin during an intermission of the Israeli show at Severance Hall. (Courtesy author's collection.)

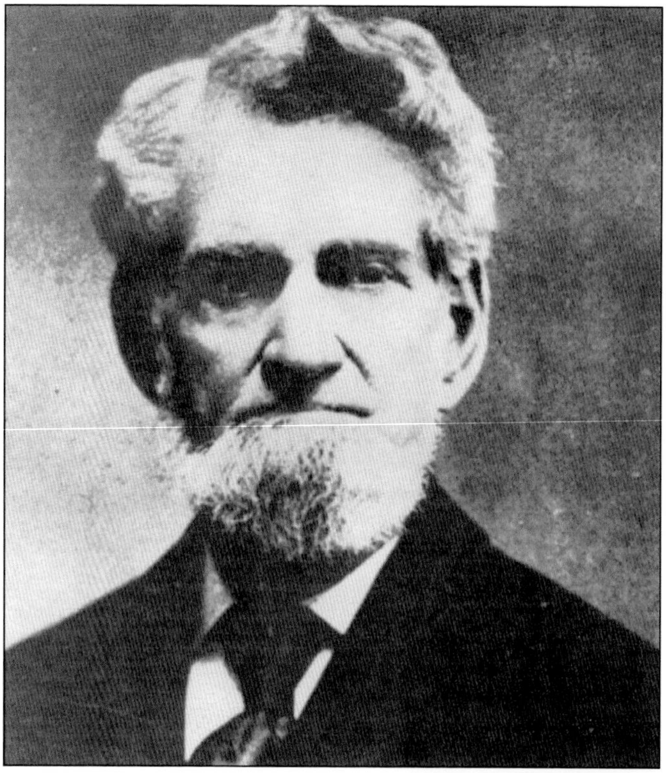

Gov. Preston Hopkins Leslie was a native of Clinton County, Kentucky, but made Glasgow his home as a young attorney. He later went to on represent the county in the Kentucky Legislature and eventually became the commonwealth's governor. Later Pres. Grover Cleveland appointed Leslie the territorial governor of Montana. Glasgow's Leslie Avenue bears the family name, though the street is said to be named in honor of the governor's daughter, Emily, a founder of the Glasgow Ladies Matinee Musicale. (Courtesy South Central Kentucky Cultural Center.)

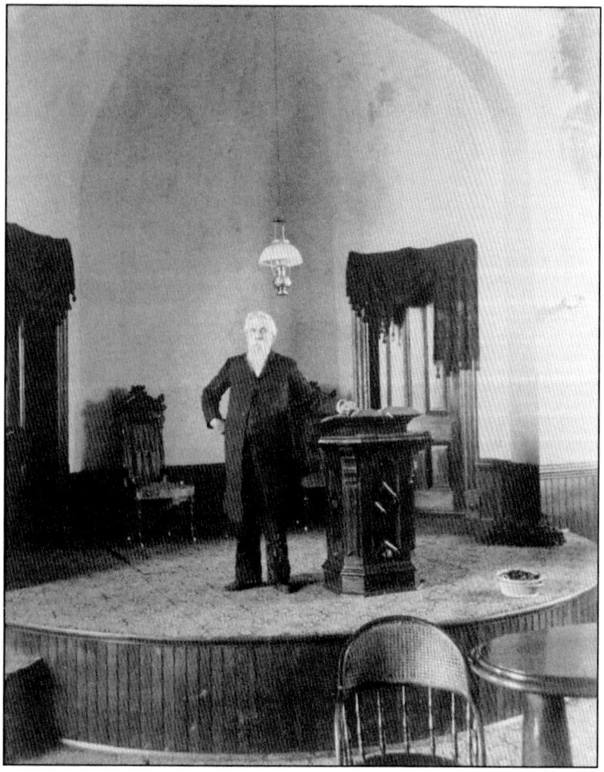

The Reverend Nathaniel Gorin Terry was one of the most prolific and best-known Baptist preachers in Glasgow and Barren County. In this image, Reverend Terry stands at the pulpit in the Glasgow Baptist Church on the corner of Green and College Streets. The frock coat Terry wears is said to be his "preaching" coat and is preserved and displayed at the South Central Kentucky Cultural Center. (Courtesy Jane Terry Goodman.)

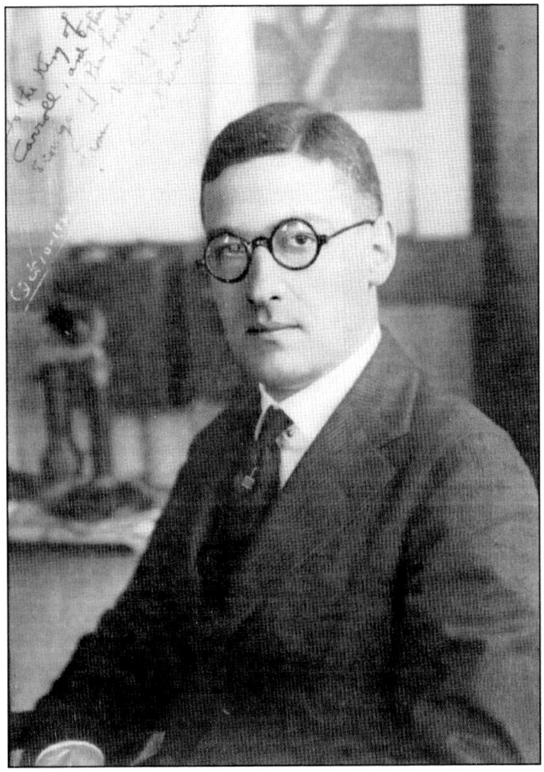

Glasgow native Arthur Krock began his career in the newspaper field when he worked for the *Glasgow Times*. He was a reporter for the *Louisville Herald*, later worked for the *Louisville Times*, and was for a time editor of the *Courier-Journal* before becoming an assistant to the editor of the *New York World*. He later became Washington bureau chief of the *New York Times*. During his career, he three times won the Pulitzer Prize and one Pulitzer Prize citation. (Courtesy the Kentucky Library.)

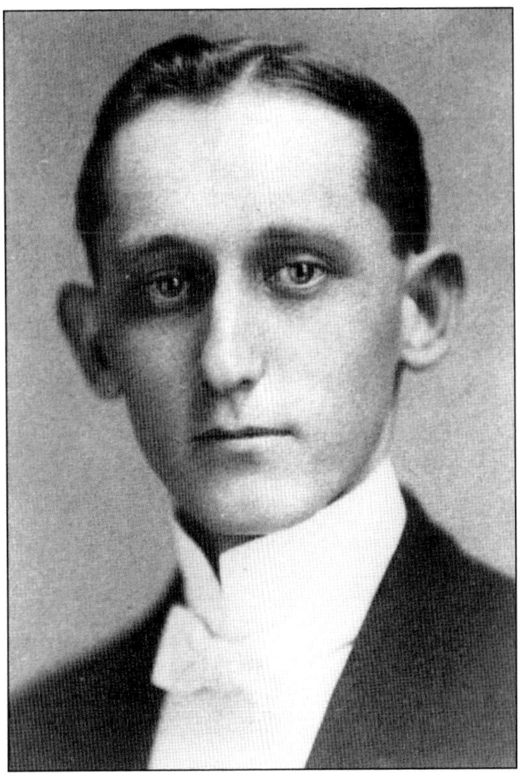

Dr. Carl Clifford Howard established Glasgow's first hospital, Maplewood Infirmary. He later was instrumental in helping establish T. J. Samson Community Hospital and was the driving force in creating the Tuberculosis Hospital with the aim of eradicating TB from the commonwealth. He created the Howard Medical Clinic on West Washington Street, now home to the Barren County Health Department. (Courtesy Mary Lloyd Lessenberry.)

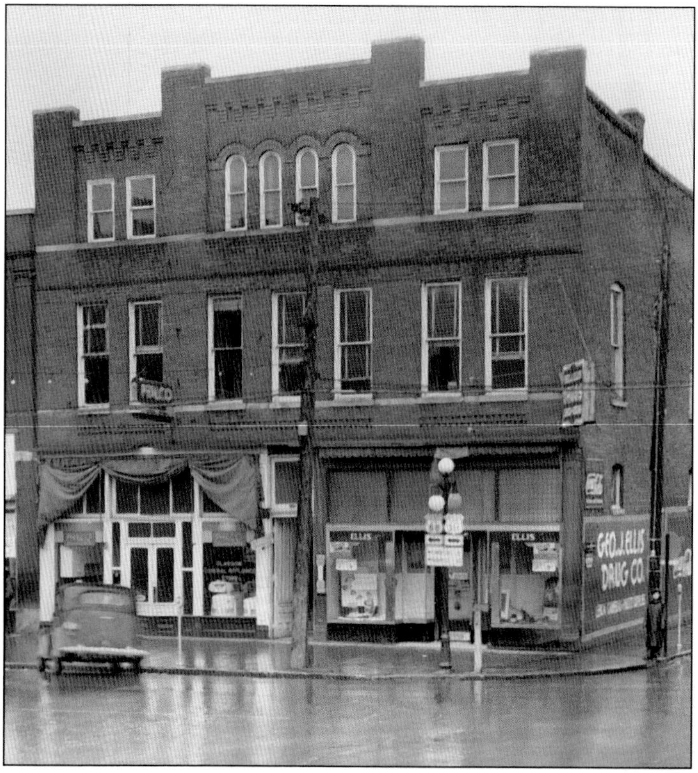

George J. Ellis Drug Company was one of Glasgow's longest-running business concerns and the ubiquitous "corner drugstore" that virtually everyone knew. George J. Ellis Sr. was an enterprising businessman who had a number of partners over the years before settling into the business that carried his name. His son, J. Mitchell Ellis, was a pharmacist and succeeded his father as owner of the company. Under the son's ownership, the store branched out into other areas, such as home appliances, quality cameras, and guns and gun supplies. (Courtesy author's collection.)

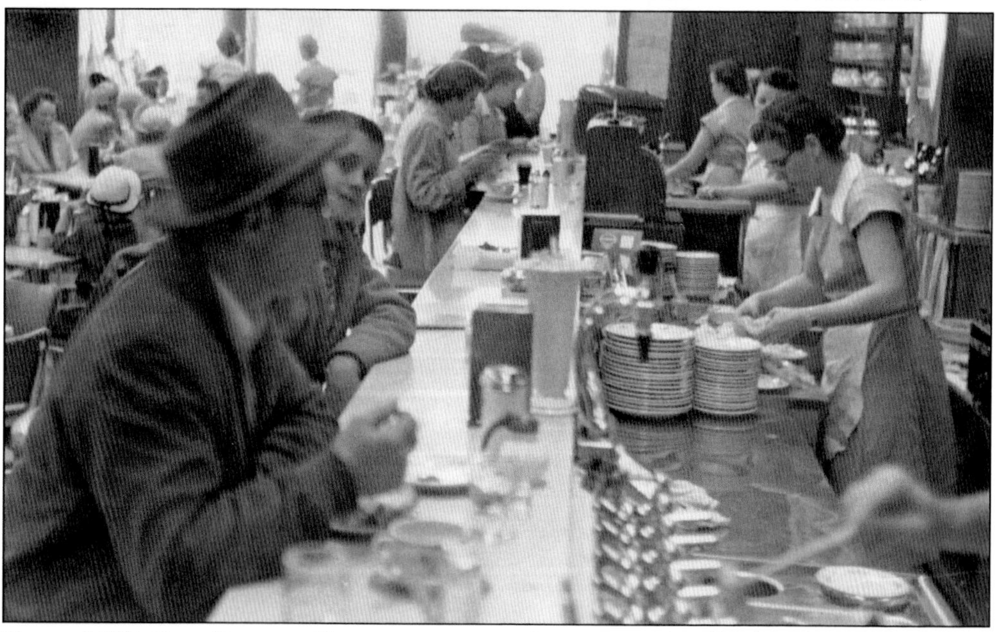

George J. Ellis Drug Company Fountain was a popular eatery and coffee shop for decades, giving the business its notoriety. The cooks and wait staff served up hundreds of breakfasts and plate lunches throughout the week and gallon after gallon of piping hot coffee and tasty ice cream. Today the pharmacy is gone, but the tradition lives on through a restaurant known as George J.'s on the Square. (Courtesy author's collection.)

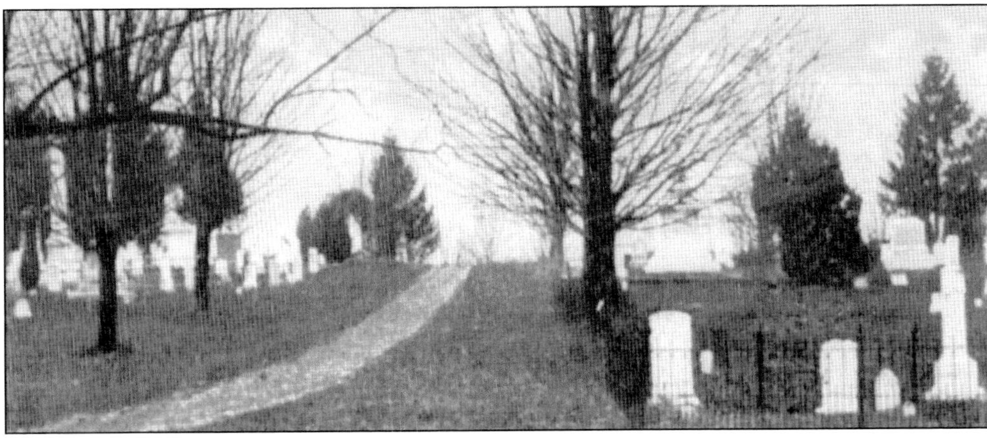

In the late 19th century, the International Order of Odd Fellows (IOOF) Lodge created a cemetery in Glasgow to serve the needs of its members and the community. Ultimately, the cemetery was sold to the City of Glasgow in the early 20th century and remains under the city's auspices. Since its earliest days, the cemetery has been a peaceful and beautiful place of repose for the dead and visitation for the living. Adjoining the cemetery is Fort Williams, a restored Civil War fort built by Union forces in 1863. (Courtesy author's collection.)

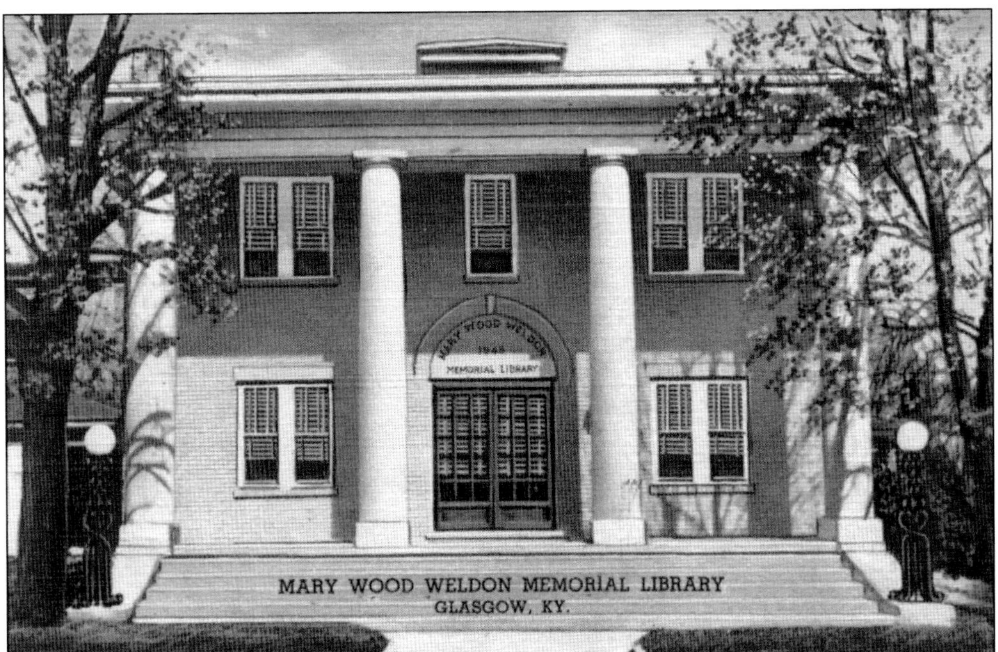

Mary Wood Weldon Memorial Library was the name given to Glasgow's public library when Dr. William A. Weldon presented a building for use as a library. The structure was actually two apartment buildings with a connecting wing. Glasgow's efforts to have and maintain a public library reach back to the dawn of the 20th century. (Courtesy author's collection.)

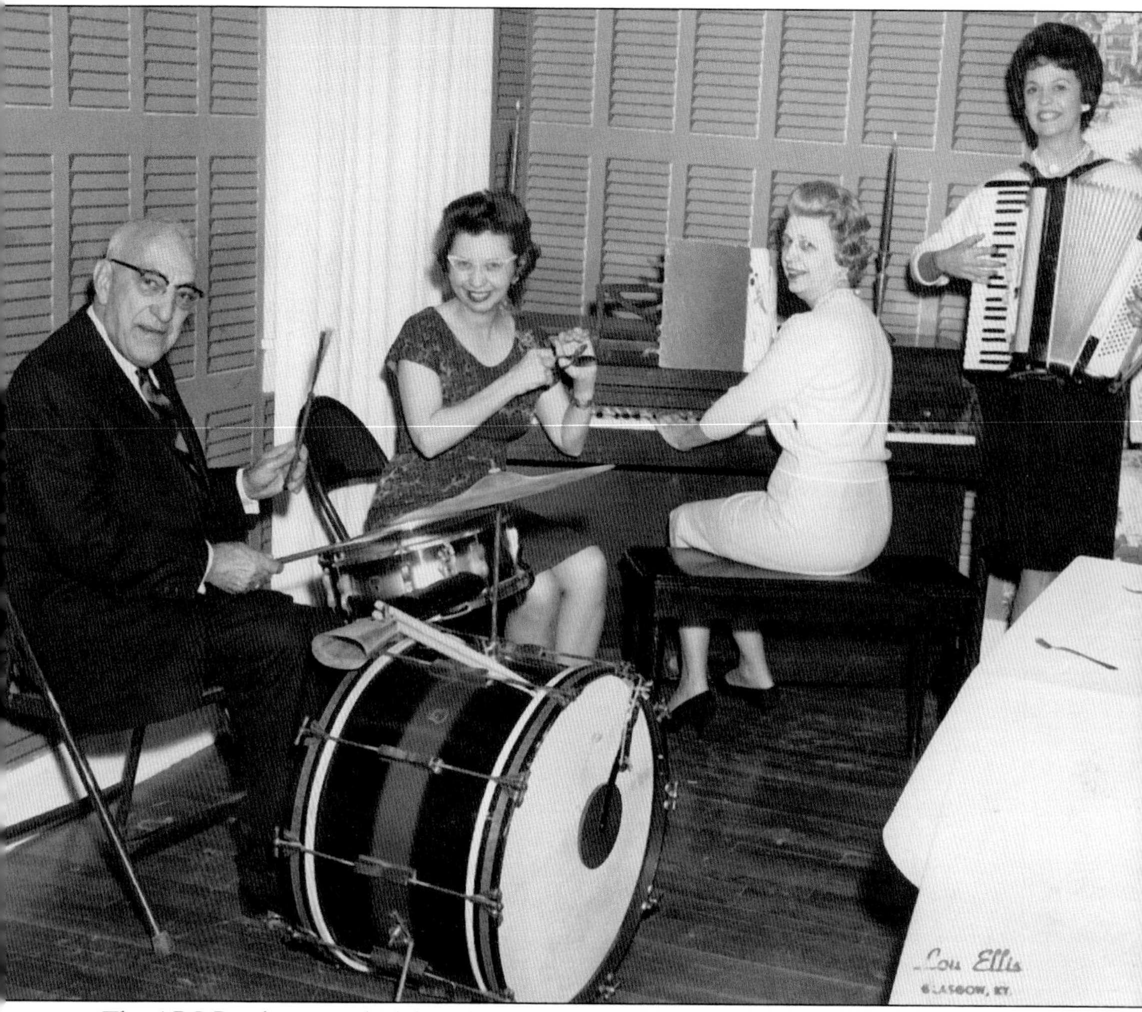

The ABC Band consisted of three local ladies with a penchant for music and fun. Ann Wells, Bertie McGuiar, and Christeen Snavely entertained various local groups and gatherings for several years. The name of the band came from the first letters of their first names. Wells shared her talents on the accordion while McGuiar played the piano. Snavely played spoons and the drums. In this photograph, Anthony "Papa" St. Charles plays the drums. (Courtesy author's collection.)

Two

At Home in Glasgow

Glasgow has seemingly always had a love affair with old homes—to this day, they are sought after, bought, sold, bequeathed, and most of all cherished as tangible parts of our past. South Green Street, once known as Maple Driveway, is certainly the most storied of picturesque streets lined with homes both quaint and great. The house in the far right is the Maples, then home of the Hascal Mitchell family. (Courtesy author's collection.)

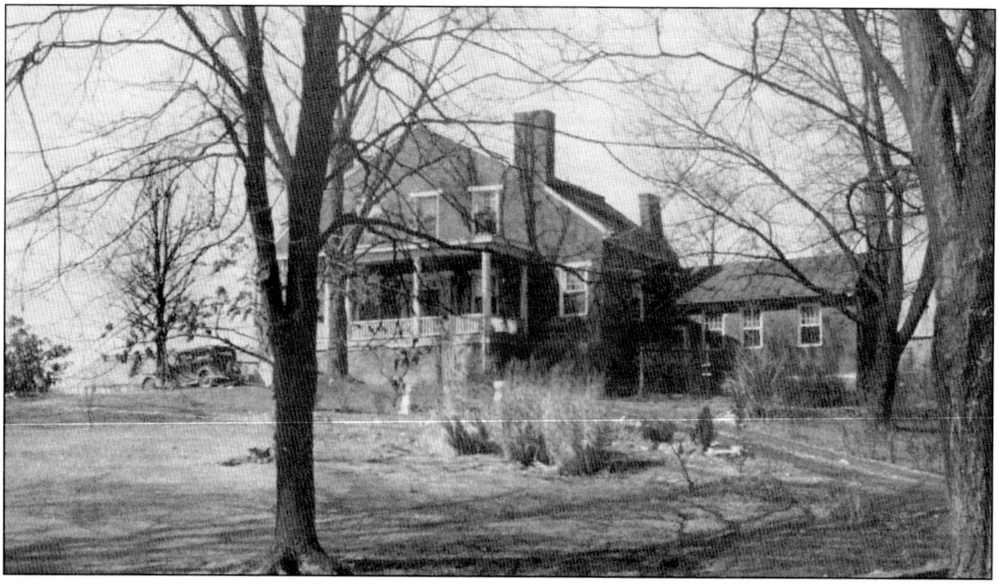

The Spotswood House, bounded by Front, Race, and Mitchell Streets, is one of Glasgow's most fabled historic places. It is believed to be the oldest house in Glasgow and was built for the great-nephew and great-niece of George Washington, Alexander E. Spotswood and Elizabeth W. Lewis. In addition to its storied first owners, the Spotswood House has been home to Will T. Bush, Glasgow's first real estate developer; Confederate general William Thompson Martin during his childhood; Confederate general and commander of the famed Orphan Brigade, Joseph H. Lewis; U.S. Representative James M. Richardson; Lucy Rogers Richardson, who operated a florist shop from her home; and many others. (Courtesy author's collection.)

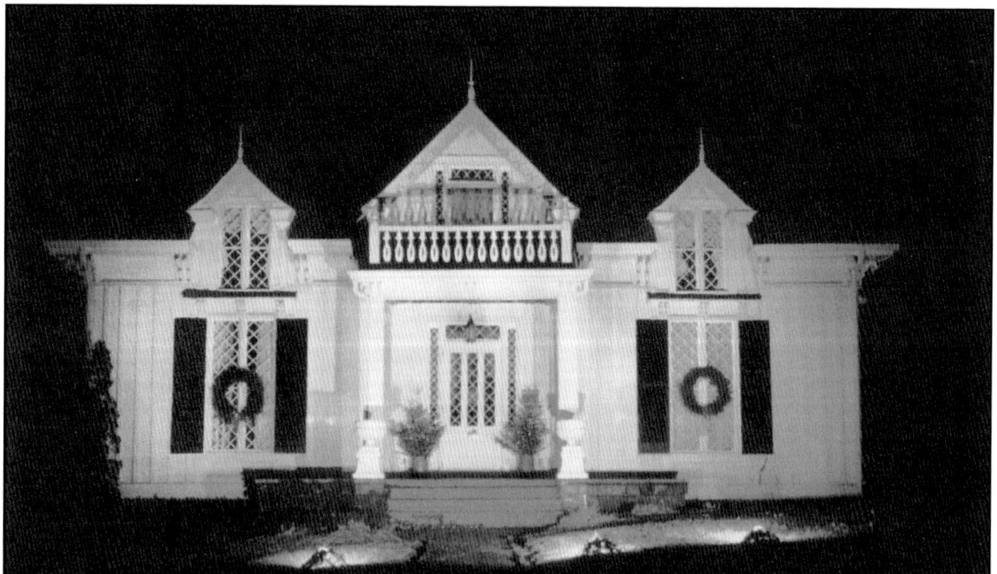

Seven Gables is one of only a handful of Gothic Revival–style homes surviving in south-central Kentucky. Built for Wilburn and Lucinda Bybee in the 1850s, the home is one of Glasgow's architectural gems and has been painstakingly maintained by the Wilson and Garmon families. (Courtesy author's collection.)

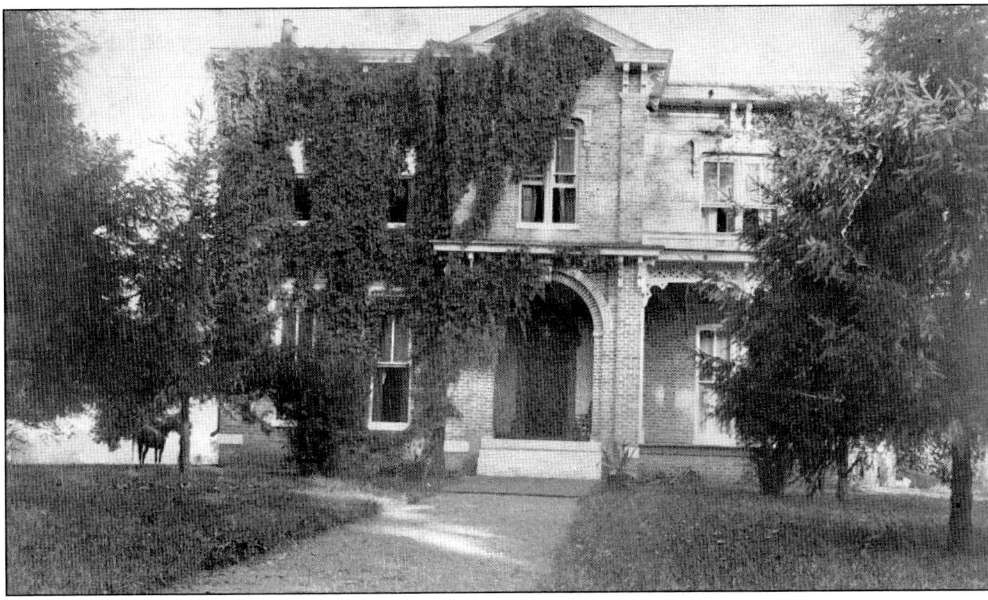

The Italianate-style Haiden C. Trigg home stood in what is now Trigg Court. Trigg was one of the organizers of Gorin, Trigg, and Company Bank, predecessor of Trigg Bank. Trigg was also the breeder of the famous Trigg foxhound, one of the sought-after breeds of hounds to this day. Local lore reveals that a room in the Trigg home was known as "The Prophet's Chamber" where local business leaders gathered. The home burned many years ago, and Trigg Court was developed on its grounds. (Courtesy author's collection.)

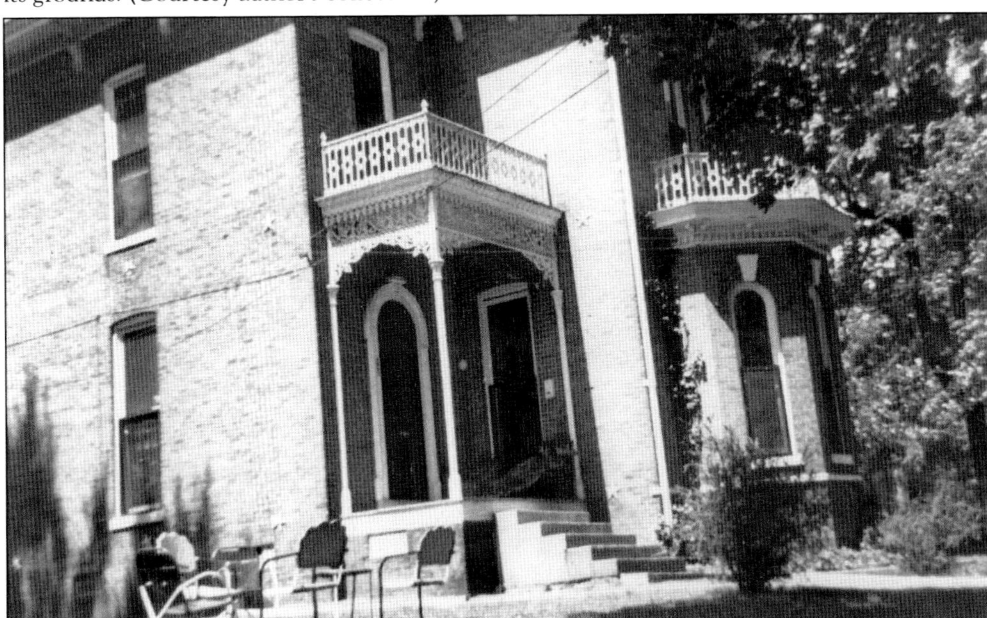

Eugenia and John A. "Old Reb" Murray built this lovely Italianate-style home and later sold it to the Gorin family. Annie Gorin, daughter of the Honorable Franklin Gorin and granddaughter of one of Glasgow's founders, resided here and taught generations of young people to play the piano within these walls. The house was later converted into the Howard Clinic Hospital. The structure was demolished in the 1990s. (Courtesy South Central Kentucky Cultural Center.)

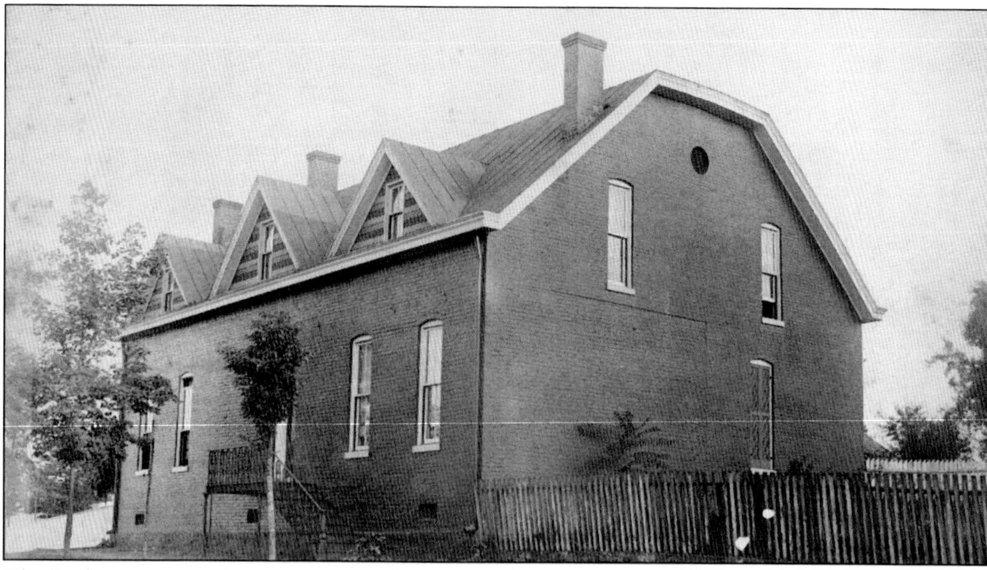

The Dickinson-Greer house is one of Glasgow's oldest surviving structures. Property records indicate that a portion of this house was standing by the 1820s, and it was treated to an enlargement and remodeling by Thomas Childs Dickinson in the 1880s. Dickinson's daughter, Lillie, married John Baptiste Delvaux; their daughter, Jeanne, married Paul Greer, whose son Delvaux Dickinson Greer was the last occupant of the structure. The Flounder-style house is presently being restored and renovated by the Renaissance–Main Street Glasgow organization. (Courtesy South Central Kentucky Cultural Center.)

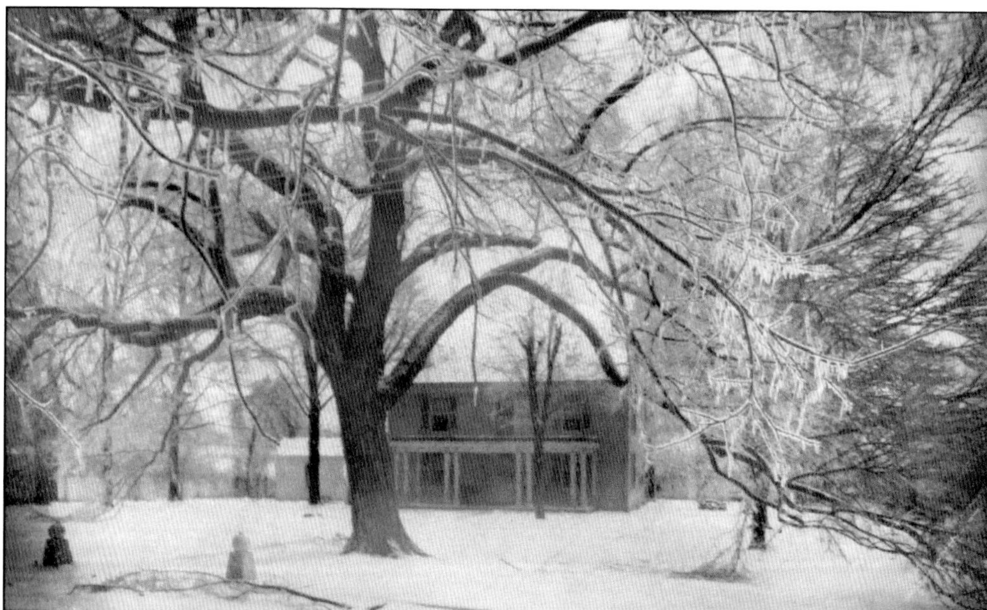

Local builder James Thompson constructed this home for Benjamin Nuckols in 1855. It later became the home of Michael Hall Dickinson and, even later, his son T. P. Dickinson. This 1906 image of the home was captured by Adolph Rapp following a winter storm, which left a crystal coating of ice on all of nature. The West Brown Street property once adjoined several acres on which the Dickinson family had stables and pasture for horses. (Courtesy author's collection.)

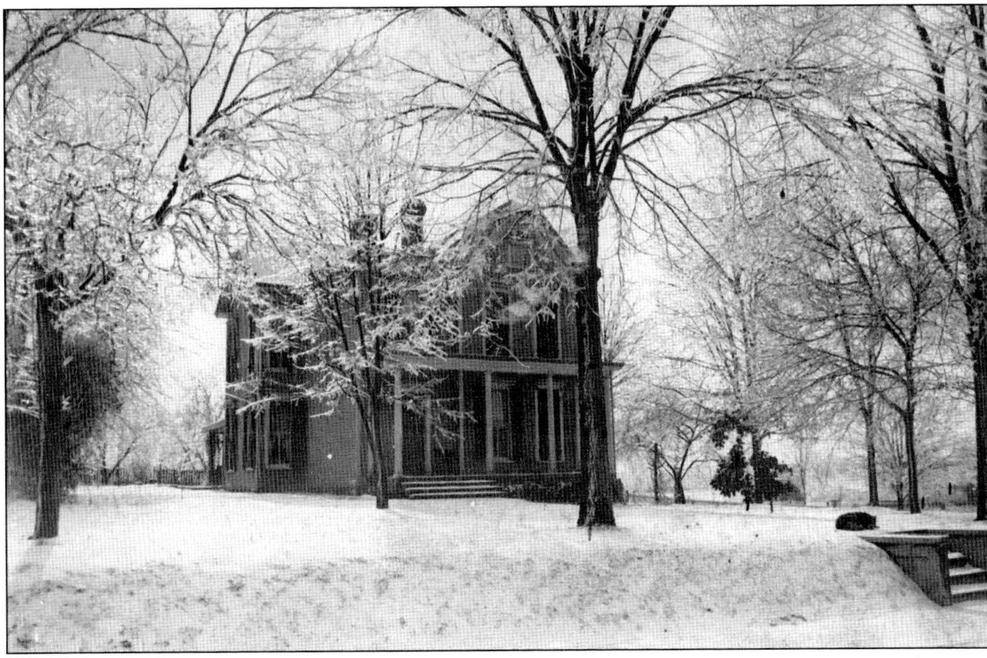

The Elisha and Sophie Dickinson Dickey house on West Brown Street is but one of Glasgow's Victorian gems with amenities such as colorful stained glass, corner fireplaces, and tall, narrow windows. Dated February 1910, this image emphasizes the lack of surrounding structures that now fill the neighborhood. (Courtesy South Central Kentucky Cultural Center.)

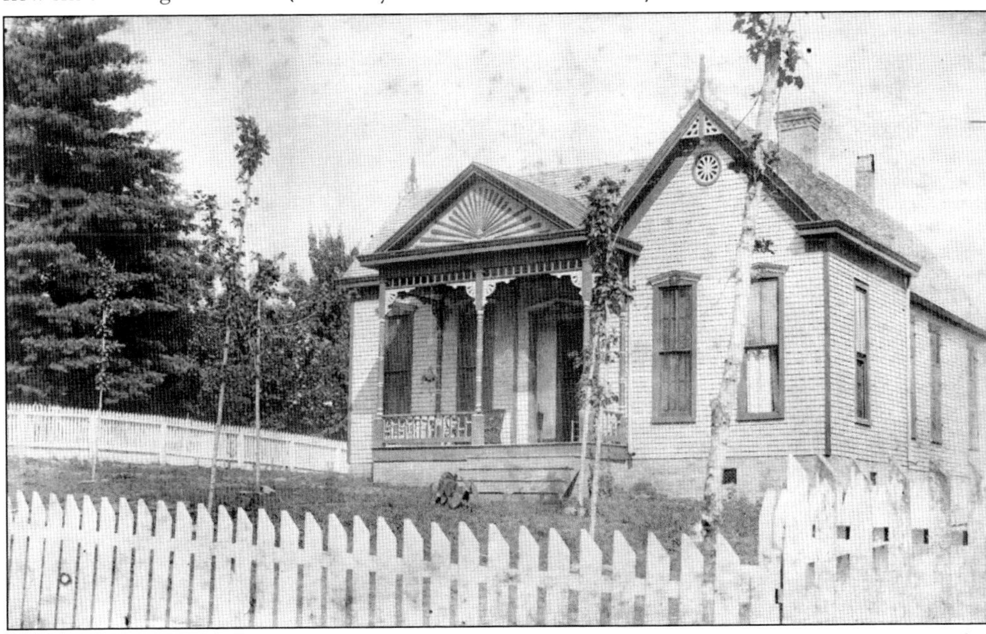

The Allie Smith House on South Green Street is captured in this photograph possibly soon after its construction. An 1890 deed for this home states that Allie Smith was to build a house on this lot within one year or it would revert back to the previous owner. The exuberant Victorian millwork greets the viewer with a T-angle porch with a sunburst overhead. (Courtesy South Central Kentucky Cultural Center.)

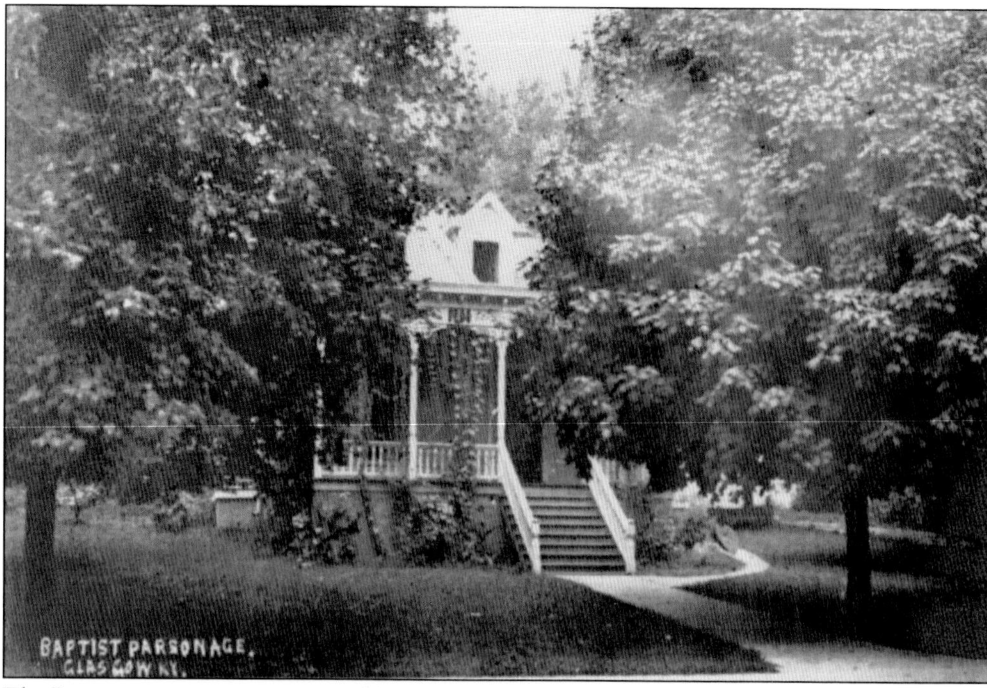

The Baptist parsonage was captured by Adolph Rapp at the height of summer when various vines have worked their way up the facade to shade front-porch visitors from the burning sun. The cottage was the home of the Jack Reynolds Leech family for many years and has now been transformed into a restored "painted lady" by the Vincent Foushee family. (Courtesy author's collection.)

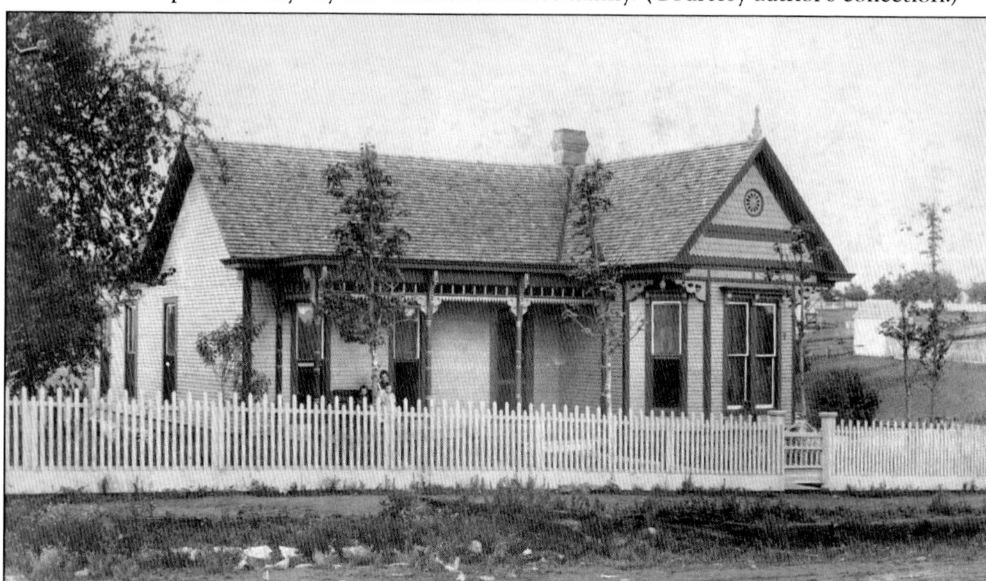

This Victorian cottage represents a large segment of the type of architecture found in Glasgow during the late 19th century and early 20th century with detailed millwork ornamenting the porch and front gable areas of the structure. While the exact location of the structure is unknown, it illustrates the type of comfortable homes found in south-central Kentucky. (Courtesy South Central Kentucky Cultural Center.)

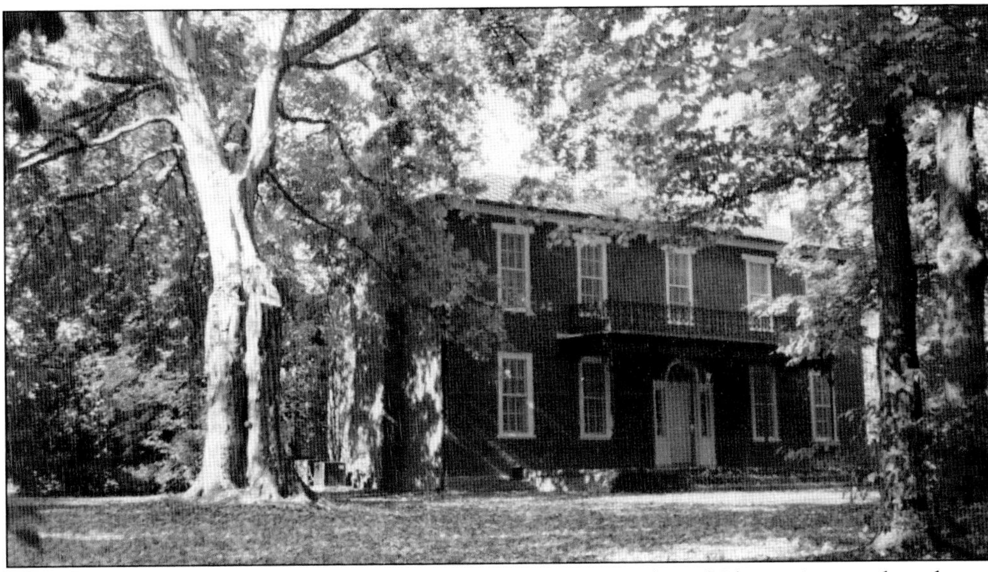

The Christopher Tompkins house on North Race Street is another of Glasgow's storied residences steeped in history. Tompkins received his legal training under the tutelage of John Breckinridge of Lexington before coming to Glasgow, where he gained a reputation as a noted jurist and statesmen. Tompkins's wife, Theodosia Logan, was the aunt of Stephen T. Logan, one-time law partner of Abraham Lincoln. In addition to living here, Tompkins taught law to young would-be lawyers in this house. Between 1850 and 1860, the home was used as a girls boarding school, and during the War Between the States, it became a hospital. (Courtesy South Central Kentucky Cultural Center.)

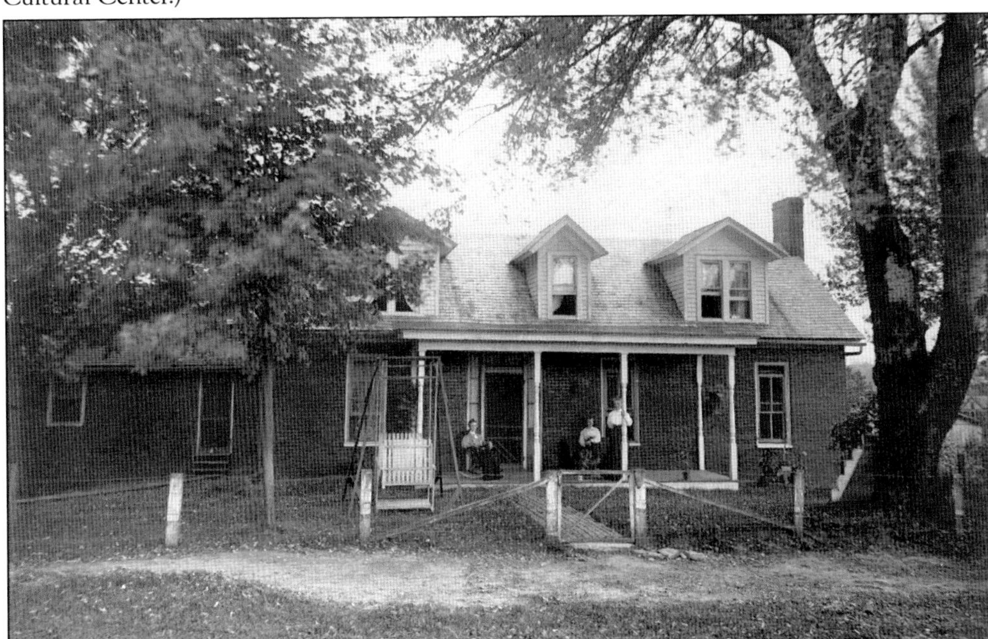

The Ford sisters (Ellen, Edna, Fannie, and Polly) were each "unclaimed treasures" who made use of their fine sewing skills as dressmakers. Their quaint house was built in the 1850s and was home to a number of families over the years. (Courtesy South Central Kentucky Cultural Center.)

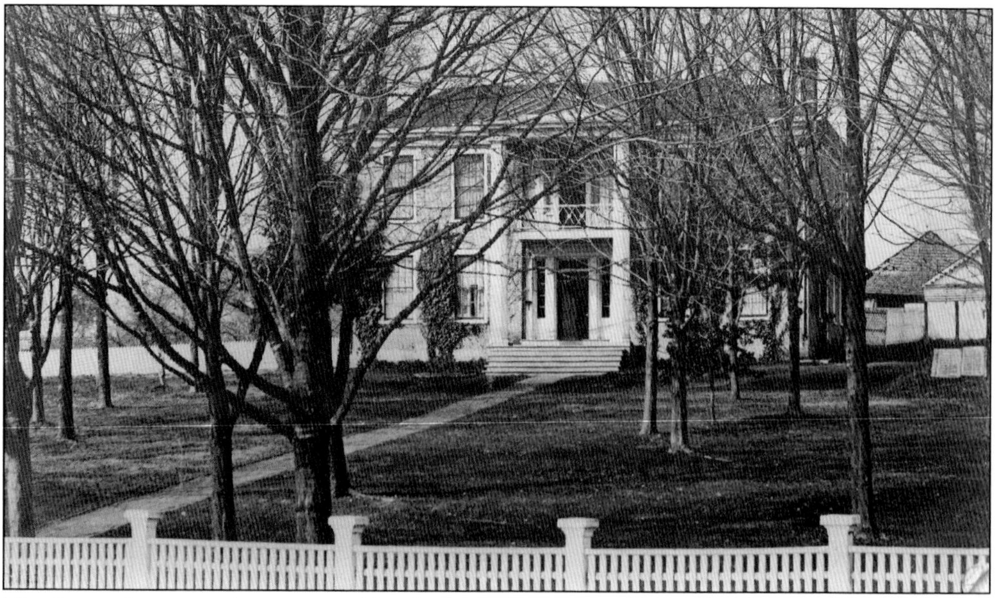

The Brents home on the corner of South Green Street and Leslie Avenue was at least partially constructed in 1850 by the Dodd family. Later the home was purchased by Alanson Trigg for his daughter, Eliza Trigg, who married Samuel Worley Brents. For many decades thereafter, the home was occupied by various Brents and Dickinson heirs. After a series of owners, the house has been the home of the James R. Heltsley family for several years. (Courtesy South Central Kentucky Cultural Center.)

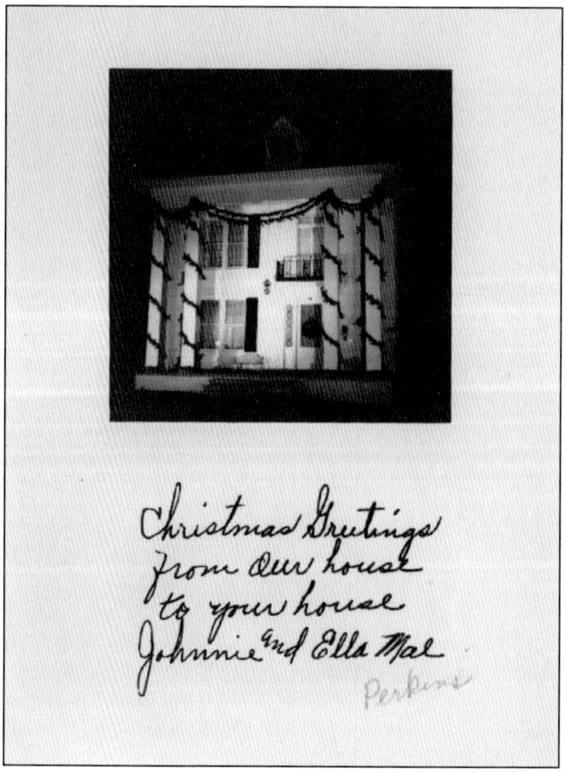

The Johnnie and Ella Mae Perkins House on South Green Street was exuberantly decorated for the Christmas holidays in this 1960s photograph. Glasgow residents have exercised great creativity since the latter half of the 20th century in bedecking their homes for the holidays in what has become an anticipated tradition. (Courtesy South Central Kentucky Cultural Center.)

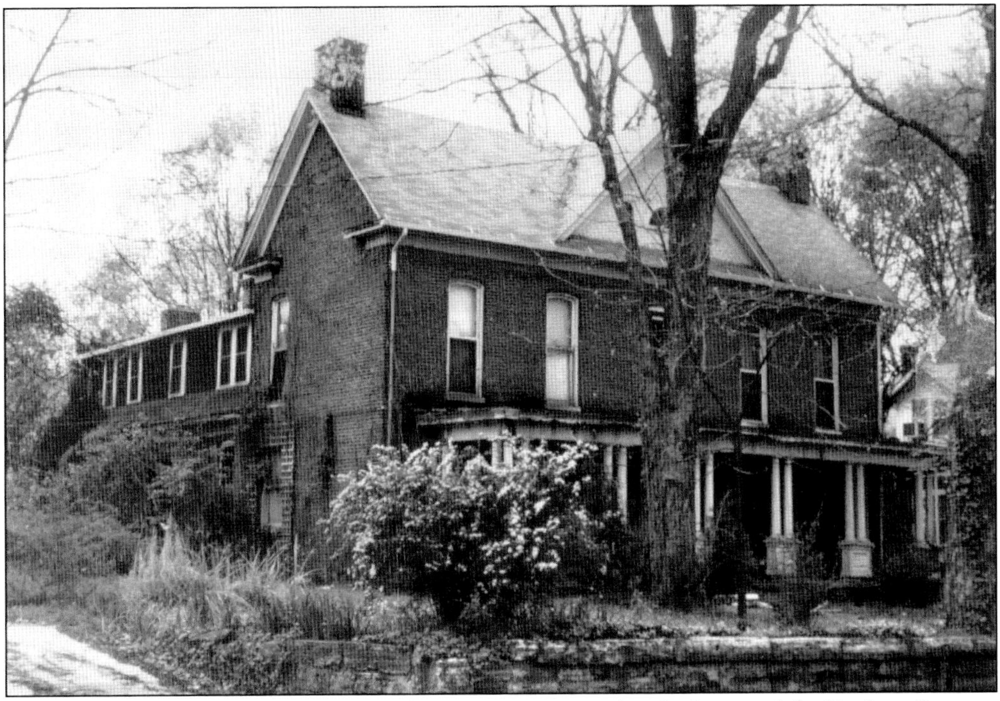

The Judge Noah Smith house on North Race Street was also the home of the Reuben Garnett family for many years. The first Roman Catholic mass said in Glasgow occurred in this house according to Annie Gorin, one of the founding communicants of St. Helen's Church. (Courtesy South Central Kentucky Cultural Center.)

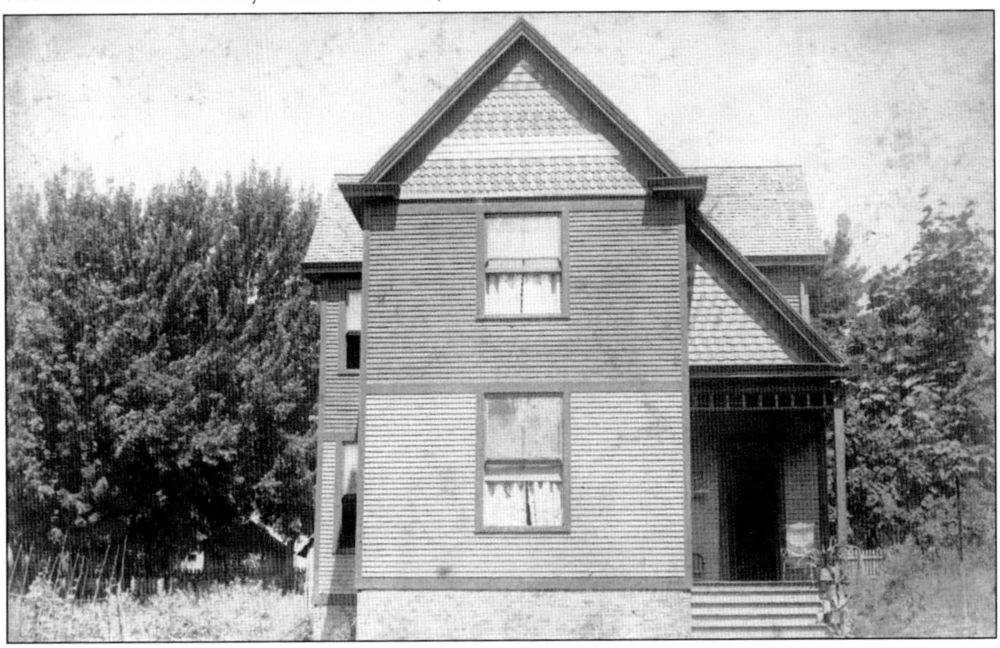

The Snoddy House on the corner of South Green and West Brown Streets is a good example of shingle-style late-Victorian architecture in Glasgow. (Courtesy South Central Kentucky Cultural Center.)

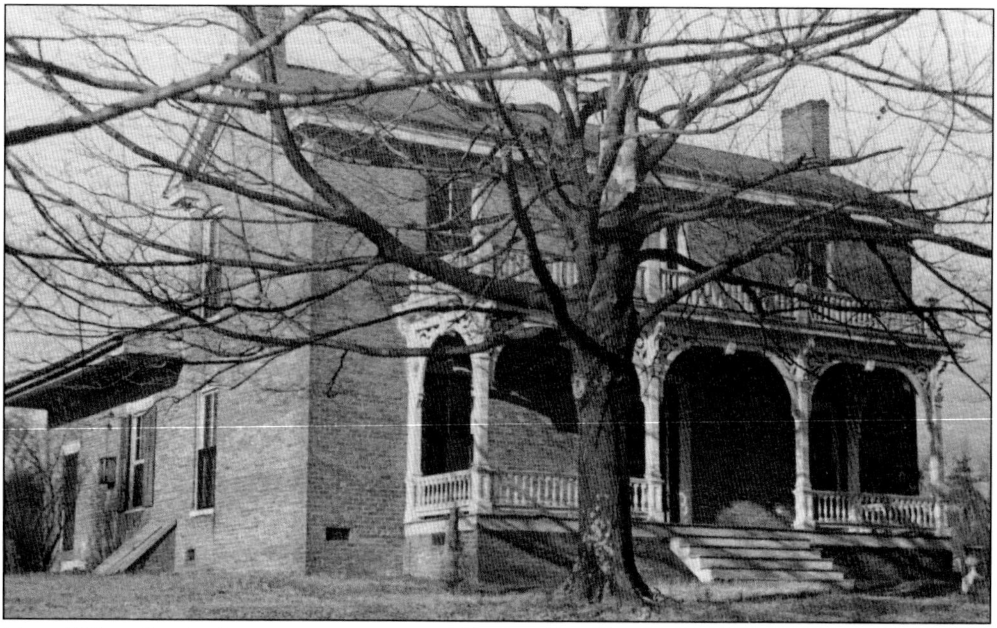

Terry Hill on Leslie Avenue was constructed by local builder James Thompson in 1866 or 1867. The home has been occupied by members of the Hall, Barlow, Yancey, Terry, Holman, and Ellis families since the 1870s. The Greek Revival–style architecture is typical of many farmhouses built in this era in the Barrens. The home had major renovations in the 1880s and 1951. The structure was originally surrounded by 22 acres and included a brickyard used by Thompson for use in his buildings. (Courtesy author's collection.)

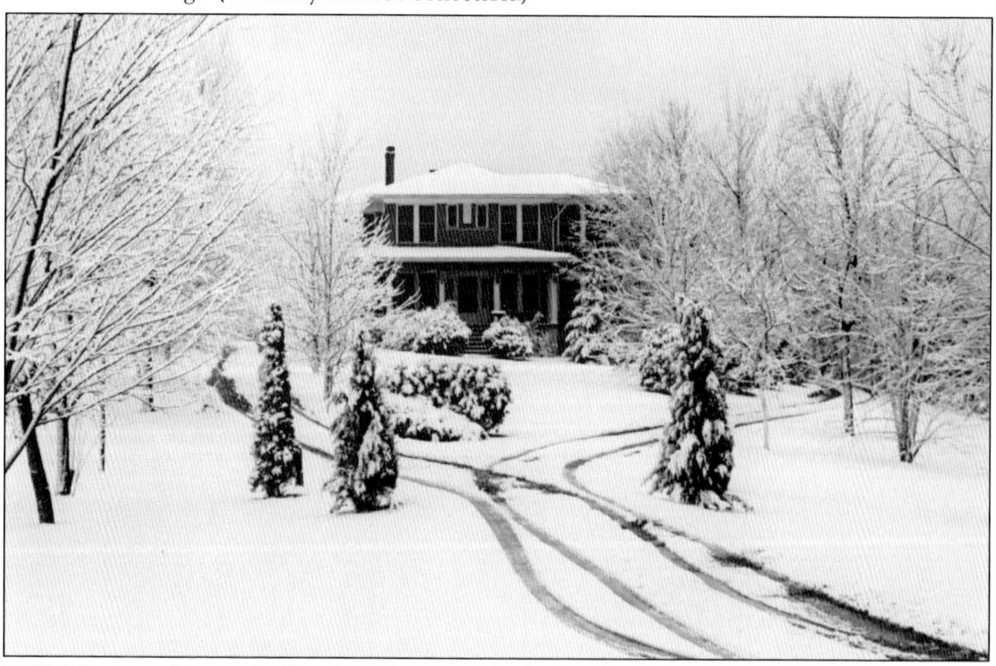

R. H. Norris and his wife, Caroline Compton, built this fine American four-square-style home on South Green Street. In what was acreage behind the house, one finds Norris, Windsor, Brice, Ridgecrest, and Wingate Avenues and Raintree Place. (Courtesy author's collection.)

Three

AT WORK IN GLASGOW

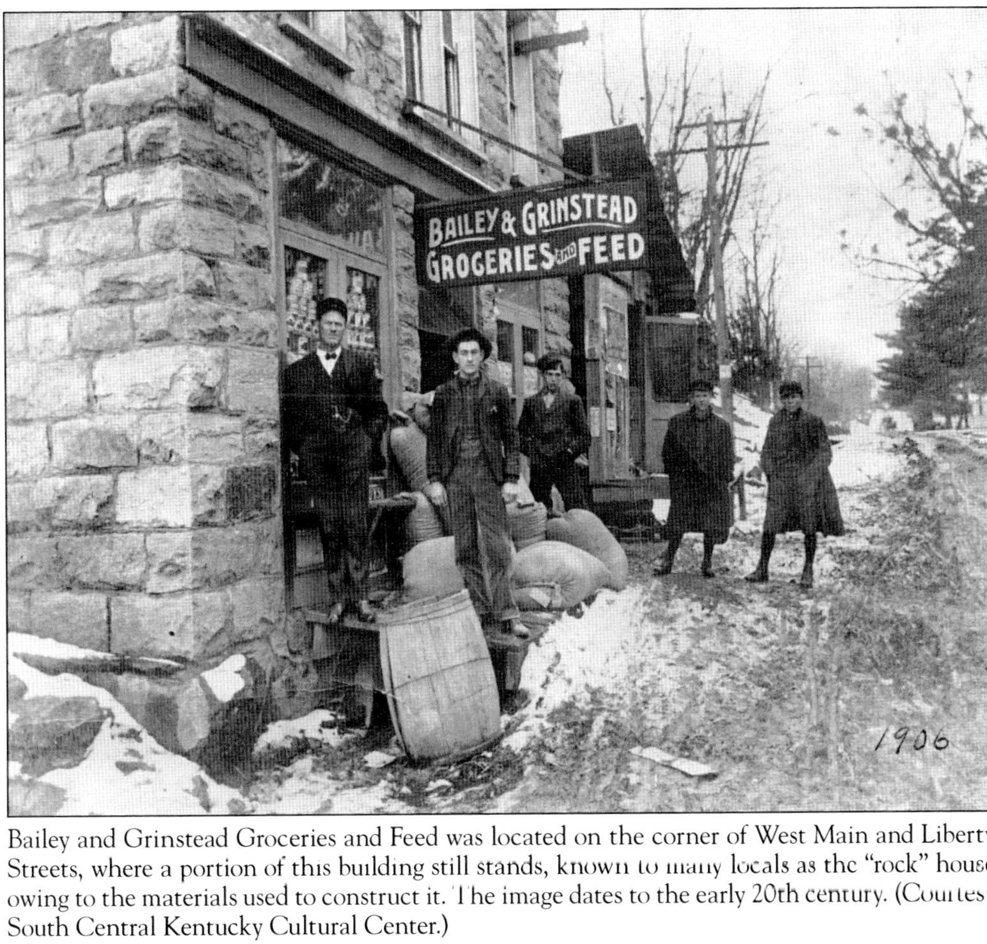

Bailey and Grinstead Groceries and Feed was located on the corner of West Main and Liberty Streets, where a portion of this building still stands, known to many locals as the "rock" house owing to the materials used to construct it. The image dates to the early 20th century. (Courtesy South Central Kentucky Cultural Center.)

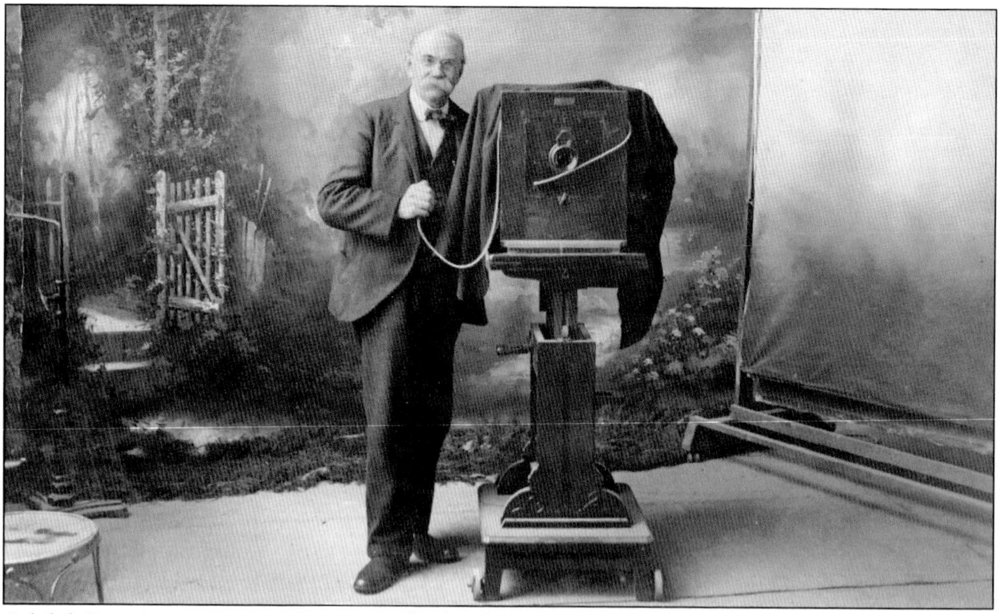

Adolph Rapp's story is one of many in which Glasgow residents lived the American dream. Rapp and others came to this country following the American Civil War and spread throughout the country to evolve into successful businessmen. Rapp's first business venture was as a confectioner; when the bakery business proved disappointing, he added photography to his repertoire. One of his newspaper advertisement states, "I guarantee my photographs to last until the end of time." Thousands of Rapp photographs have indeed survived, including this self-portrait. (Courtesy South Central Kentucky Cultural Center.)

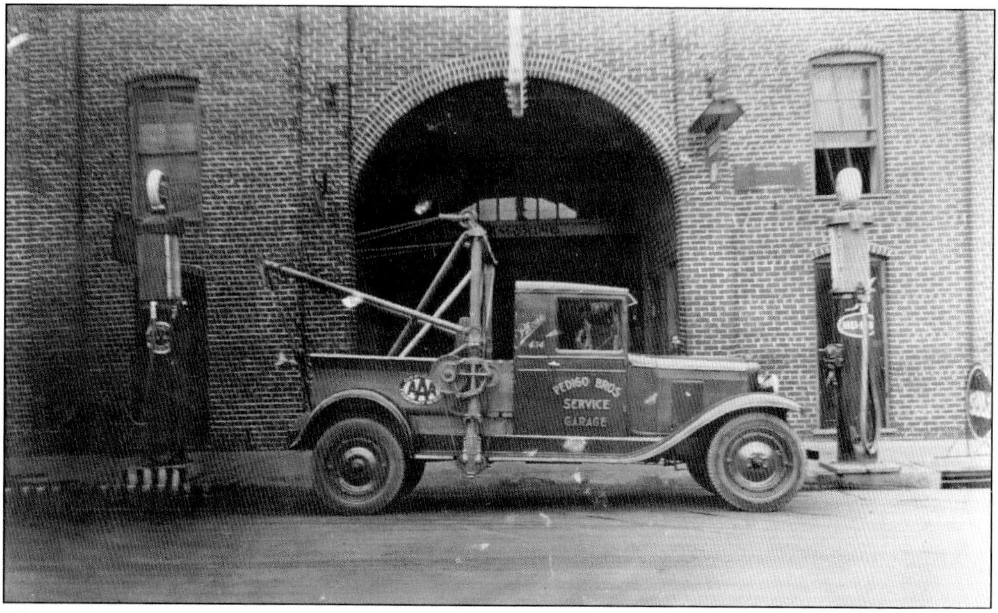

This 1929 image of the Pedigo Brothers Service Garage wrecker takes the viewer back to a time in which gasoline was pumped into glass cylinders before reaching one's car. The Pedigo family's business evolved from a livery stable to that of the modern automobile in the course of a few decades. (Courtesy South Central Kentucky Cultural Center.)

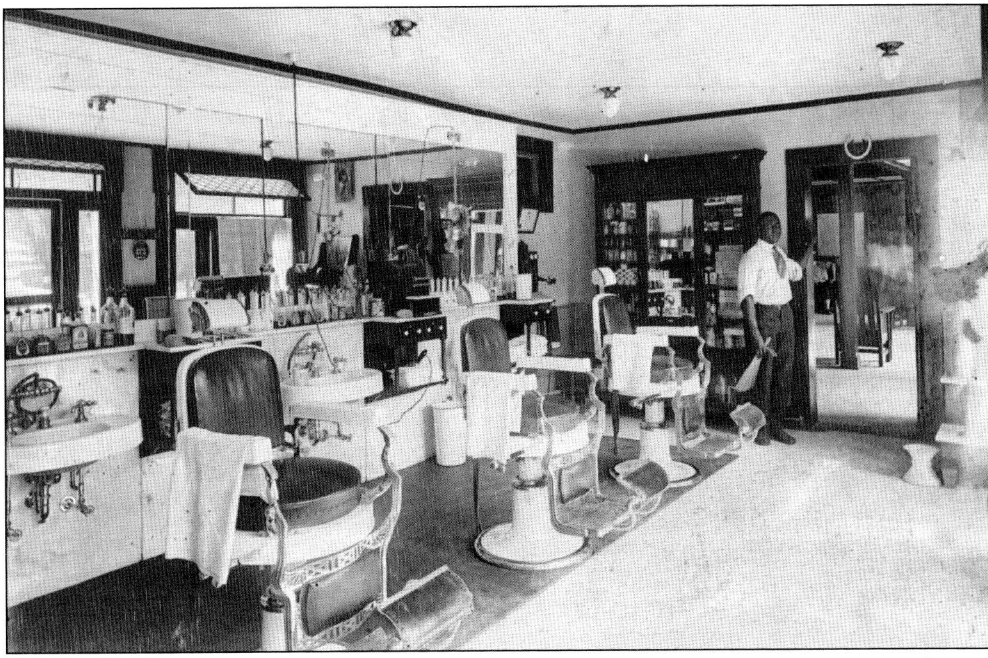

Among the amenities offered by the Hotel Spotswood was a first-rate barbershop, as seen here in the 1930s. Barbershops were not always strictly business sorts of places, but rather locations for gentlemen to meet and discuss the news of the day, the weather, the crops, and the latest political news. (Courtesy South Central Kentucky Cultural Center.)

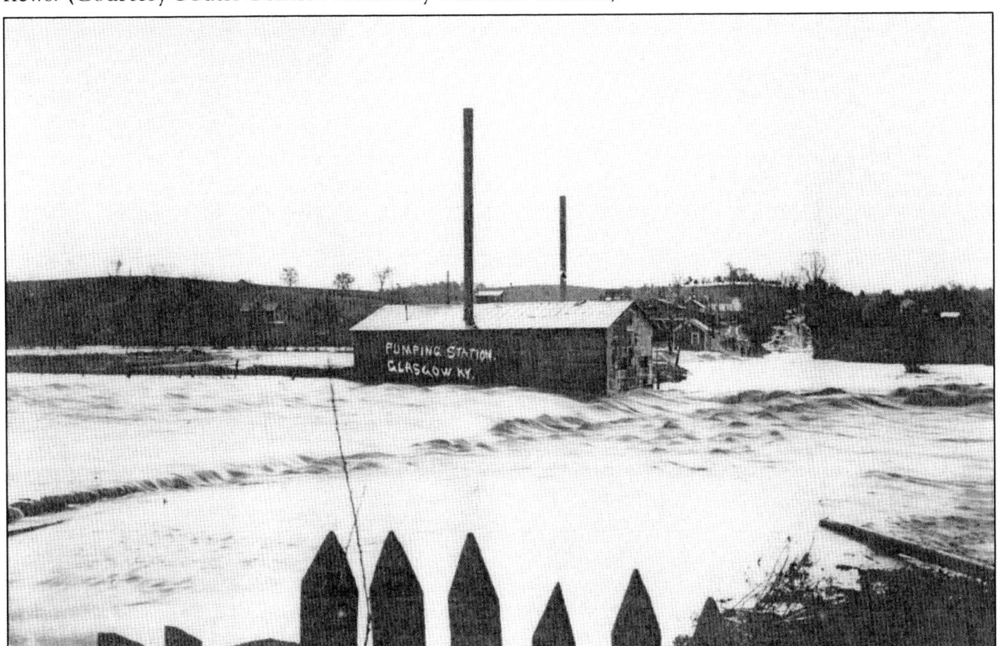

The Glasgow Pumping Station on East Main Street provided electricity for more than 2,500 electric lights in Glasgow and had cold storage for more than 100 tons of ice. This image shows the banks of South Fork Creek overflowing in an early-1900s flood. (Courtesy South Central Kentucky Cultural Center.)

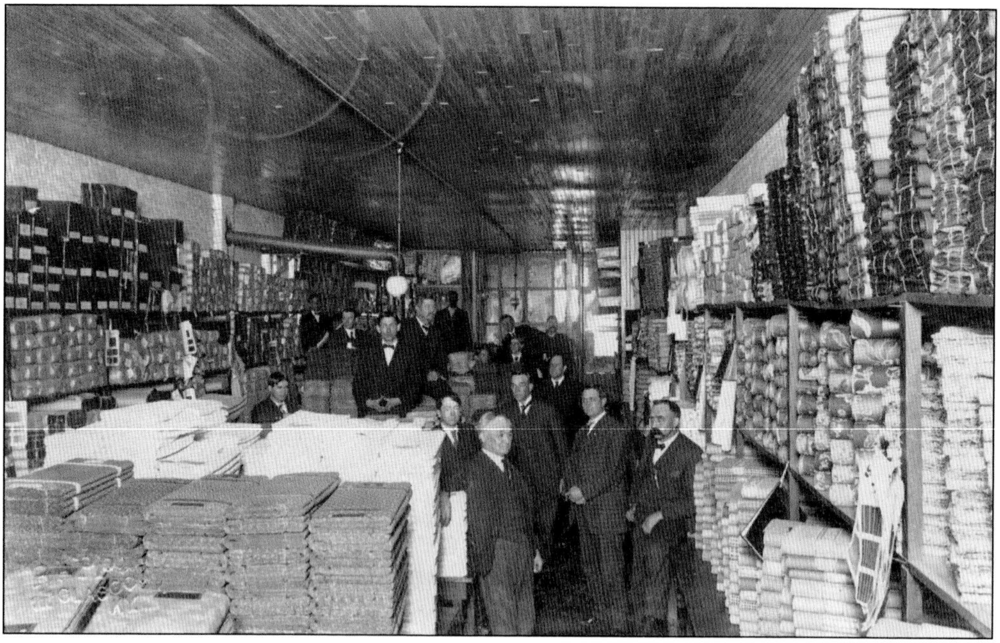

Dry goods stores of the late 19th and early 20th centuries provided a myriad of sights to bedazzle the eye. Store merchandise was limited only to the imagination and buying power of the owners, who vied for patrons in small towns such as Glasgow. (Both, courtesy South Central Kentucky Cultural Center.)

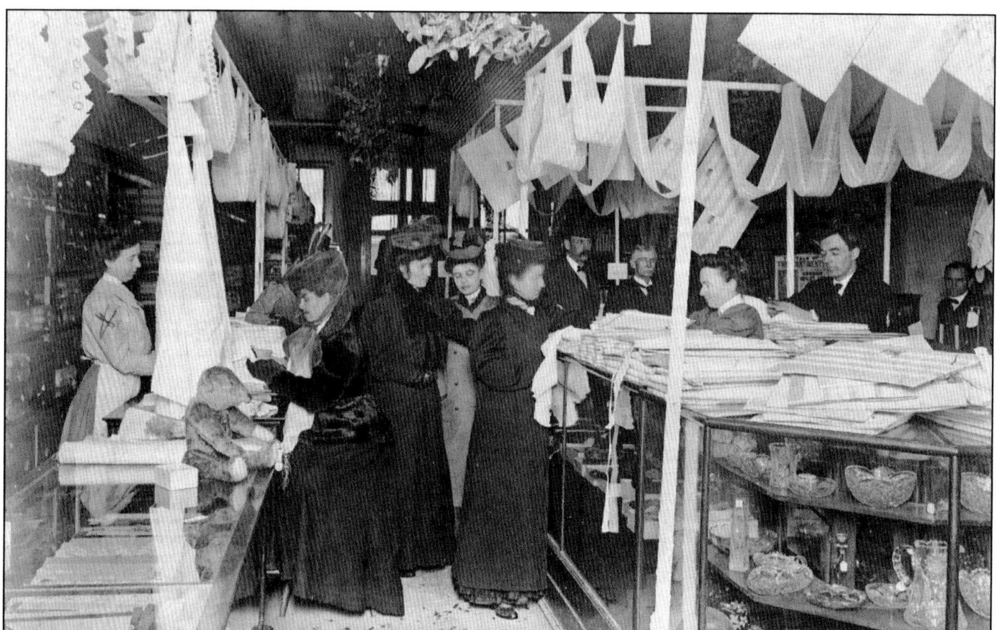

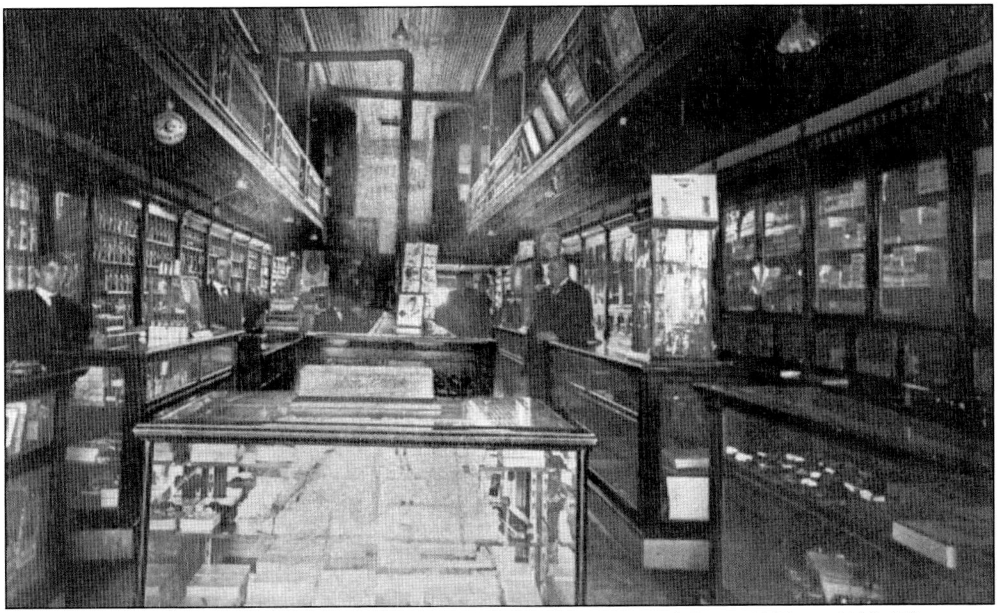

Leech and Ellis Drug Store on the East Public Square operated from 1899 to 1910. The store promoted Glasgow in new way: picture postcards of Glasgow scenes that were mailed from coast to coast and even overseas. The partnership split up, and Leech and Davis Drugs was formed in 1911 while the George J. Ellis Drug Company thrived on its own. (Courtesy author's collection.)

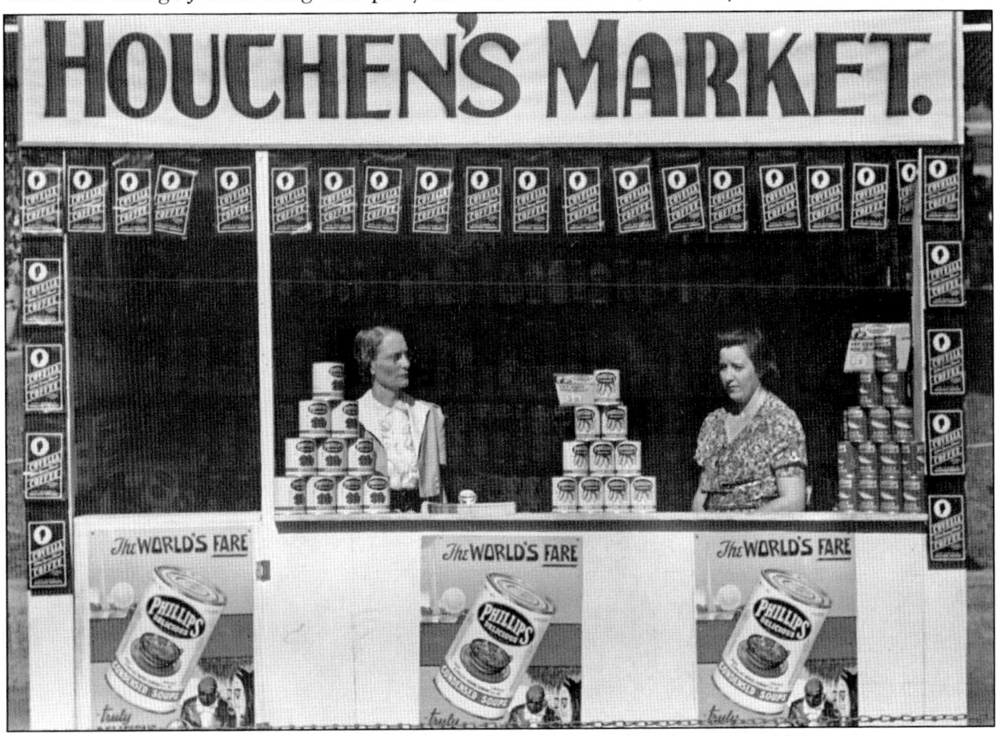

Mrs. Ervin G. Houchens is shown staffing a Houchen's Market booth at one of Glasgow's many street fairs. Ervin Houchens's first country store outside of Glasgow has now grown into a multifaceted corporation doing business in the United States and abroad. (Courtesy author's collection.)

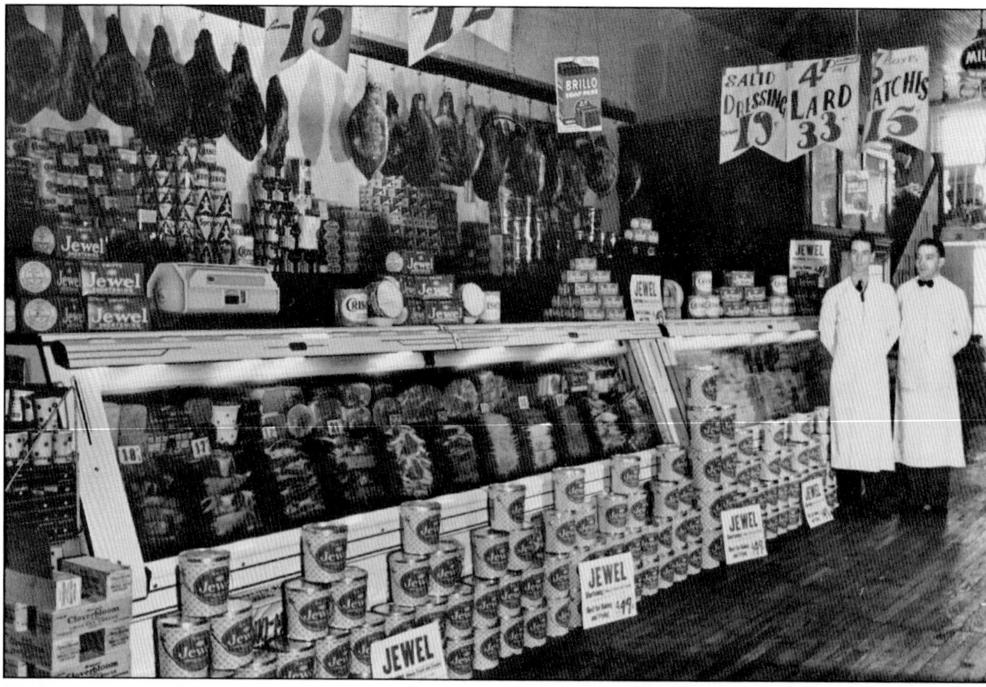

Early versions of grocery stores held a wide variety of merchandise for Glasgow and Barren County residents, as seen in this 1940s image captured by J. Mitchell Ellis. (Courtesy author's collection.)

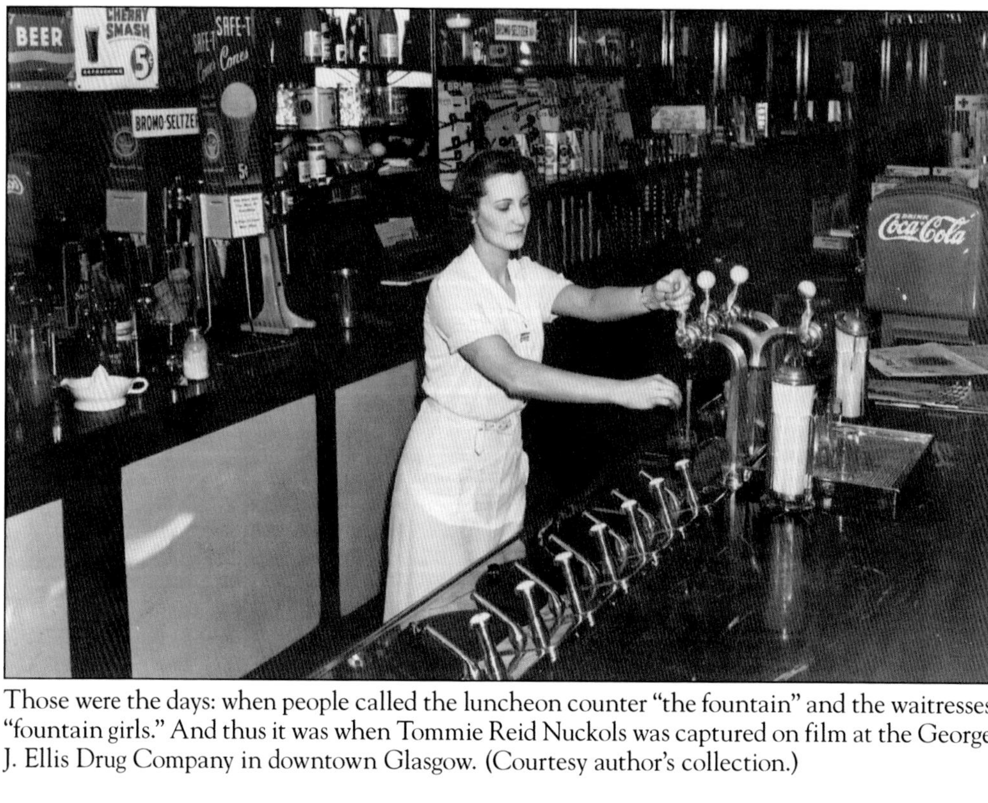

Those were the days: when people called the luncheon counter "the fountain" and the waitresses "fountain girls." And thus it was when Tommie Reid Nuckols was captured on film at the George J. Ellis Drug Company in downtown Glasgow. (Courtesy author's collection.)

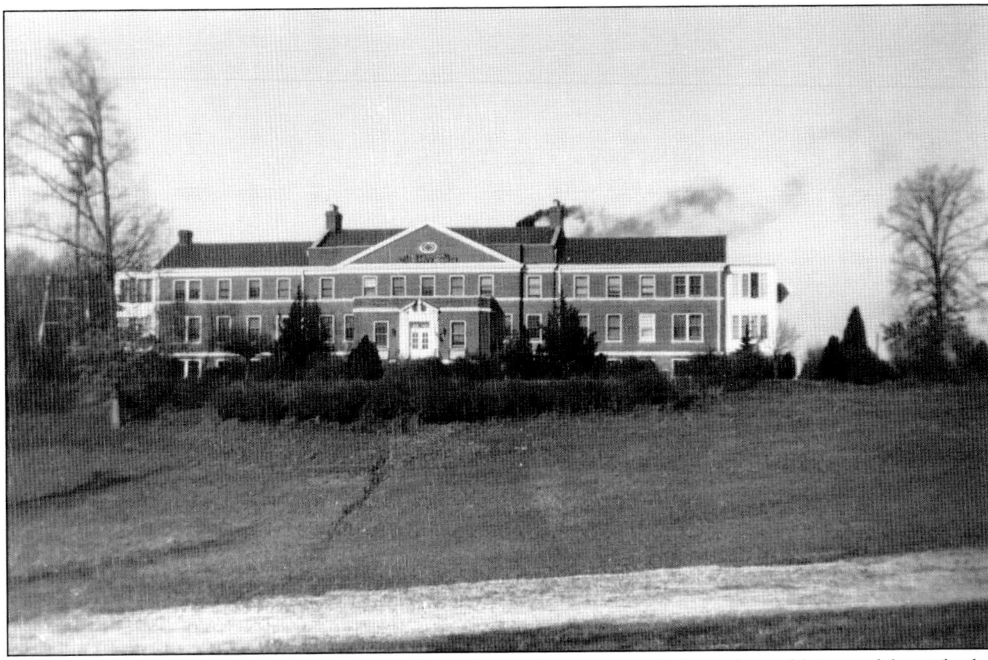

Thomas J. Samson made his fortune in the tobacco business and then shared his wealth with the community with a $25,000 gift to the community hospital that now bears his name: T. J. Samson Community Hospital. Since that 1929 gift, the hospital has grown exponentially, despite being in its original location. (Courtesy South Central Kentucky Cultural Center.)

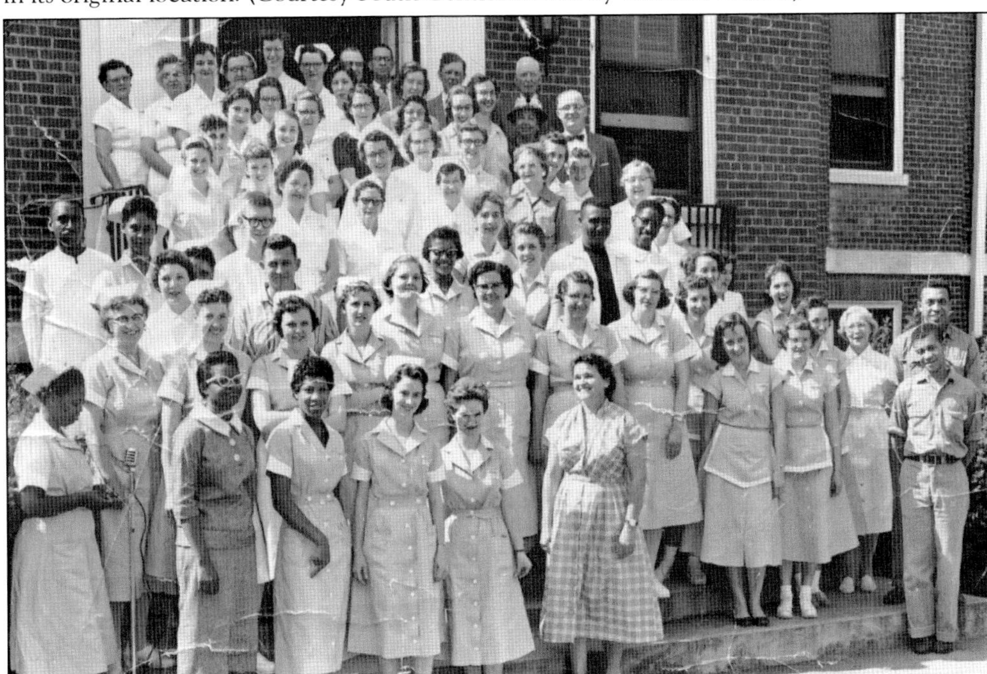

Today T. J. Samson Hospital is one of Glasgow's largest employers, a vast increase from the time this photograph of the hospital staff was made. (Courtesy South Central Kentucky Cultural Center.)

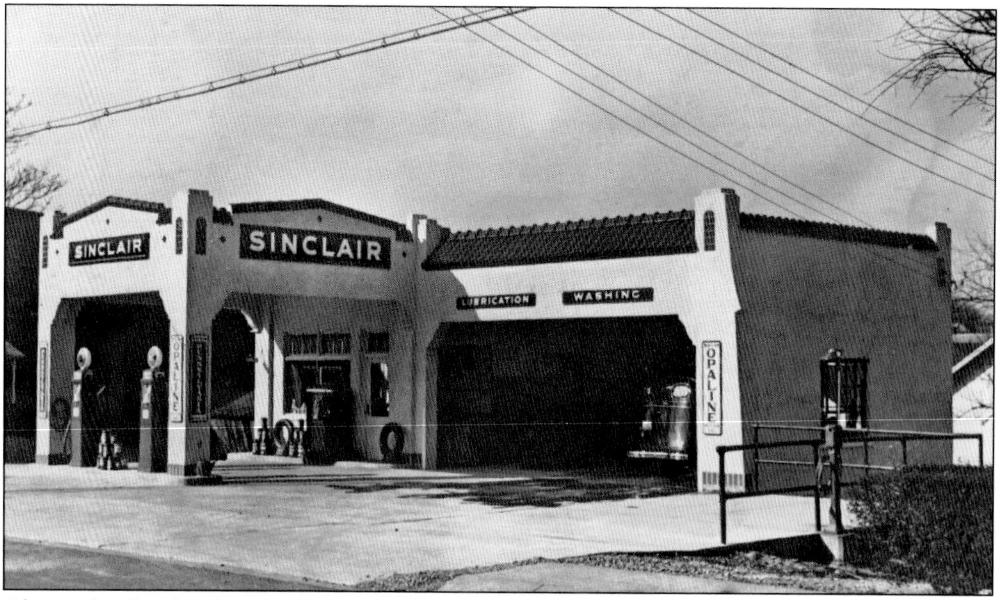

Above, this Sinclair Service Station was just one of many to pop up in Glasgow as the modern car and its necessary fuel became more widely used. The business was located on East Main Street in downtown Glasgow. A short distance away was the Gulf Service Station on the corner of North Race and Front Streets. Ironically, this mainstay to modernity shared the neighborhood with the historic Spotswood house, seen behind the service station. (Both, courtesy South Central Kentucky Cultural Center.)

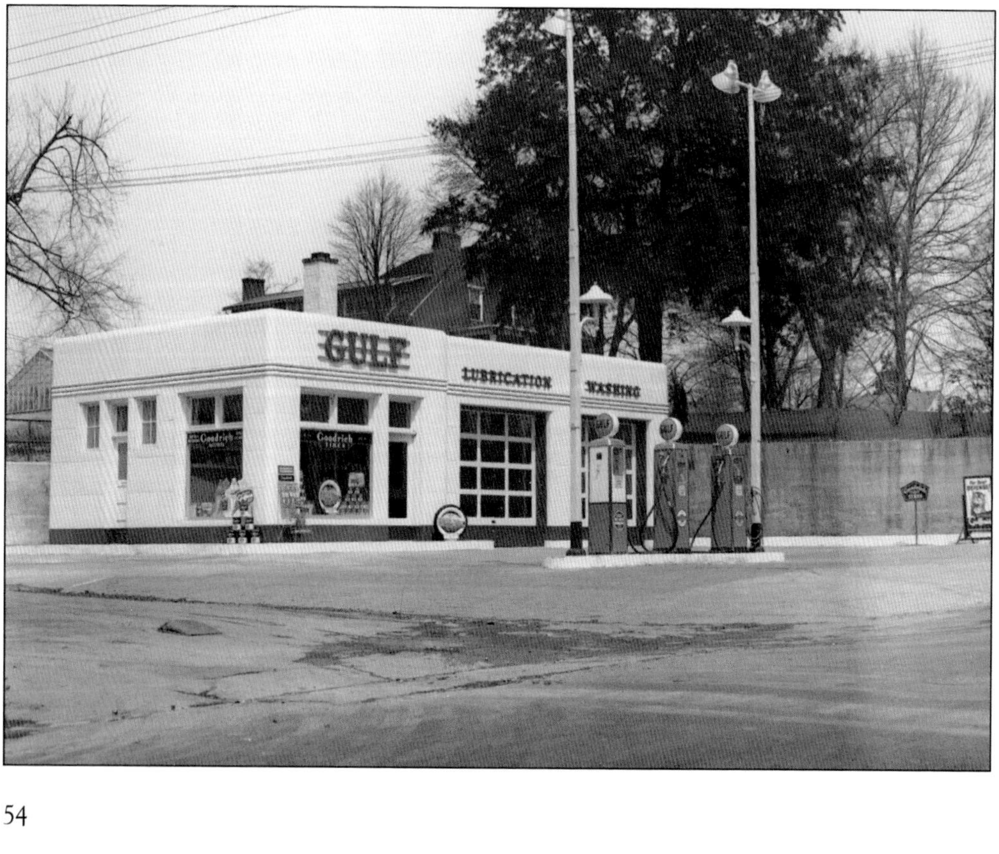

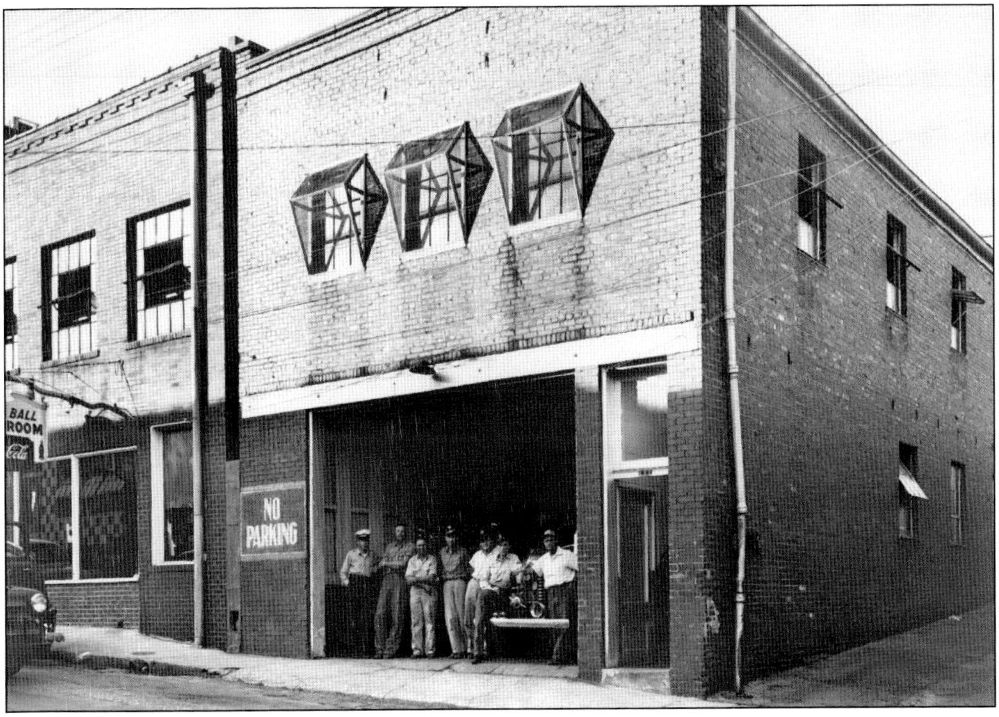

The Glasgow Fire Department building on Wayne Street was captured in this c. 1938 photograph also showing the department's staff. (Courtesy South Central Kentucky Cultural Center.)

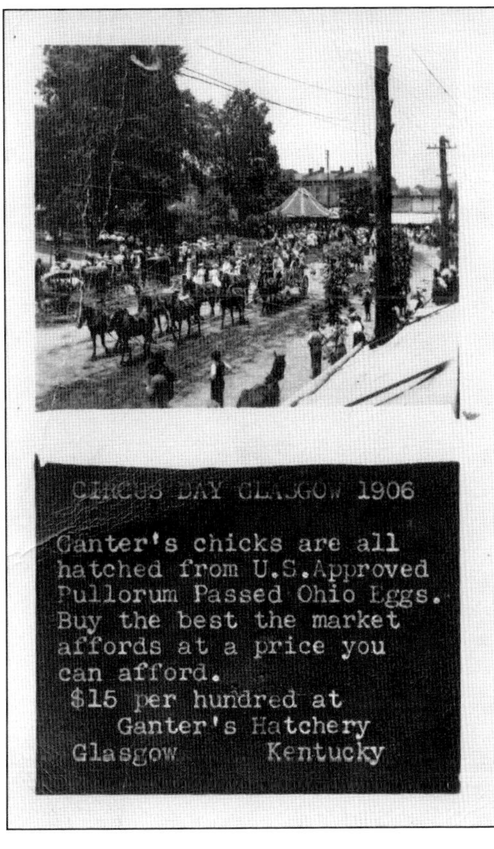

Depicted here is Circus Day in Glasgow in 1906. The typewritten message on the card explains the situation. (Courtesy South Central Kentucky Cultural Center.)

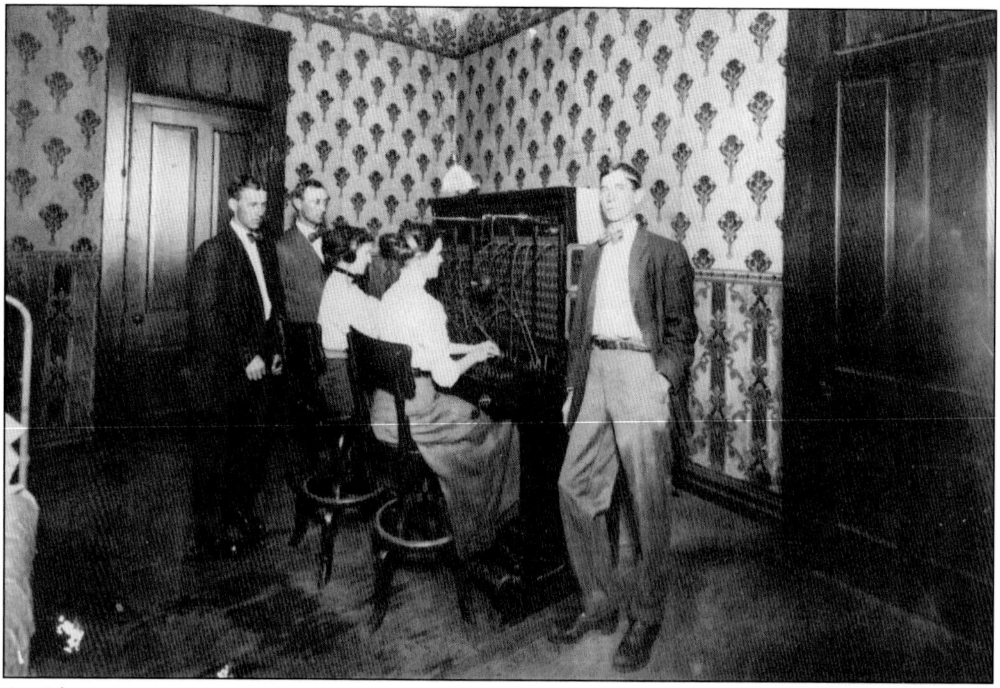

As Glasgow grew into modern conveniences, one necessary worker was the telephone operator. The back of this image simply notes "Aunt Gus and Clyde Nelson" at the switchboard. (Courtesy South Central Kentucky Cultural Center.)

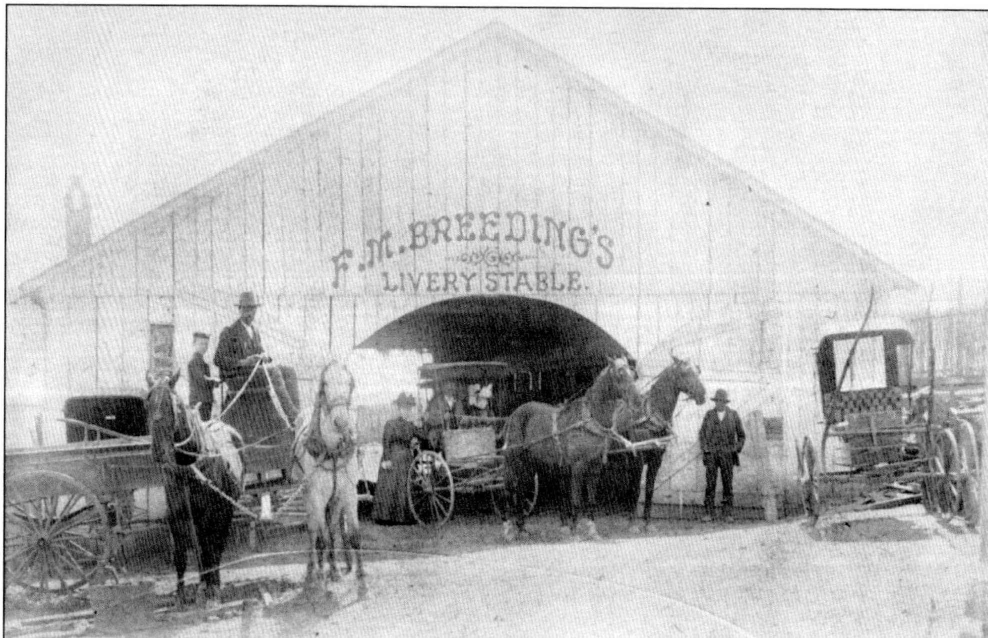

Finis M. Breeding's Livery Stable was but one of several in Glasgow that provided a necessary service to Glasgow's residents and visitors. The image is filled with what were likely Breeding's best offerings of carriages and conveyances available to his patrons. (Courtesy South Central Kentucky Cultural Center.)

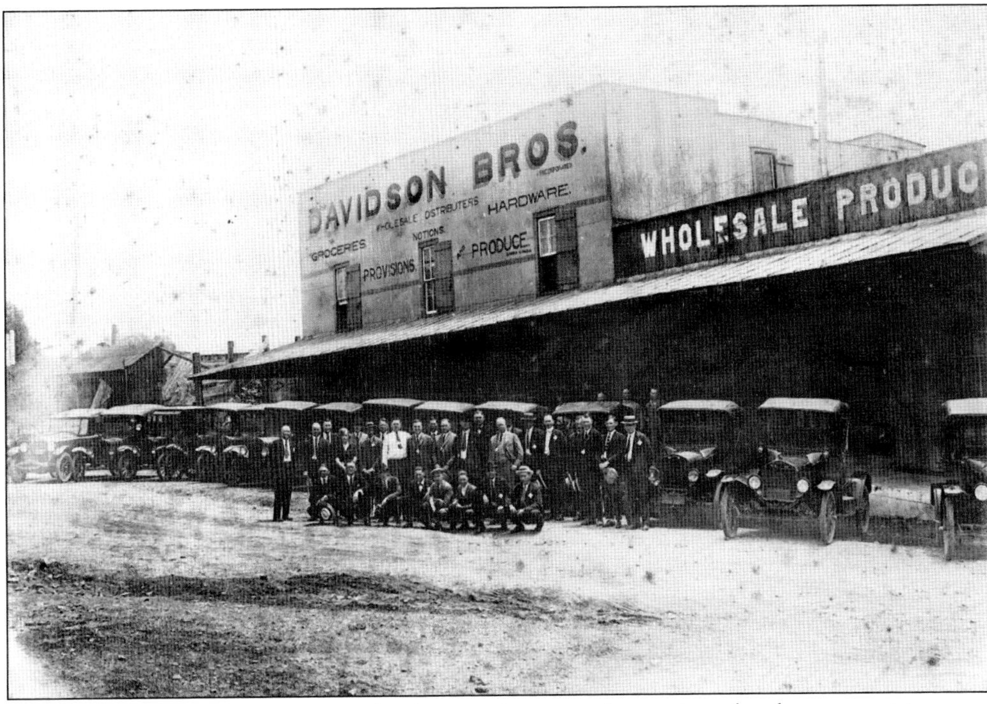

Davidson Brothers was a major wholesaler carrying groceries, notions, hardware, provisions, and produce as noted in the above image. Below, the unnamed sales force gathered for dinner and a photograph—ironically, most of the gentlemen have their eyes closed. (Both, courtesy South Central Kentucky Cultural Center.)

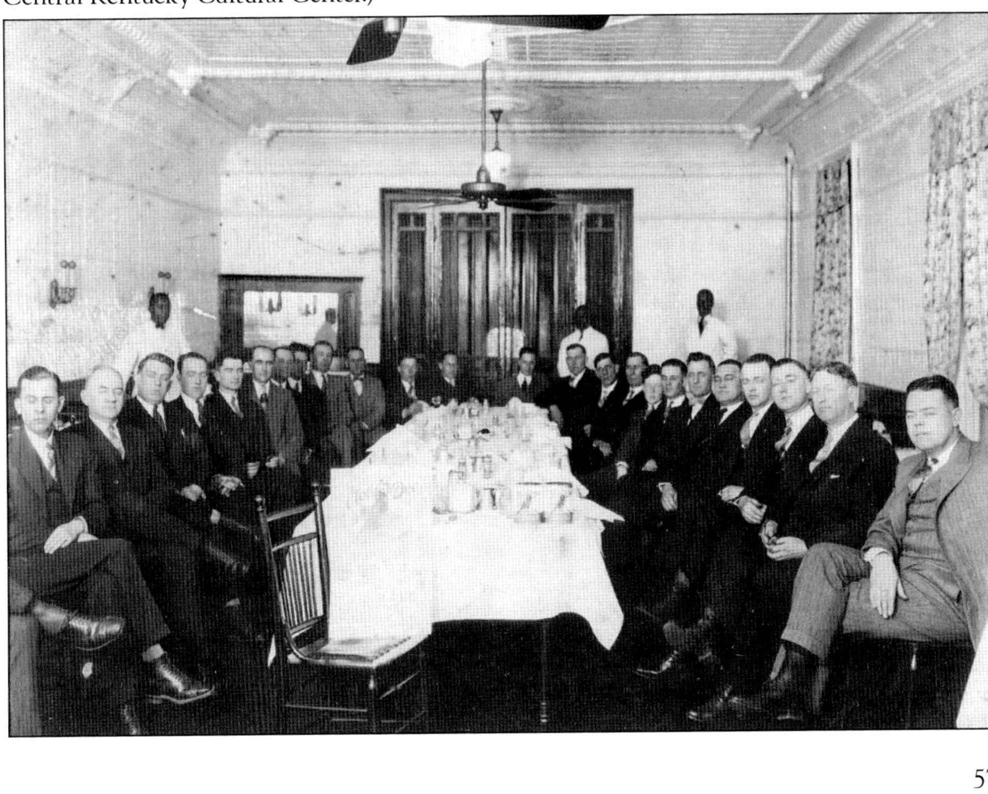

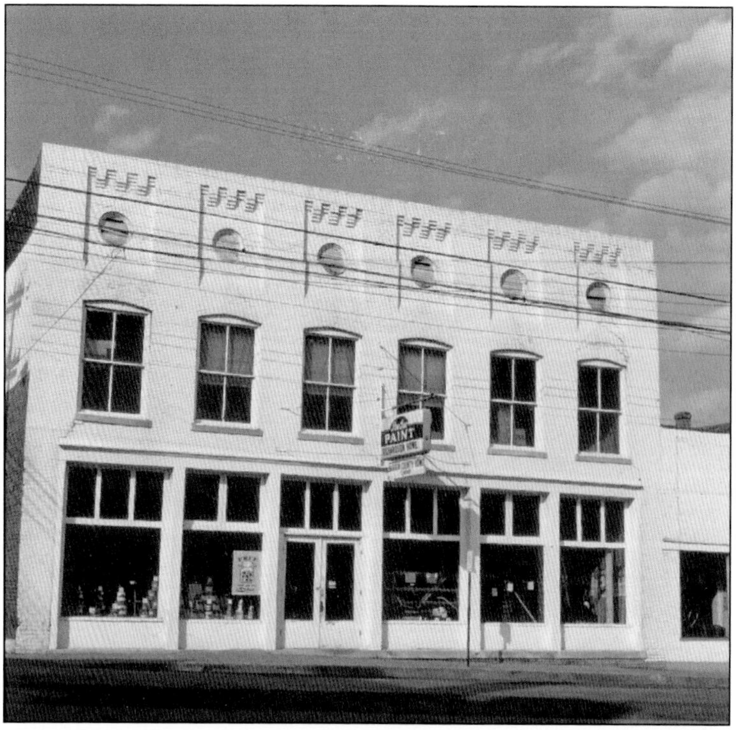

Richardson Hardware was located on East Washington Street, where for several decades Barren Countians could find a plethora of hardware needs for the home, farm, and business. (Courtesy South Central Kentucky Cultural Center.)

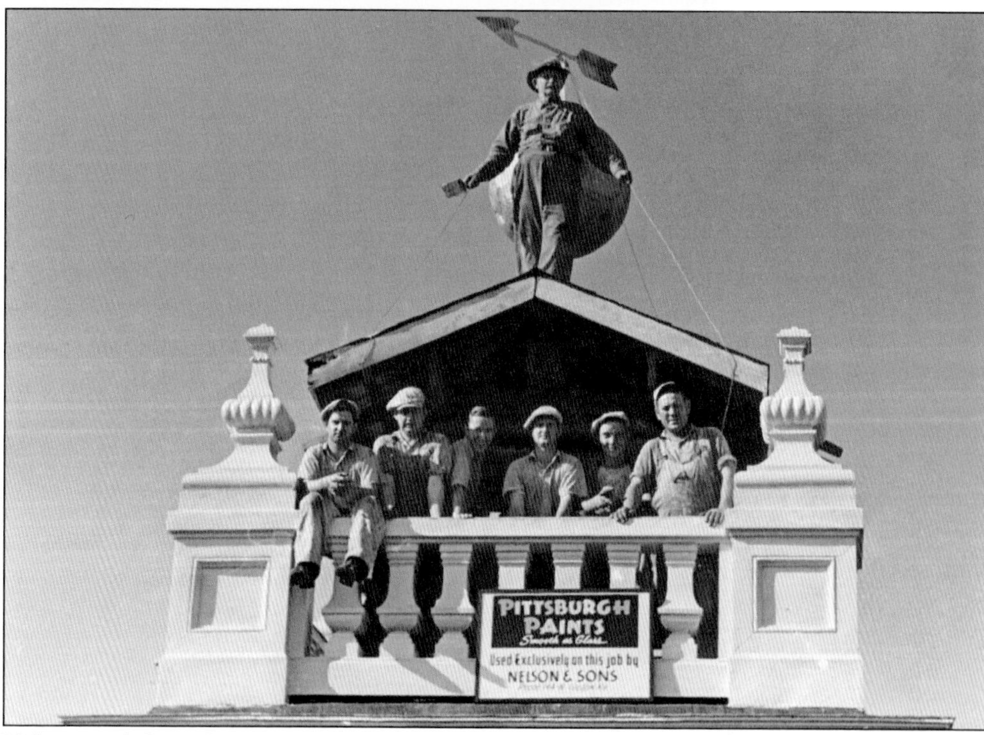

Nelson and Sons Painting crew posed atop the old courthouse cupola promoting their work and Pittsburg Paints. John "Pa" Nelson stands on top of the cupola roof. (Courtesy author's collection.)

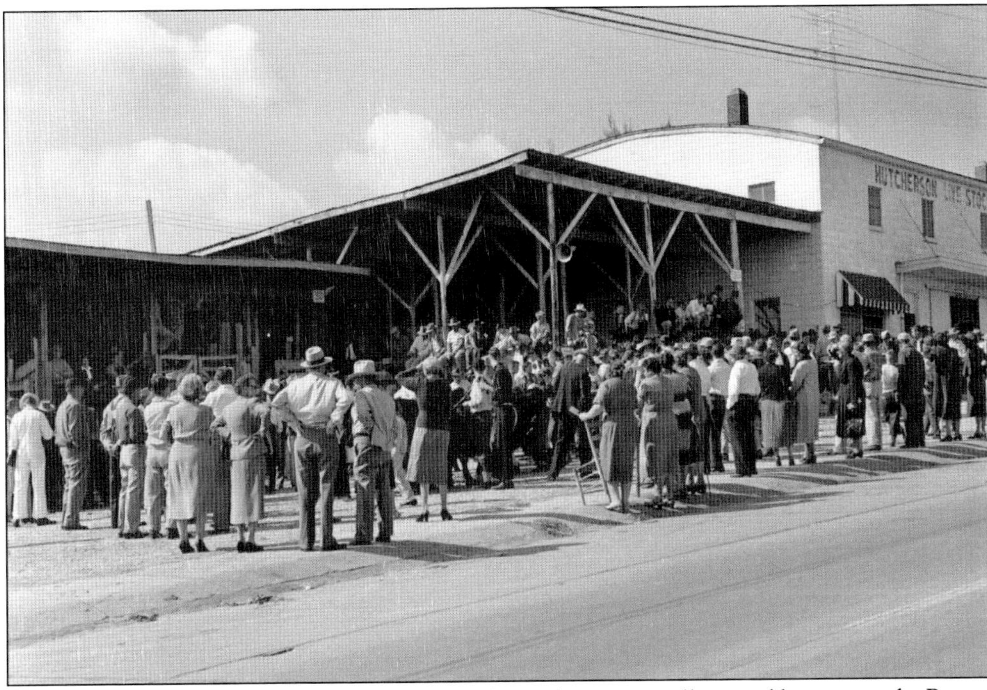

Hutcherson Livestock Market in Glasgow aided area farmers in selling and buying cattle. Barren County remains the top dairy producing and top beef producing county in the commonwealth. (Courtesy author's collection.)

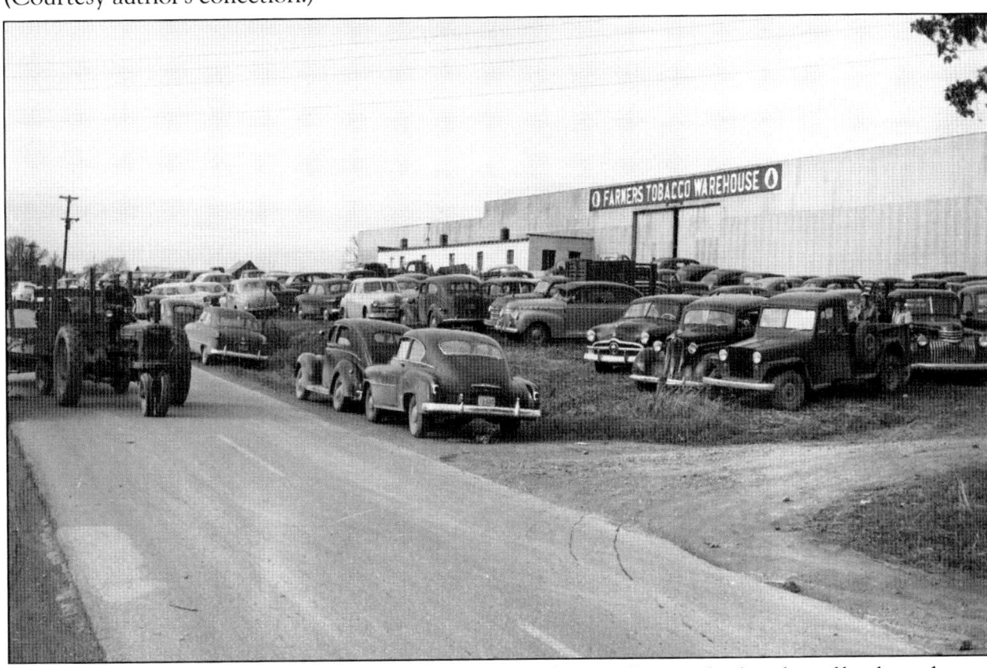

Farmer's Tobacco Warehouse was one of several in Glasgow during the heyday of burley tobacco. The Glasgow tobacco market was considered one of the best in Kentucky for gaining top prices. Barren County was the top burley tobacco producing county in Kentucky. (Courtesy South Central Kentucky Cultural Center.)

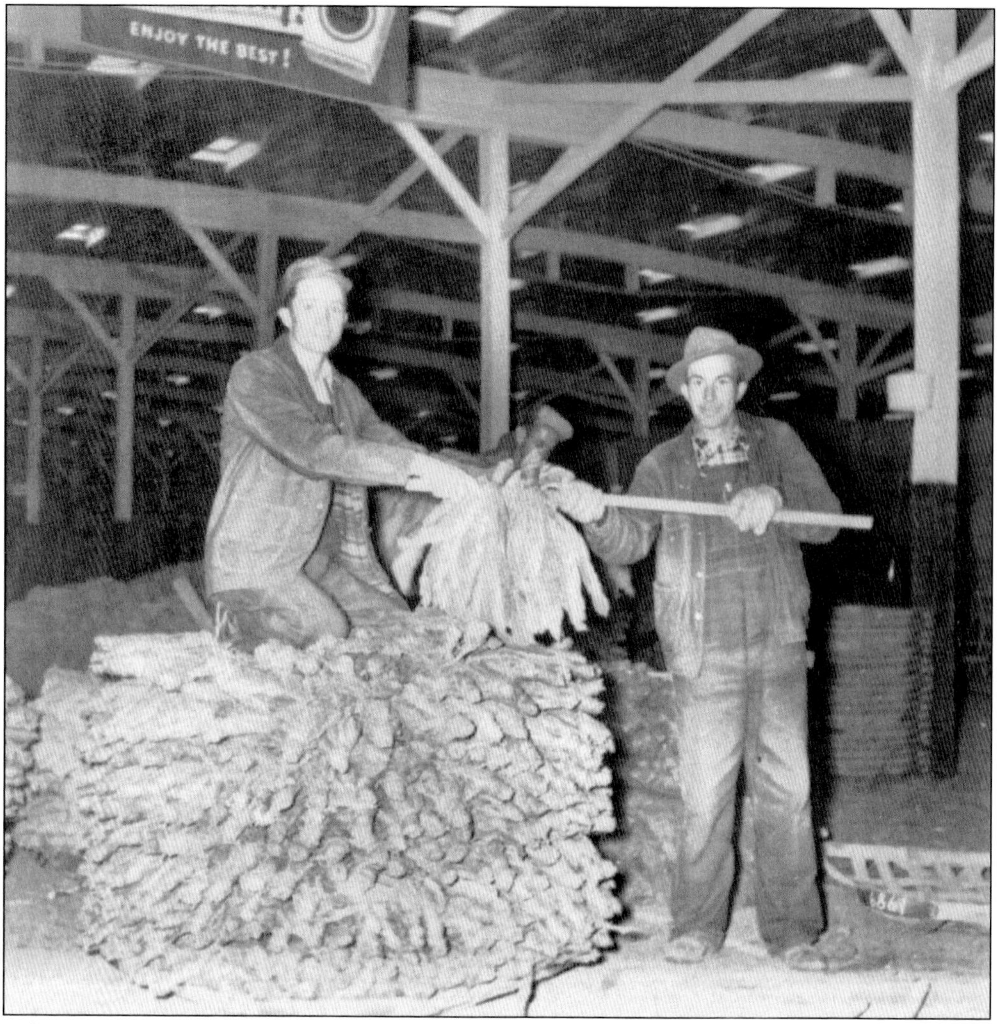

Tobacco provided livelihood for many Barren County farm families, but that extended to other laborers on farms as well as in tobacco warehouses and processing plants. Here tobacco workers remove hands of tobacco from the stick to be packed into baskets for sale at auction time. (Courtesy the Kentucky Library.)

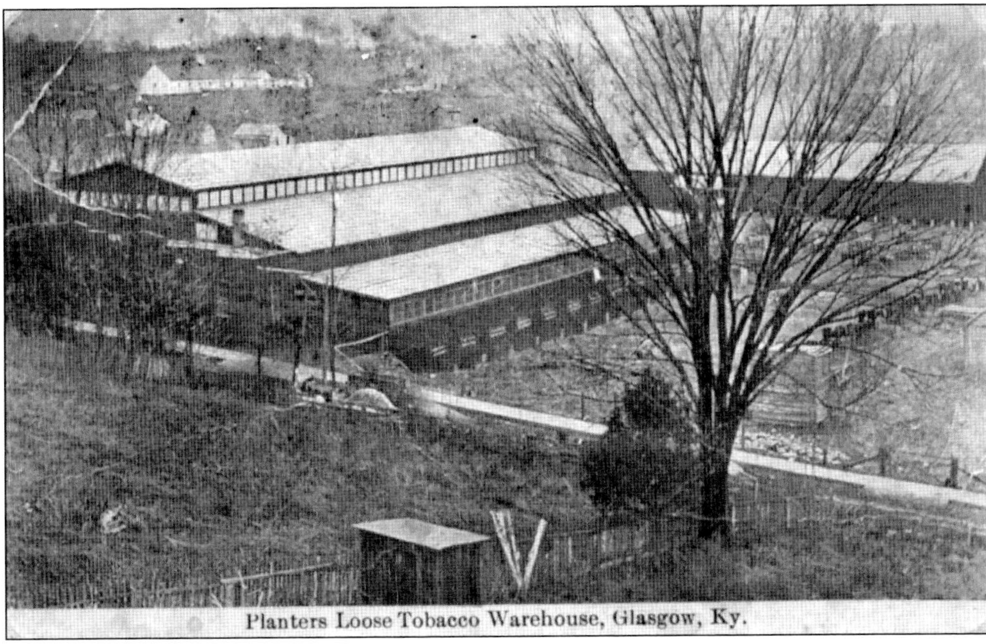

Planters Loose Tobacco Warehouse used picture postcards to promote its services to area farmers, from the impressive exterior spread to the thoroughly up-to-date interior. (Both, courtesy South Central Kentucky Cultural Center.)

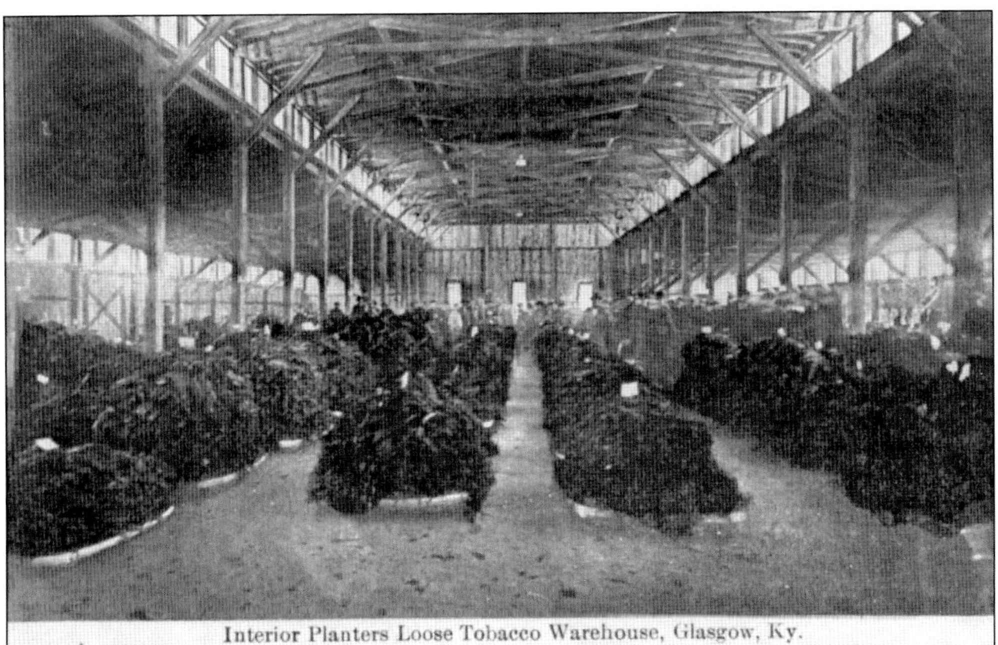

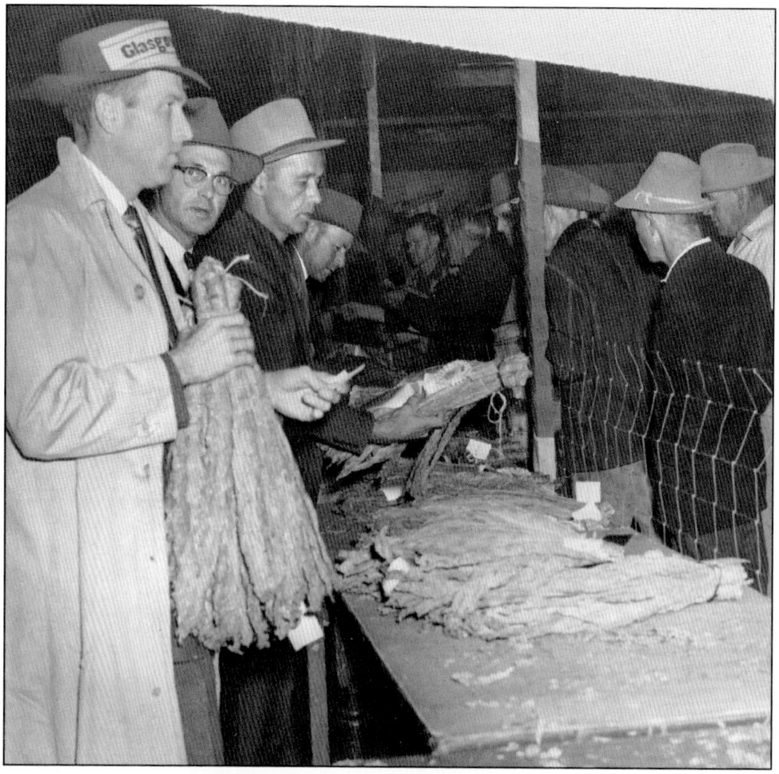

Tobacco buyers, such as Phil Wells (left), might work local markets but also use their expertise in other areas of the country, such as North Carolina and Virginia, as well. (Courtesy South Central Kentucky Cultural Center.)

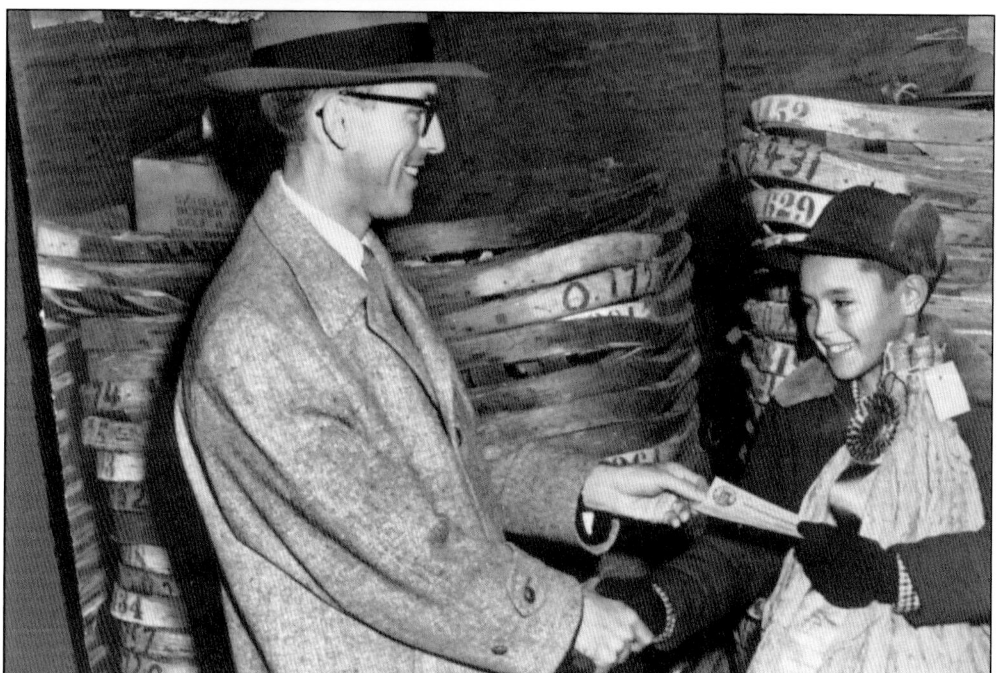

Excellence in tobacco production extended to 4-H and Future Farmers of America organizations. Here Rotary Club president Lyle Snavely presents a U.S. Savings Bond as a premium for a youth tobacco project. (Courtesy author's collection.)

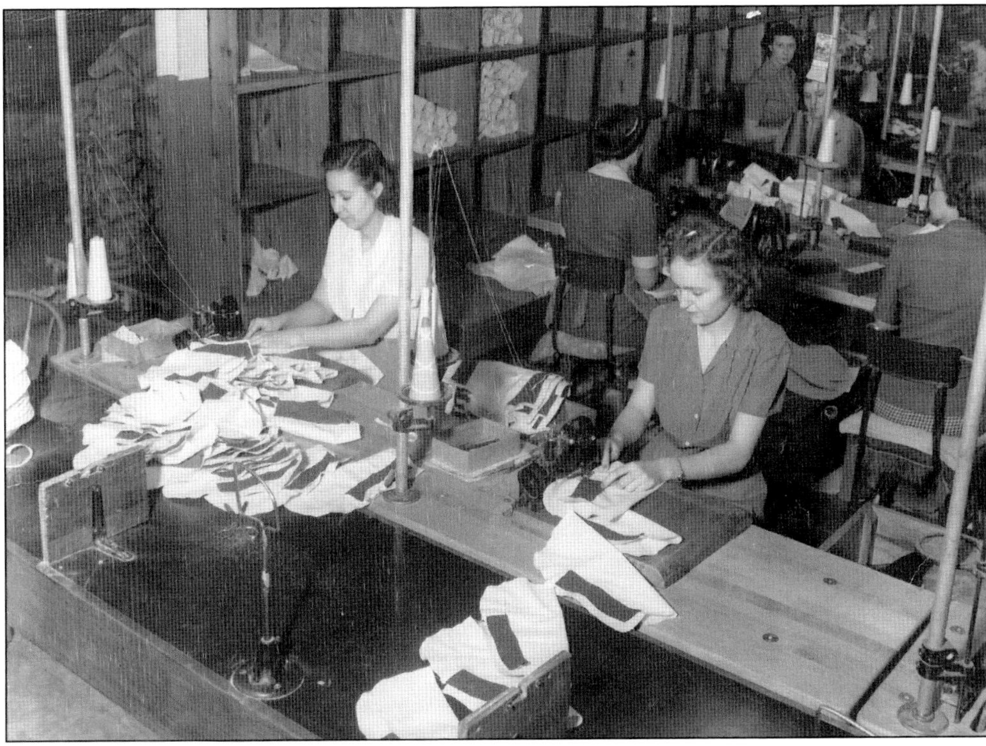

The Kentucky Pants Factory opened in 1929 and provided many women with sewing jobs for several decades. The building is now the renovated South Central Kentucky Cultural Center. (Both, courtesy South Central Kentucky Cultural Center.)

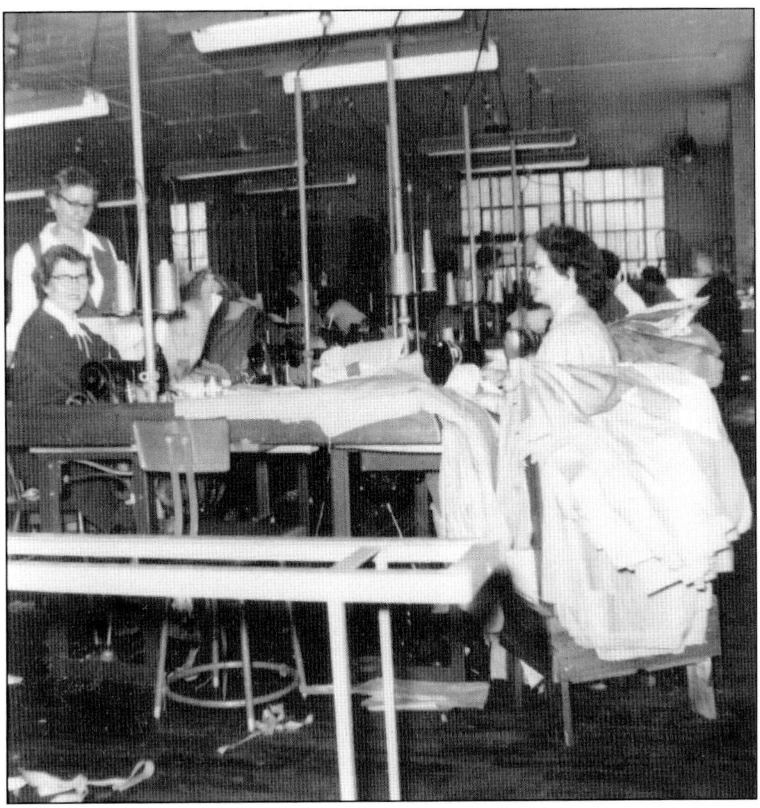

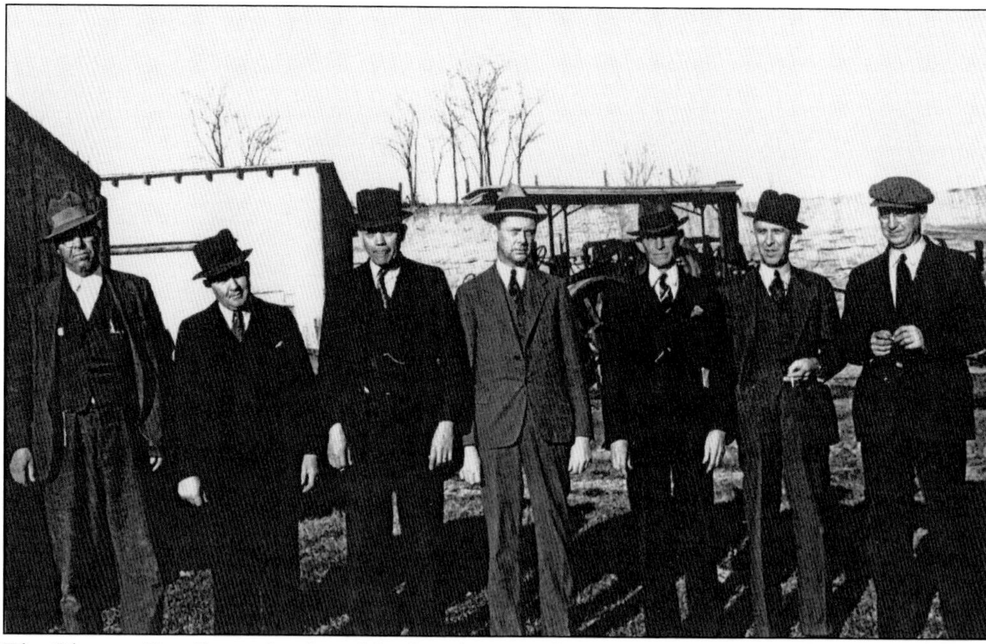

The Glasgow City Council gathered for this photograph in 1938. From left to right are councilmen J. D. Walbert, George W. Pedigo, and Ernest Leech Myers Sr.; Mayor Winn Davis; and councilmen O. F. Curd Sr., Mosby Woodson, and Bruce Aspley. (Courtesy author's collection.)

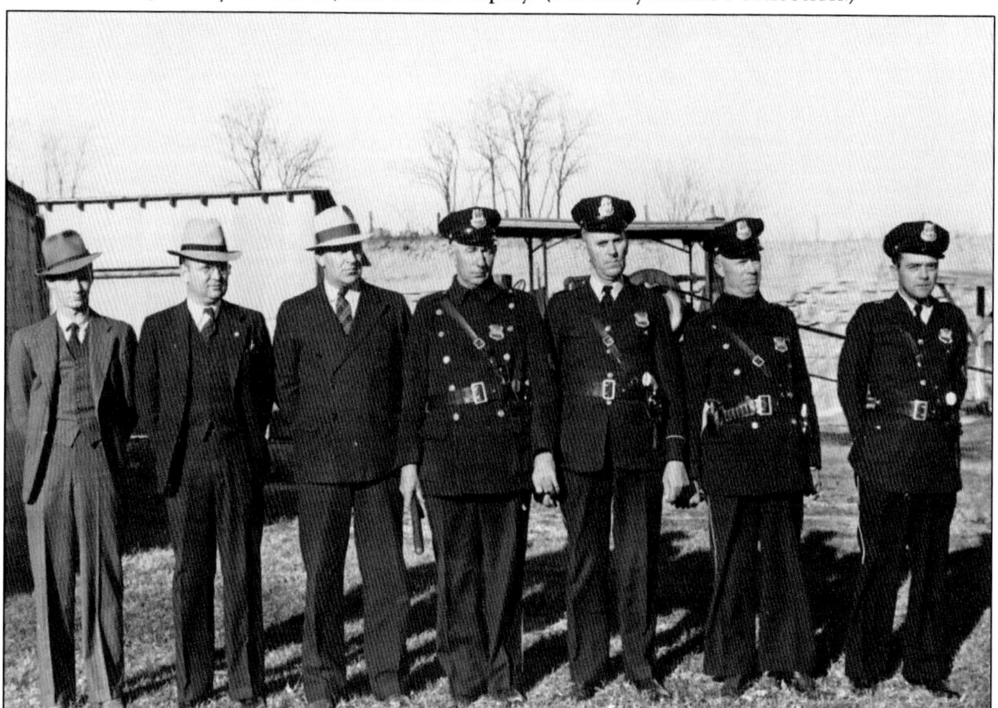

Also gathered in 1938 was the Glasgow Police Force. From left to right are Aubrey Crow, assistant city clerk; George J. Ellis Jr., city judge; George B. Berry, chief of police; and policemen Pate Walkup, Luther Lowe, Melvin Cravens, and Jake Eatman. (Courtesy author's collection.)

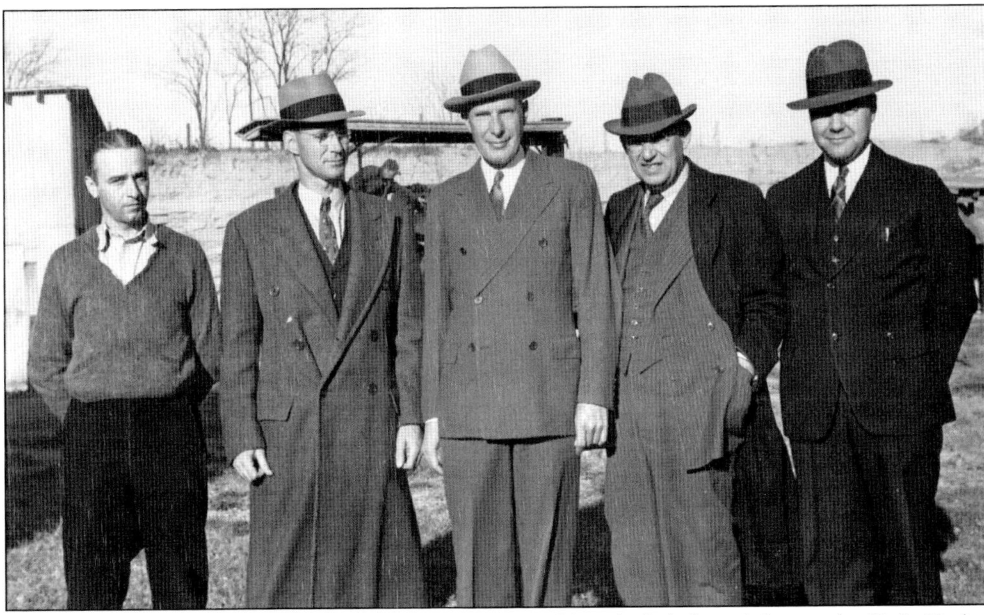

The Glasgow Water Commission and assistants in 1938 included, from left to right, E. L. Kerley, auditor; R. L. Beatty, manager; and commissioners R. H. Norris, Brice R. Leech, and Terry L. Hatchett. (Courtesy author's collection.)

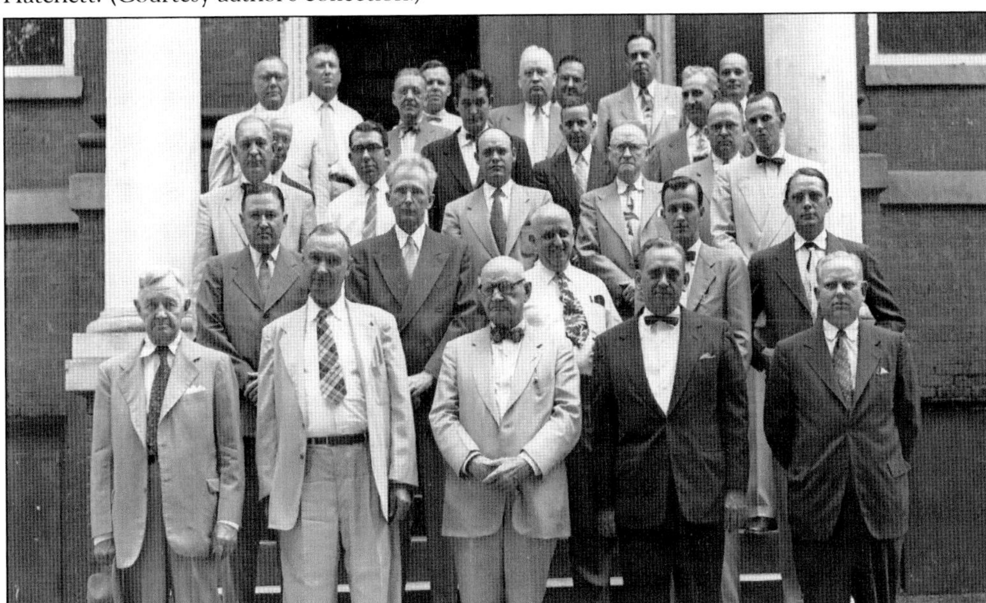

Members of the Bar gathered at the September 1952 Barren Circuit Court for this photograph. Shown are, from left to right, (first row) V. H. Jones, Paul Greer, Robert White, Cecil Wilson, and Carroll M. Redford Sr.; (second row) Frank Jones, Basil Preston, Richard Garnett, Harry Berry, and William Beatty Jones; (third row) Brents Dickinson, Uhel O. Barrickman, J. Wood Vance Jr., Will Jones, and Jack Longshore; (fourth row) J. Martin of Edmonton, John Richardson, Marion Vance, Maxie Harlin of Bowling Green, George J. Ellis Jr., and Phil Wilson; (fifth row) Terry L. Hatchett, P. Carter of Tompkinsville, James Gillenwater, Ross Settle, L. Logan of Bowling Green, R. M. Coleman of Bowling Green, and Cass Walden. (Courtesy author's collection.)

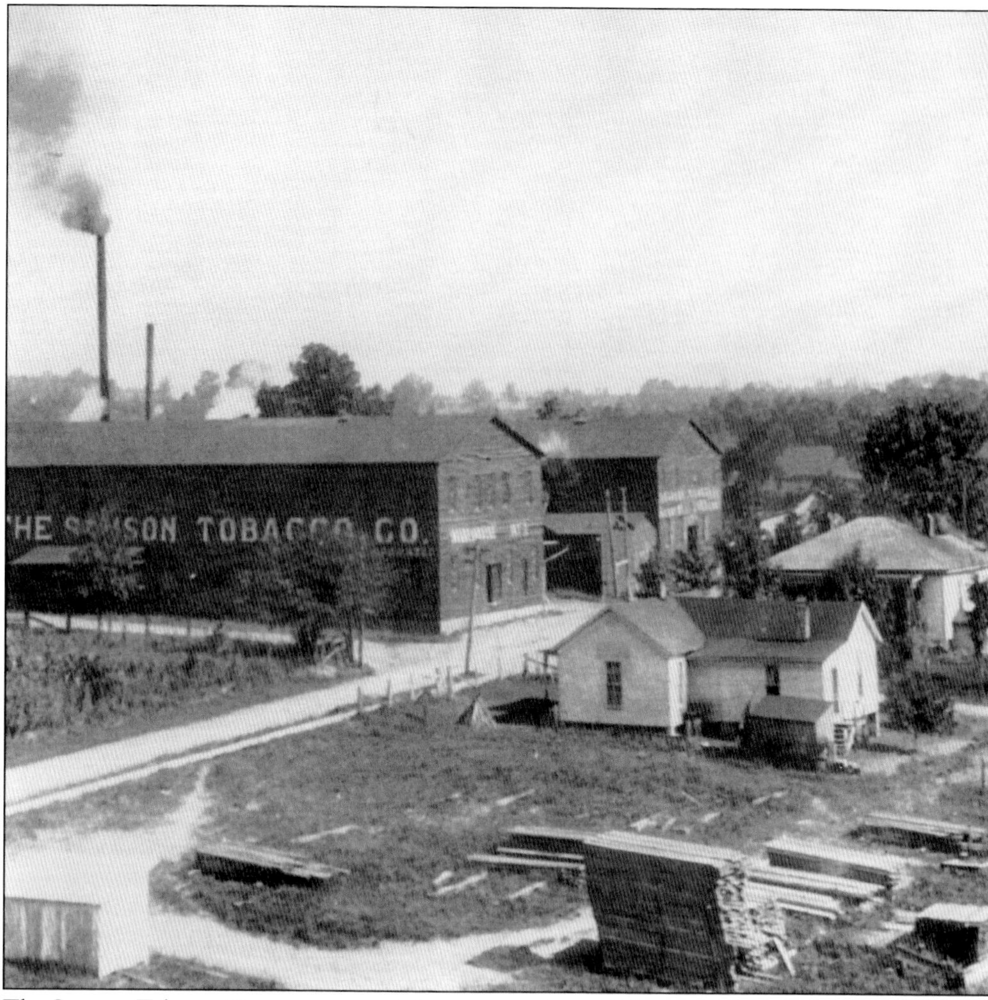

The Samson Tobacco Company occupied a vast area just off Glasgow's West Main Street corridor. T. J. Samson used his good fortune to help establish the T. J. Samson Community Hospital. (Courtesy author's collection.)

Four

AT WORSHIP IN GLASGOW

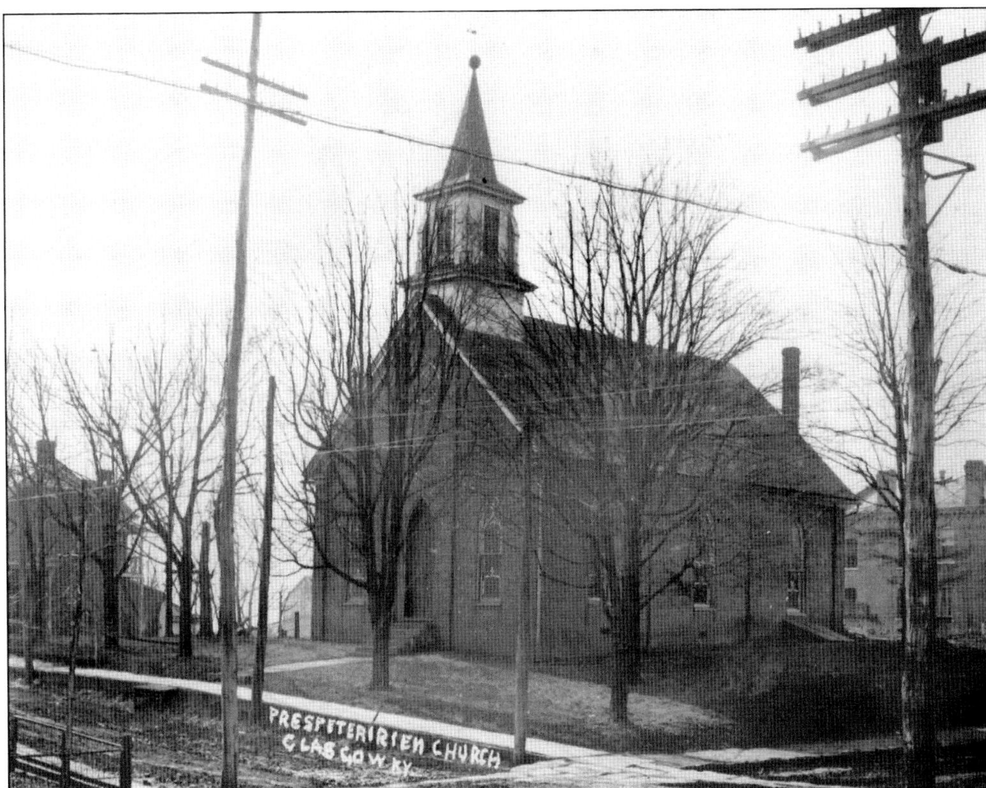

Organized in 1802, First Presbyterian Church was the first religious group organized following the designation of Glasgow as county seat. The congregation was the only religious group in Glasgow for several years and the only house of worship for nearly 25 years. This is the third structure to house the congregation and dates to 1853; it is one of few Gothic Revival buildings remaining in south-central Kentucky. (Courtesy author's collection.)

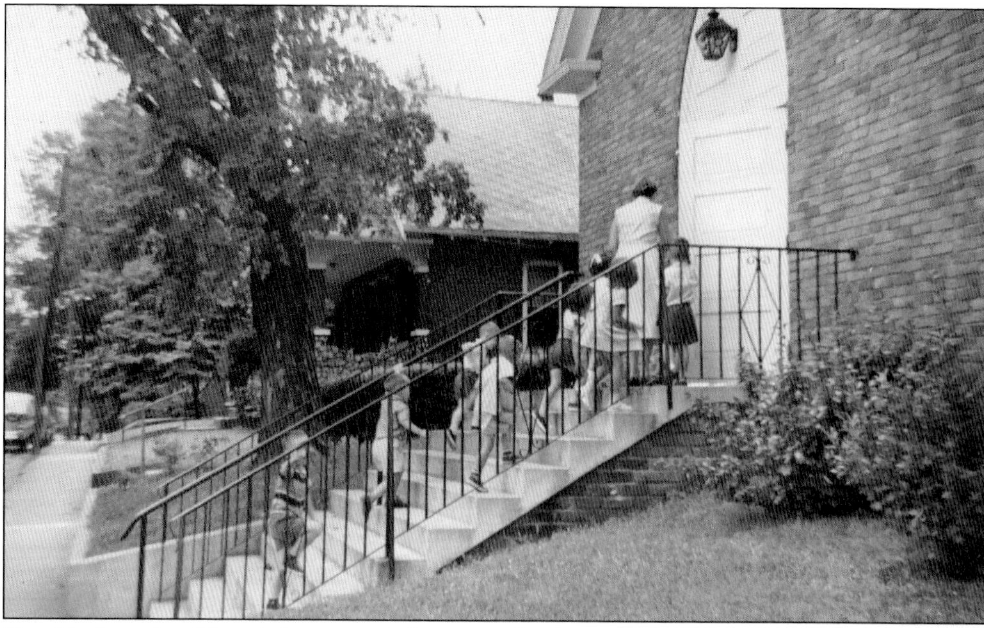

First Presbyterian Church has occupied its same lot since 1802, when it was donated by Isaac Robertson, a member. The 1850s building was enlarged in 1929 with an education wing, a project that caused Glasgow's first burying ground to be moved to make way for the expansion. Another enlargement and renovation occurred in 1953 and produced a front vestibule addition. (Courtesy First Presbyterian Church.)

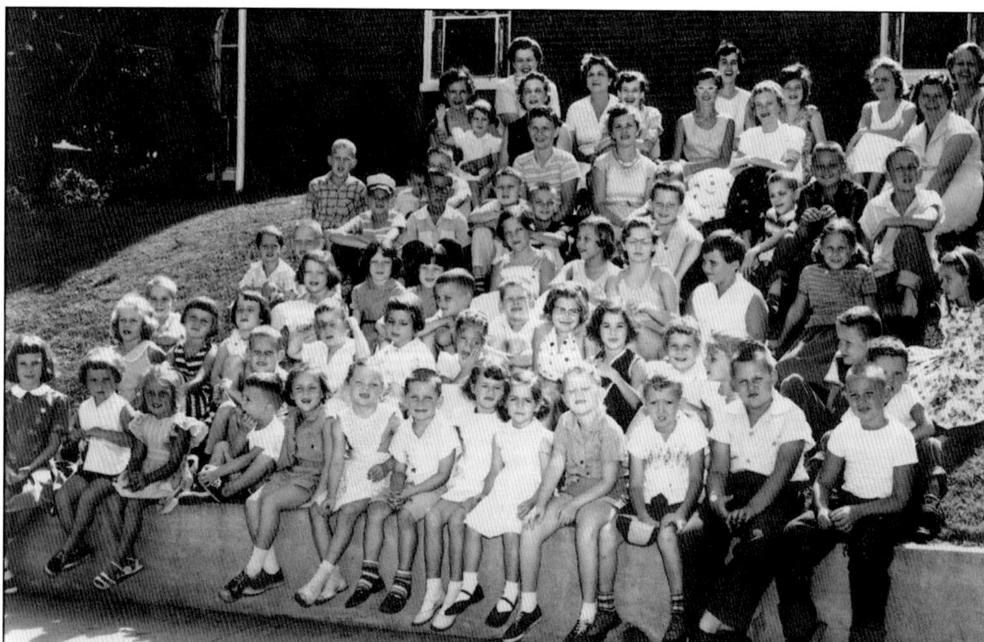

As with most churches in the post–World War II era, First Presbyterian Church saw an explosion of young families coming through its doors. This photograph captures a 1950s Vacation Bible School group posed on the side lawn of the church building during the pastorate of William L. Huntsman. (Courtesy First Presbyterian Church.)

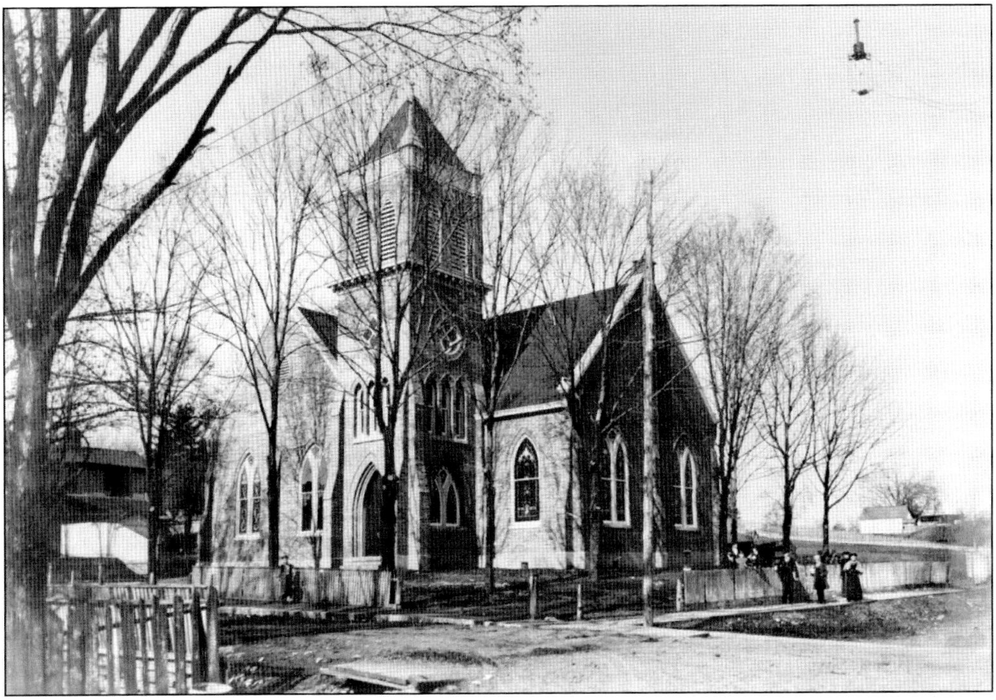

Glasgow Baptist Church is the second oldest religious group in town, tracing its organization to 1818. These images are of the congregation's second structure, which was dedicated in 1895. The lot on which the church stands was donated by Richard Garnett. (Above, courtesy author's collection; below, courtesy South Central Kentucky Cultural Center.)

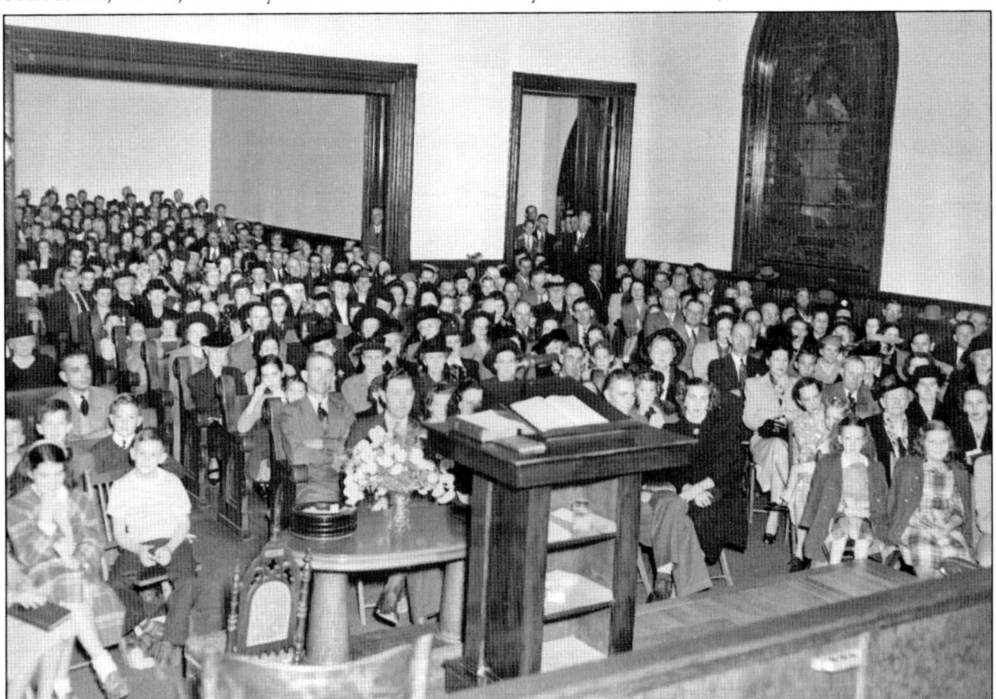

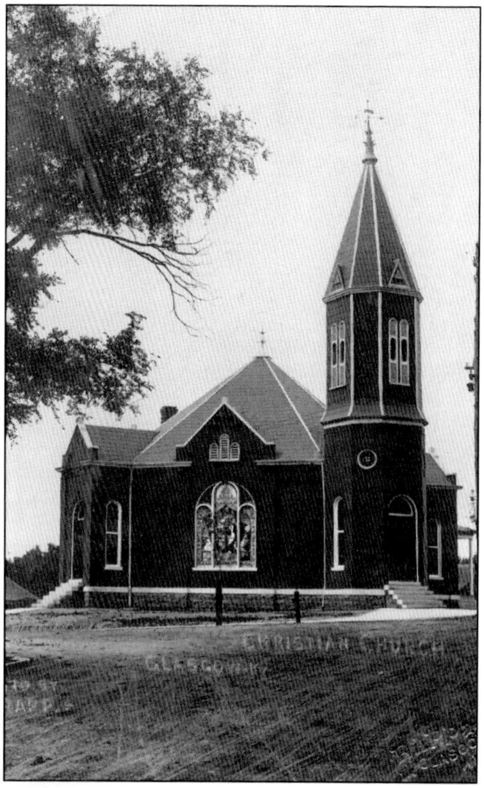

Glasgow's First Christian Church was organized in 1830, following efforts by the Reverend Alexander Campbell, thus the nickname "Campbellites" refers to Campbell's followers. The first and second houses of worship erected by the group were located on South Green Street (present-day Church of Christ) at the corner of Wayne Street. The "church on the square," as it was lovingly called, was dedicated in 1902 when First Christian and Second Christian Churches reunited. (Courtesy author's collection.)

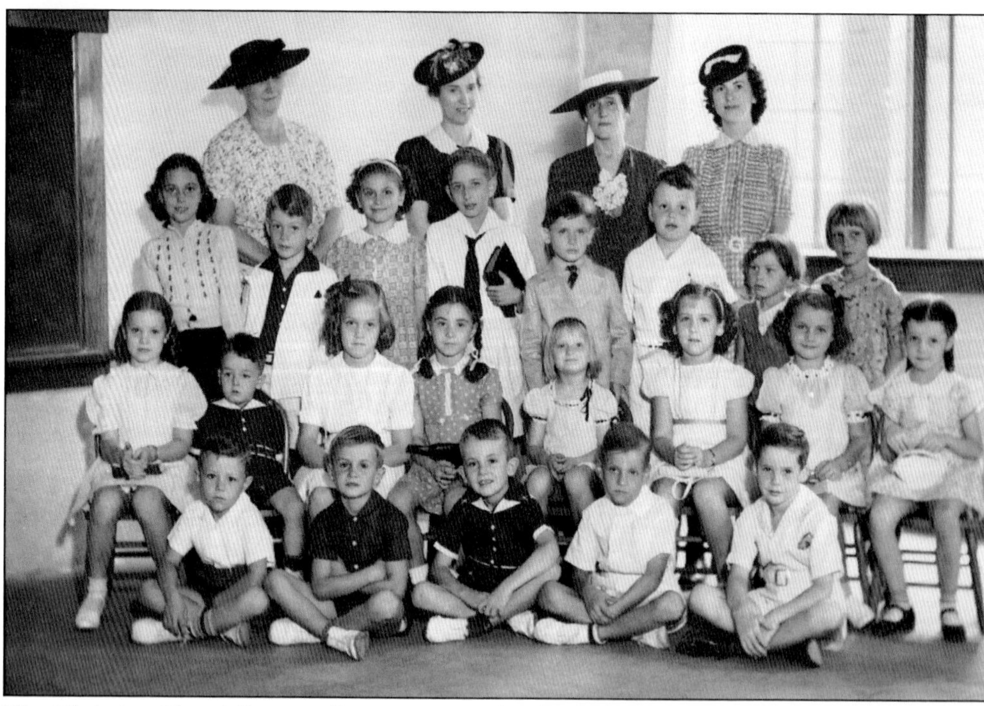

The Christian Church Primary Department under the direction of Ruth Terry Fant gathered for this photograph in the 1940s. (Courtesy author's collection.)

The Coombs Bible Class of First Christian Church sat for this composite photograph of class members in 1933–1934. Beginning at the top left to right, the gentlemen included Ernest Houck, P. L. Samson, R. E. Courtney, Joe Wade, G. W. Reynolds, J. D. Smoot, Col. W. J. Ford, J. W. Gramlin, J. B. Bunch, K. Y. Boyd, A. R. Vaughn, Cass R. Walden, J. T. Frank, Burley Neeley, Louie P. Stout, J. T. Sherfey, Flem Harrison, Dr. Palmore, B. C. Baker, M. R. Wilkinson, Curtis Jump, William Henry Jones, W. C. Turner, Judge J. F. Allen, D. W. Wilson, W. L. Porter, Ernest Myers, Alvin A. Berry, Paul D. Bushong, V. H. Baird, Dr. P. S. York, L. T. Oliver, John H. Beals, C. A. Turner, Brice Leech, Dr. Turner, W. P. Mansfield, O. F. Curd, G. H. Fant, Lewis W. Jones, Rev. T. H. Alderson, Dr. C. C. Howard, and T. R. Palmore. (Courtesy South Central Kentucky Cultural Center.)

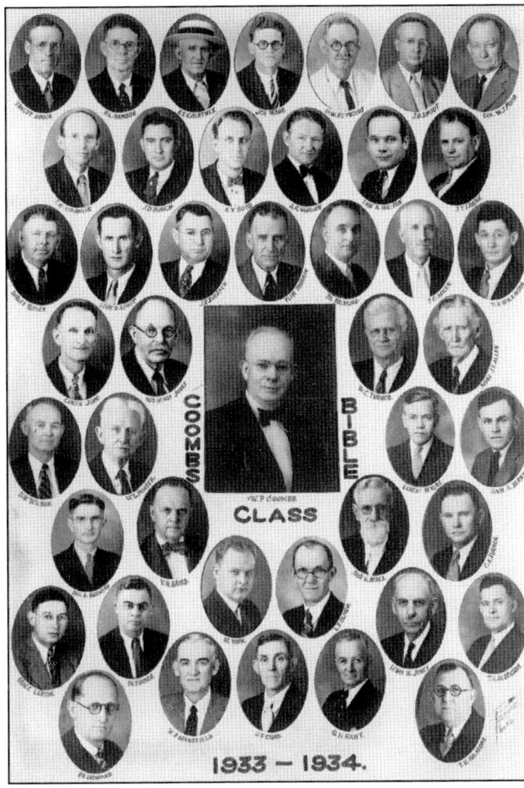

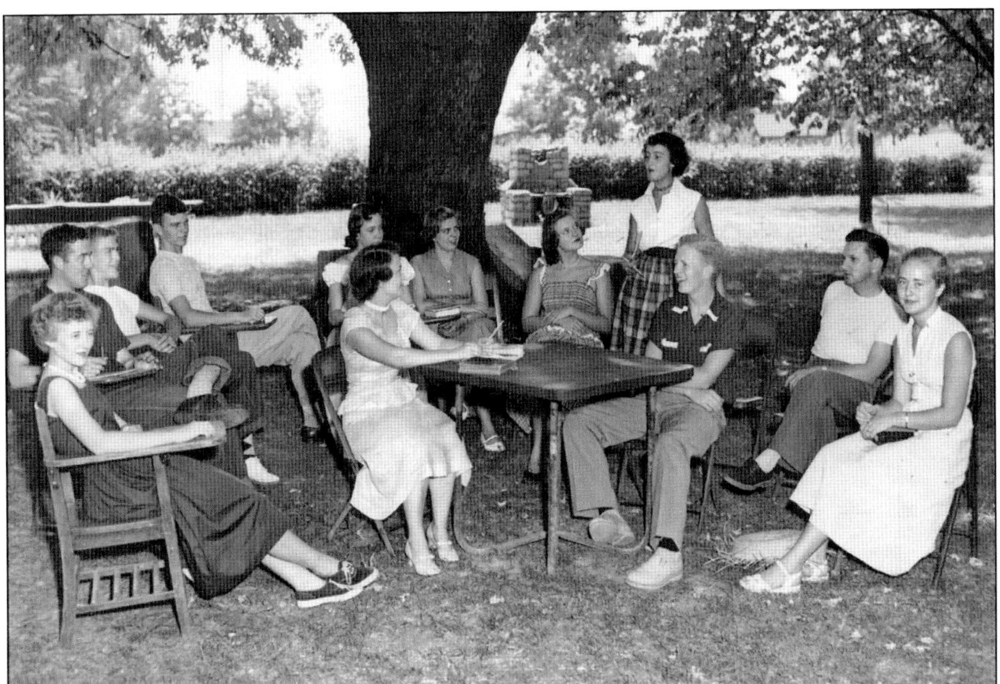

The Christian Youth Fellowship of First Christian Church joined with other Christian churches in the area for various activities such as church camp. (Courtesy author's collection.)

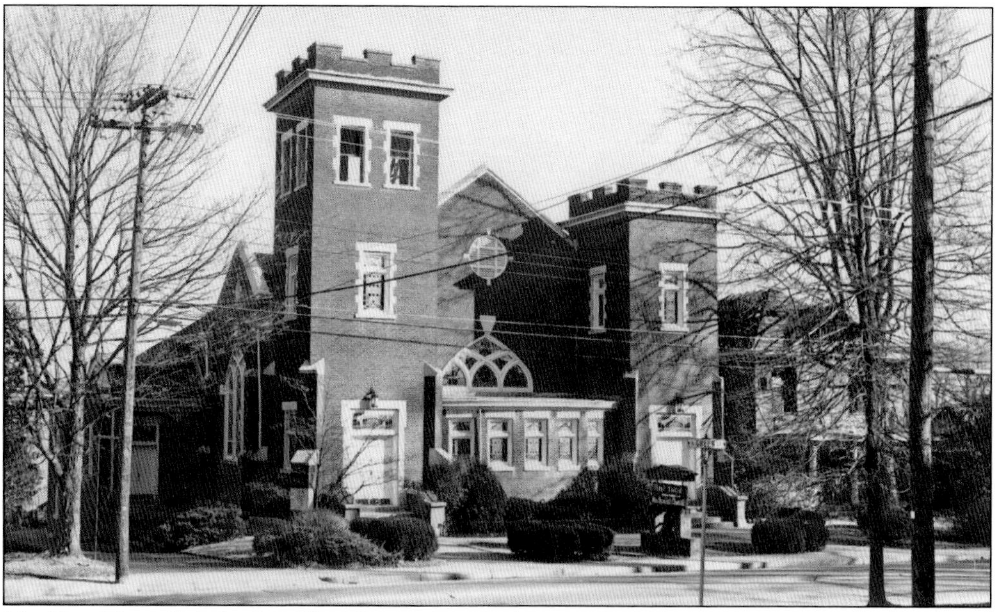

The First United Methodist Church was organized in 1822. Its first and second houses of worship were erected on West Washington Street where the telephone company is now located; the third building was on the south side of East Main Street. The Methodists then purchased the old Christian church on South Green Street (present site of South Green Street Church of Christ) and worshipped there until the current building was completed in 1913. (Courtesy South Central Kentucky Cultural Center.)

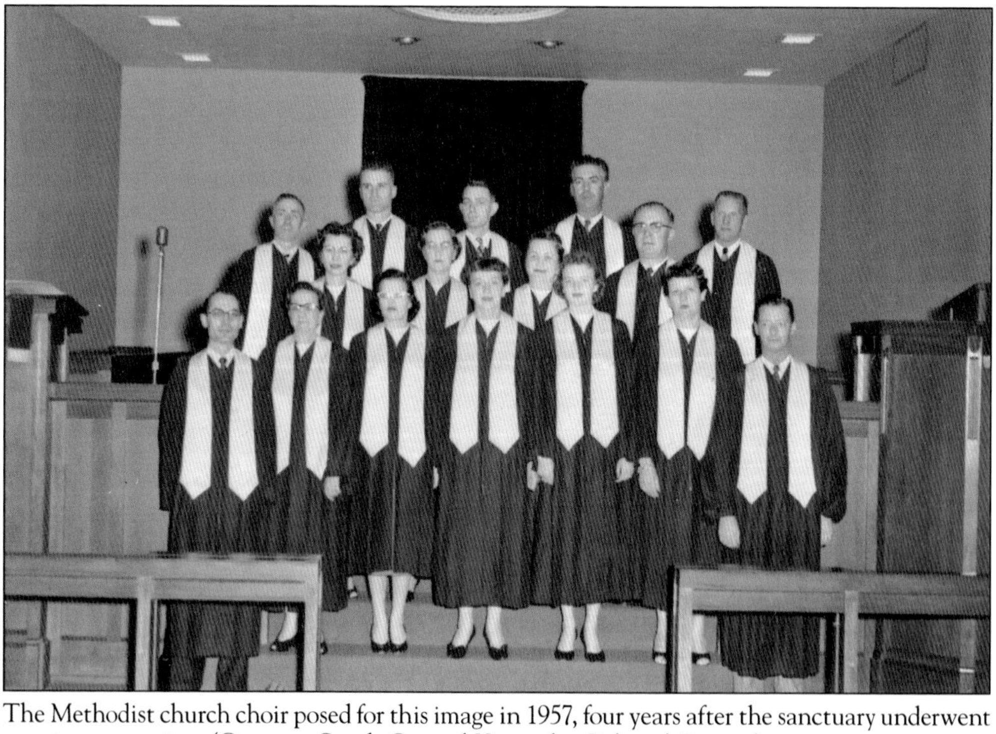

The Methodist church choir posed for this image in 1957, four years after the sanctuary underwent a major renovation. (Courtesy South Central Kentucky Cultural Center.)

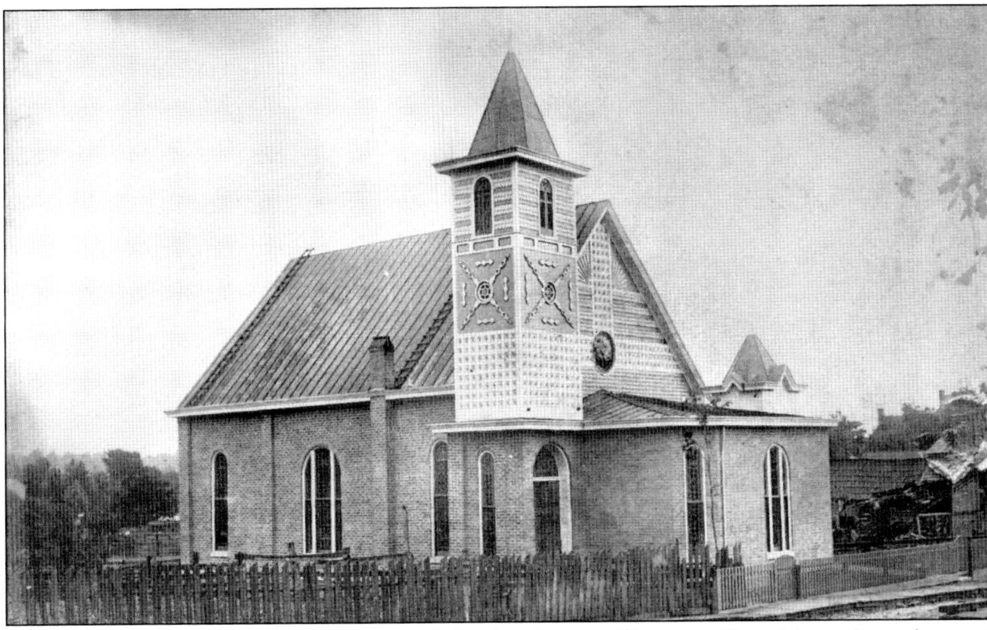

Second Christian Church (also known as Columbia Avenue Christian Church) was formed around 1890 when 44 members of First Christian Church withdrew to create a new congregation. The congregation lasted about 10 years before the two congregations reunited with a new building on the town square. (Both, courtesy South Central Kentucky Cultural Center.)

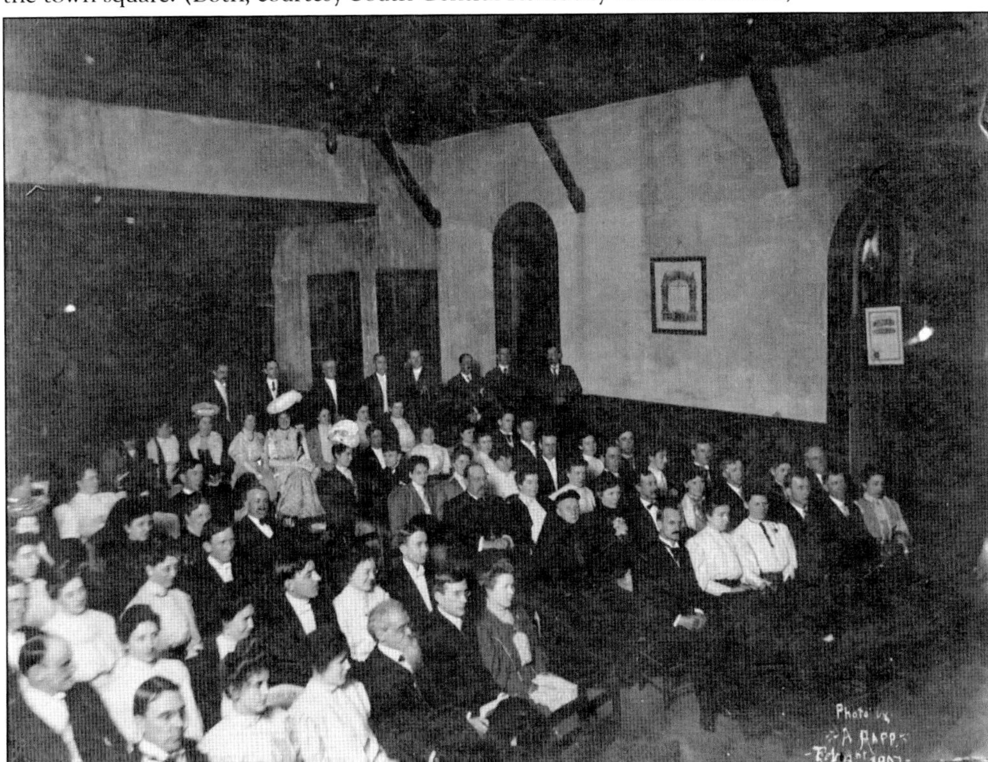

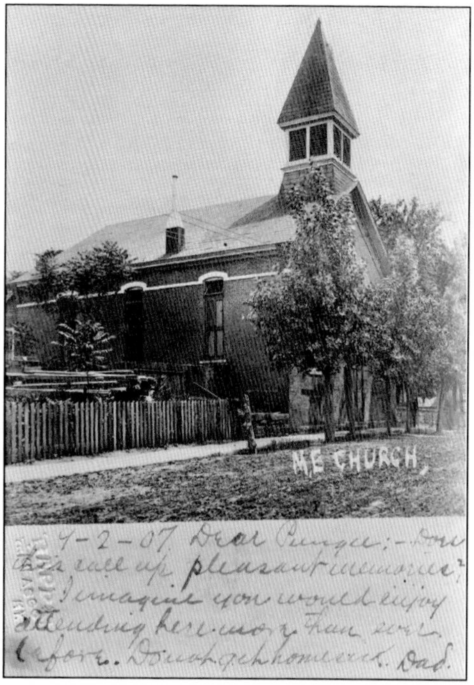

While this image is clearly marked "Methodist Episcopal" Church, it is a photograph with a history. This structure was built and used by First Christian Church until it moved to a new building on the square in 1902. The Methodist Episcopal church's building on East Main Street had suffered damage during the 1900 fire that destroyed the east side of the square. The Methodists, needing a new building, purchased the structure for $1,600. When the latter had completed a new building, this structure was sold to the South Green Street Church of Christ for $1,200. The Church of Christ later built a new structure on the lot and remains there today. (Courtesy South Central Kentucky Cultural Center.)

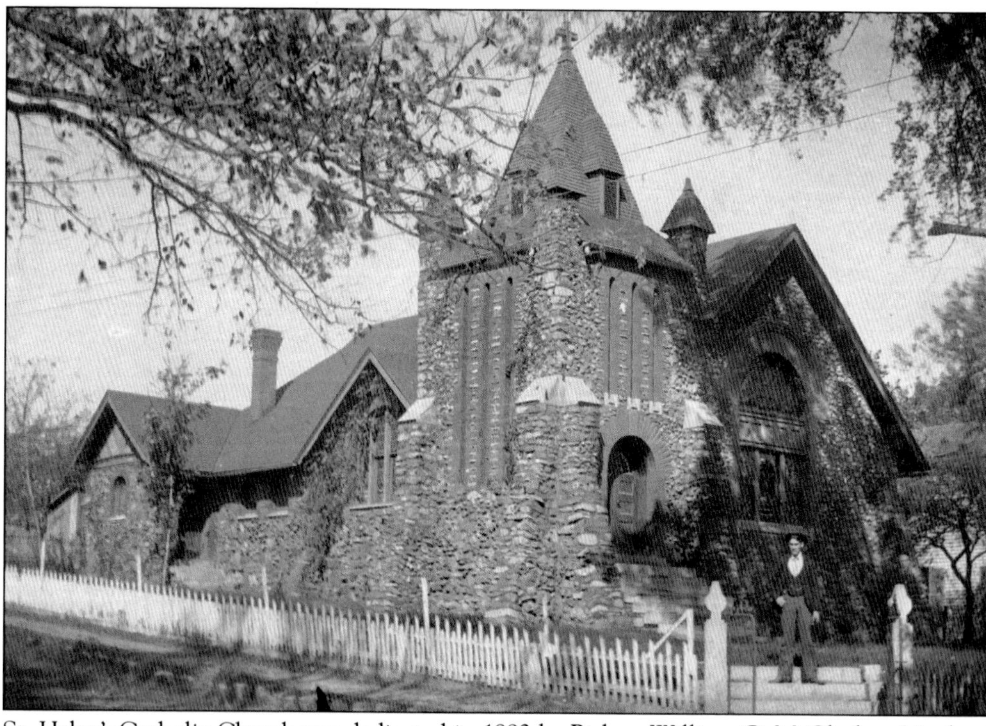

St. Helen's Catholic Church was dedicated in 1893 by Bishop William G. McCloskey. Much of the work of establishing the parish was carried out by Jennie Boles Ellison and Annie Gorin. Cora Wilson is credited with beginning fund-raising efforts to construct the building in 1889. According to local lore, the Catholic women gathered the field stones in their aprons and carts and brought them to town to be used in building the church. (Courtesy author's collection.)

Five

At School in Glasgow

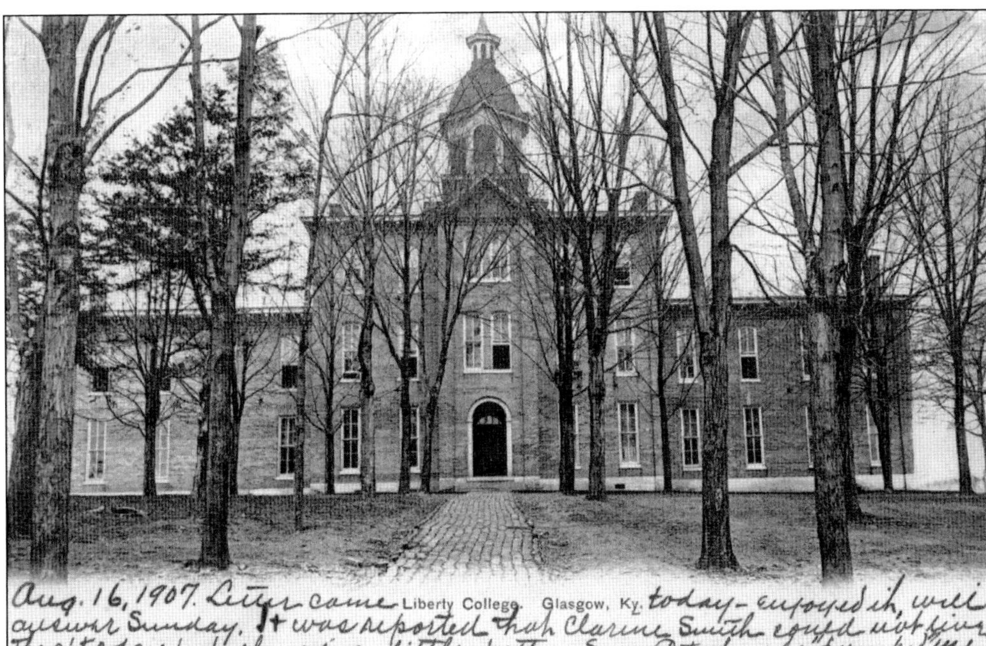

Glasgow's Liberty Female College was the result of an effort more than 10 years in the making when it finally opened as an institution of higher education in 1875. (Courtesy author's collection.)

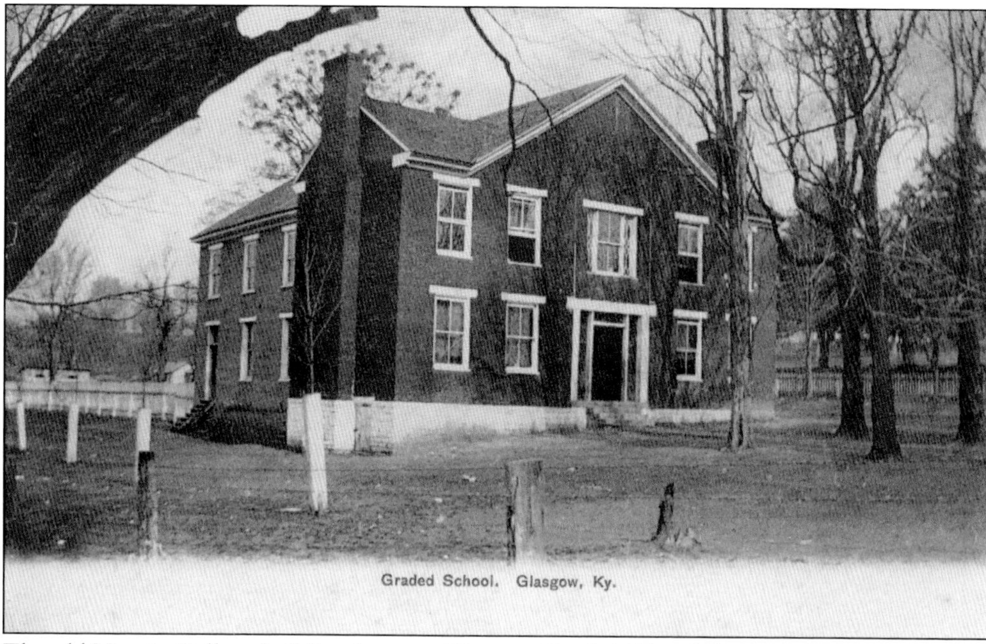

The old Urania College building became Glasgow Graded School for several years. (Courtesy South Central Kentucky Cultural Center.)

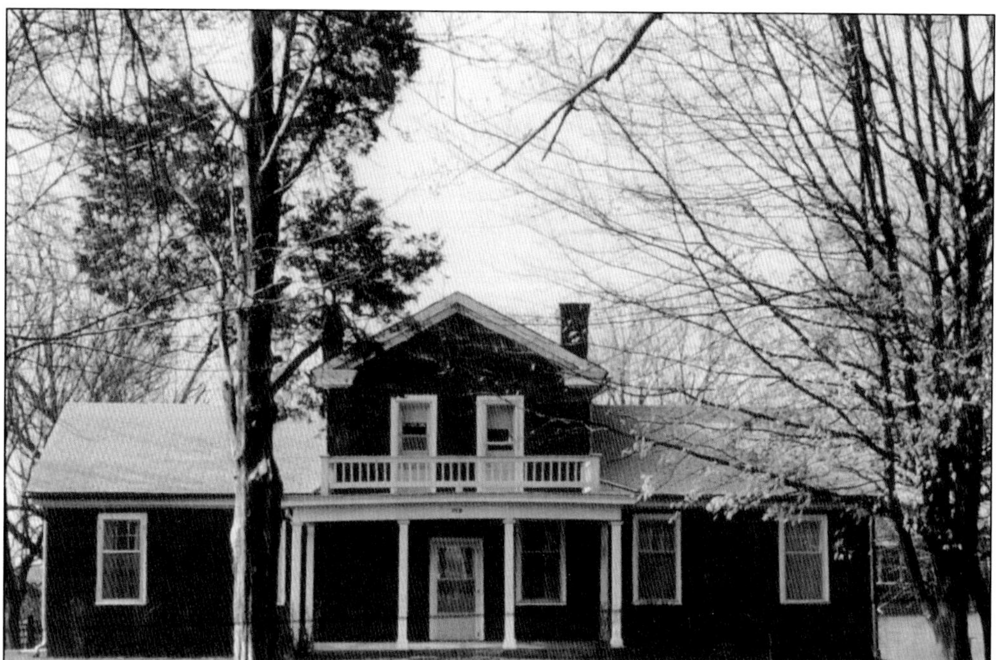
The old Glasgow Seminary was also the home of Will T. Bush, an early developer in Glasgow's history. It is among a number of schools organized in Glasgow during the first 50 years of the town's existence. (Courtesy South Central Kentucky Cultural Center.)

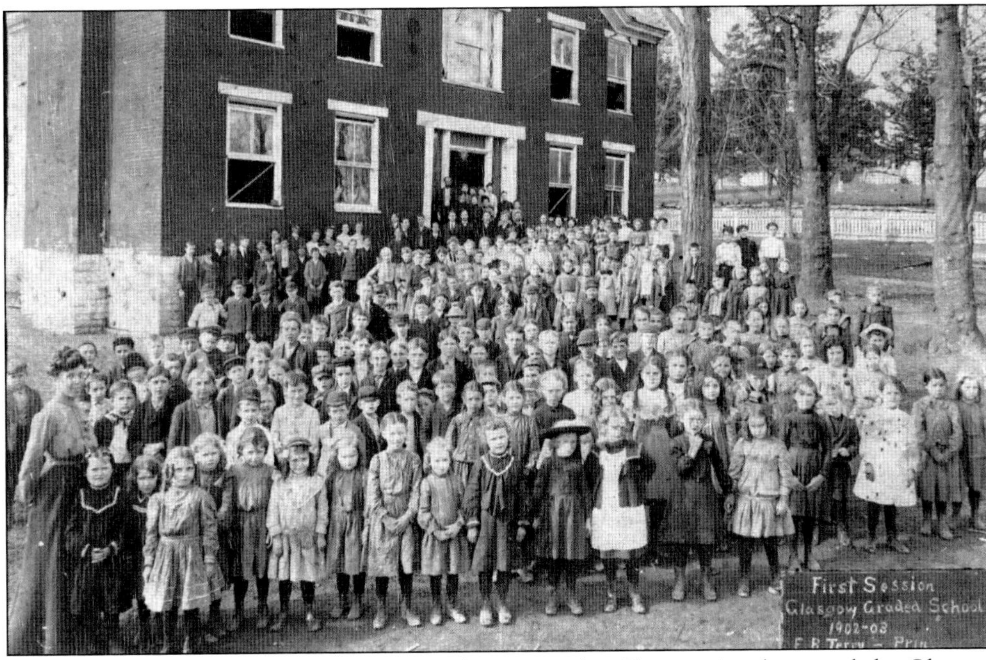

The former Urania College had also been known as the Glasgow Academy and the Glasgow Normal School before it became the Glasgow Graded School in 1902. Here the first session, under the leadership of E. B. Terry, was captured on film. (Courtesy South Central Kentucky Cultural Center.)

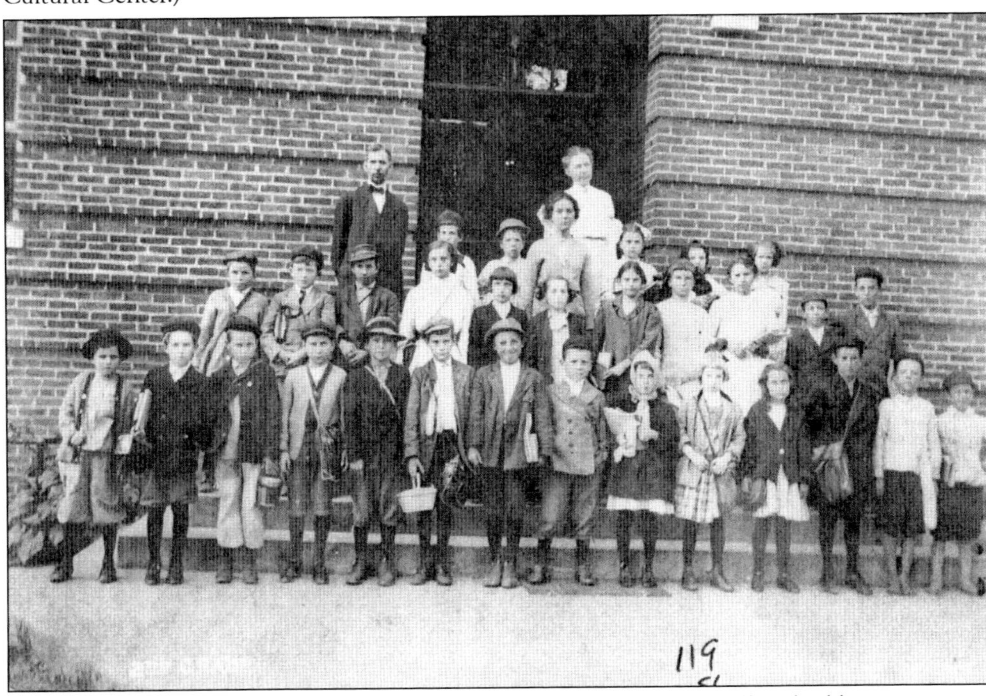

The second-grade class was posed for this image after the old Urania College building was proven inadequate for a modern school. The class is gathered in front of the new building housing the elementary grades. (Courtesy South Central Kentucky Cultural Center.)

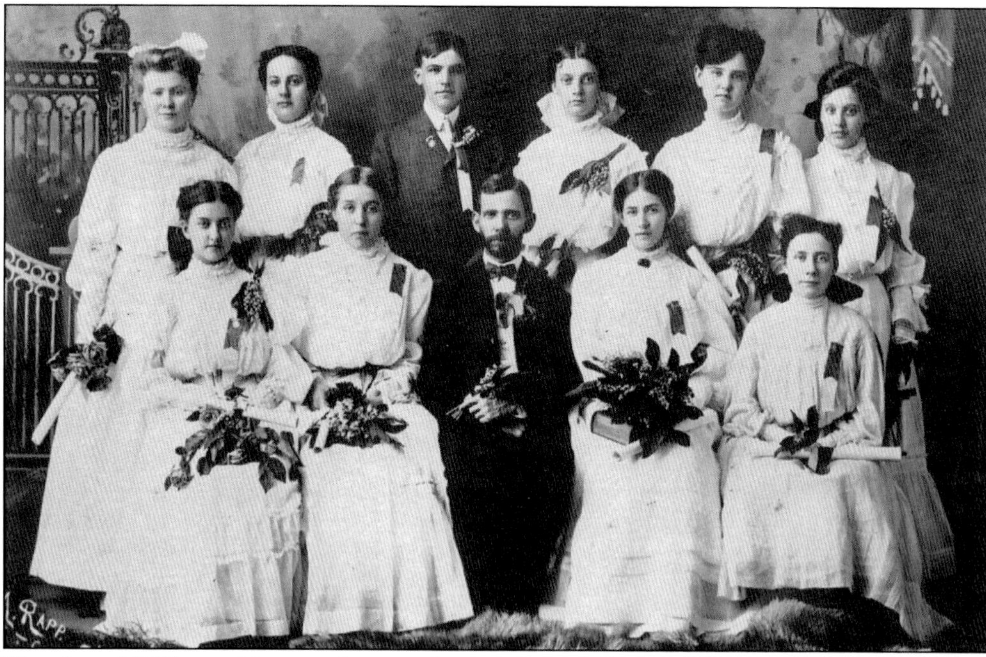

The class of 1905 posed for a graduation photograph with Prof. E. B. Terry. From left to right are (first row) Pattie Snoddy, Annie Jameson, Professor Terry, Evelyn Kilgore, and Margaret Rogers; (second row) Dora Collins, Grace Alcock, Hascal Mitchell (valedictorian), Byrd Depp, Katie Lee Peden, and Leah Jameson. (Courtesy South Central Kentucky Cultural Center.)

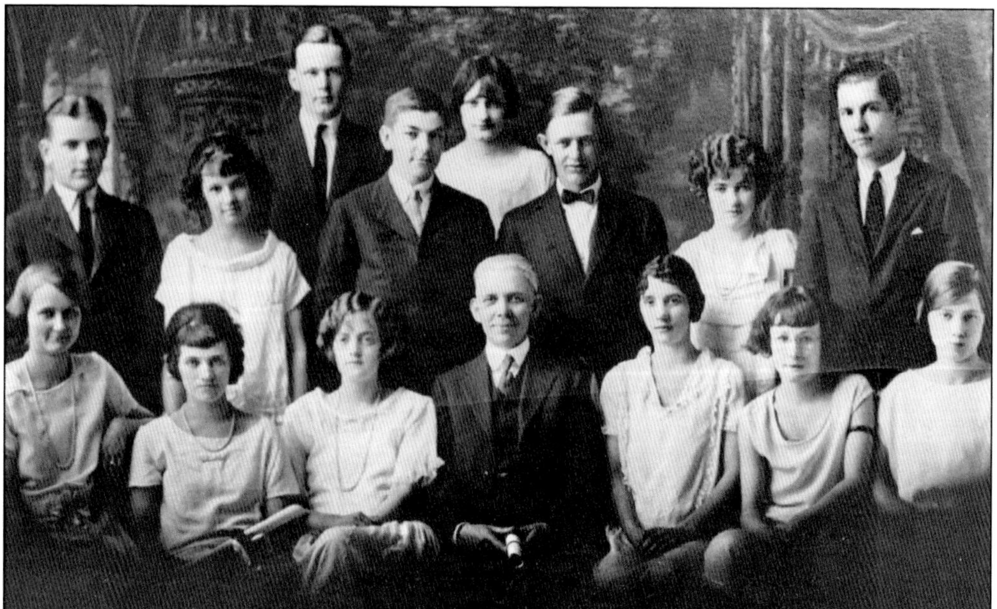

The Glasgow High School class of 1924 gathered for a graduation photograph with Prof. E. B. Terry. Class members were Carroll M. Redford Sr., Dixon Rapp, Carey Shaw, Cy Hutcherson, Garland Ford, William Pickett, Anna Bradford, Lorene LeBeouf, Nannie McDowell, Clarene Martin, Lee Smith, Vivian Taylor Rousseau, Julia Belle Jones Meador, Alice McDowell Chapman, and Hope White Doss. (Courtesy South Central Kentucky Cultural Center.)

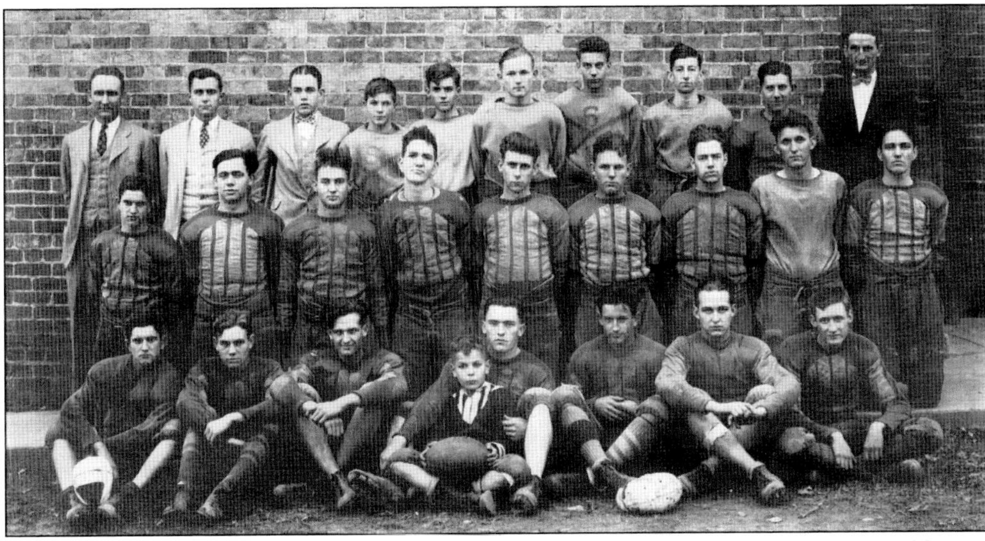

The Southern Kentucky football champions was described by James M. "Dinkum" Nelson: "They don't look bad, but they are bad medicine for the other teams!" From left to right are (first row) Loren Nelson, "Fanny" Austin, "Devil" Harpst, Capt. "Pap" Taylor, mascot Billy Vaughan, "Little One" Uri Nelson, Francis "Sunshine" Jackson, and "Peck" Jones; (second row) "Dinkum" Nelson, "Mud Eye" Brooks, Garland Reynolds, William "Silent Bill" Dickinson, "Bear" Tucker, "Socker" Hammer, Capt. Johnny Jones, Frank McGlocklin, and Charlie "Feet" Goodman; (third row) coach R. D. Ridley, assistant coach J. F. Tanner, Arthur Matthews, Billy Pedigo, Lawrence "Dusty" Miller, "Hezzy" Smith, Billy Sam Terry, Paul "Fox" Holman, Clay Barton, and ? Lynn, manager. The fellow on crutches in the third row got his leg broken in the Bowling Green game. (Courtesy author's collection.)

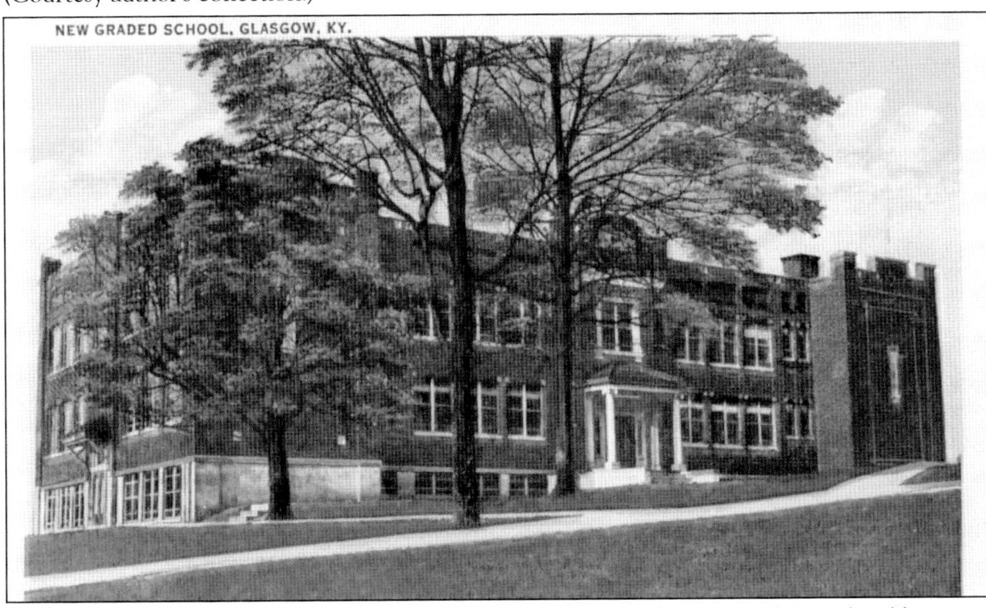

When Liberty College closed its doors, the Glasgow Public School system took over the old campus. Gradually, the old college buildings were razed and replaced with three structures: Glasgow High School, Music Hall (which included the gymnasium), and Glasgow Graded School, as pictured in the above postcard image. (Courtesy South Central Kentucky Cultural Center.)

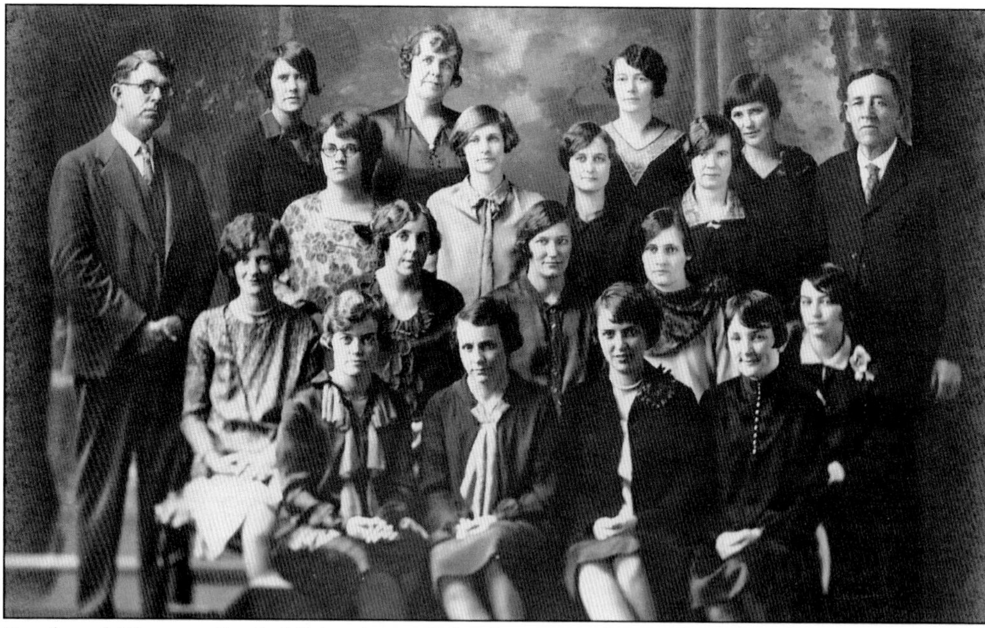

Faculty of Glasgow Graded School posed for this image for a Christmas greeting. Shown are, from left to right, (first row) Miss Goff, Mrs. Pedigo, Miss Wilkinson, and Elizabeth Sandidge; (second row) Miss Goad, Miss Akers, Miss Page, Miss White, and Miss Moss; (third row) Miss McDowell, Miss Hord, Lee Smith, and Miss Forrest; (fourth row) Superintendent Palmore, Miss Newberry, Effie Depp, Mrs. Barton, Mrs. Shirley, and J. M. Hagan. (Courtesy South Central Kentucky Cultural Center.)

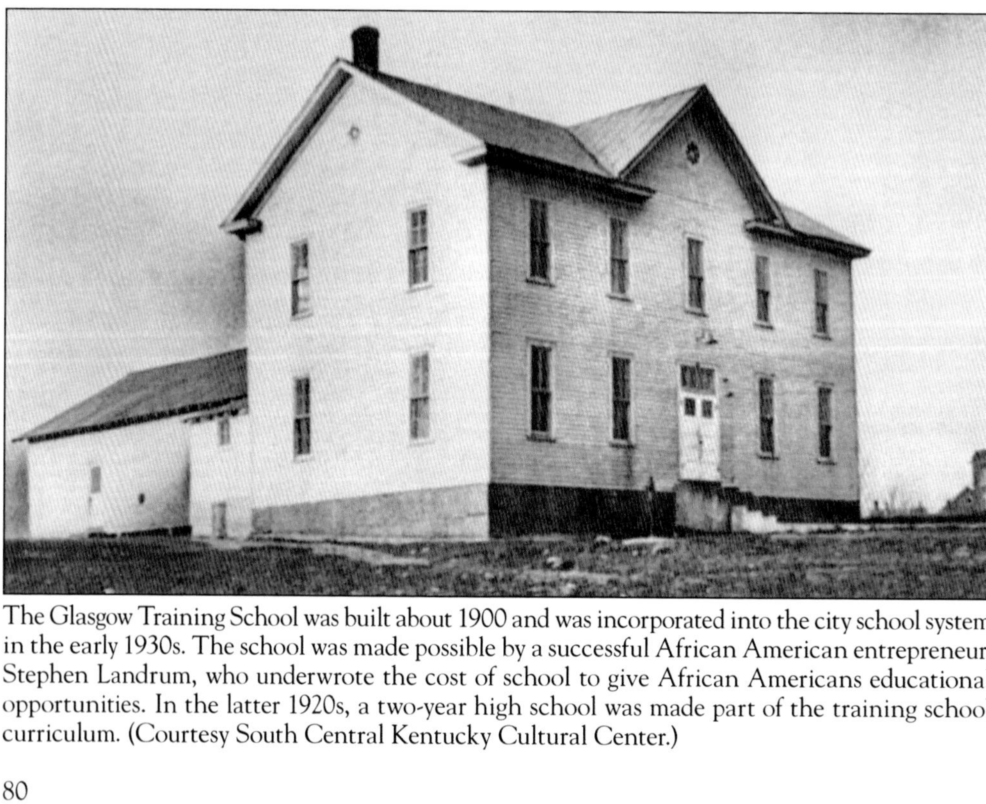

The Glasgow Training School was built about 1900 and was incorporated into the city school system in the early 1930s. The school was made possible by a successful African American entrepreneur, Stephen Landrum, who underwrote the cost of school to give African Americans educational opportunities. In the latter 1920s, a two-year high school was made part of the training school curriculum. (Courtesy South Central Kentucky Cultural Center.)

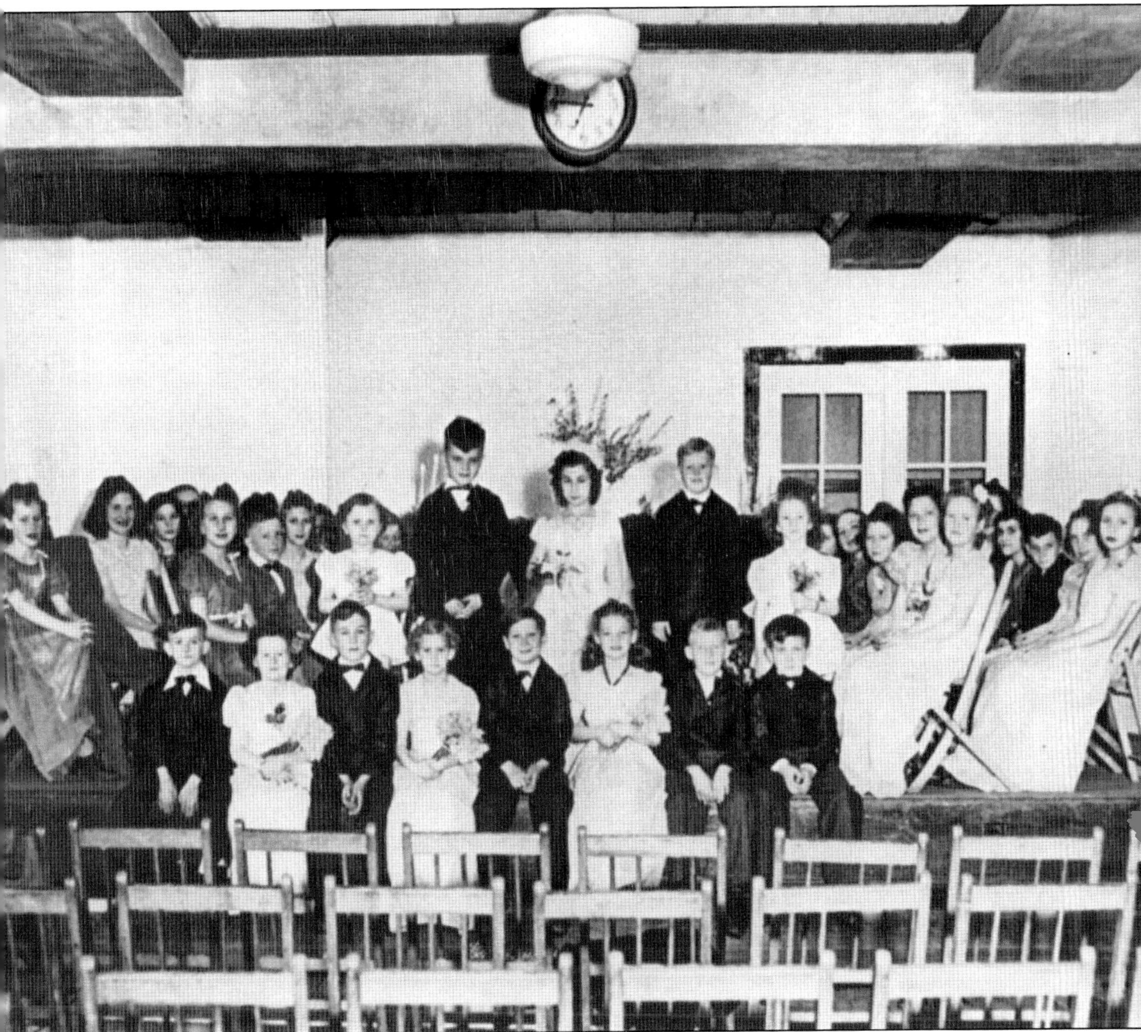

A Tom Thumb wedding took place during the 1944–1945 school year under the direction of teacher Margaret Underwood. The wedding party consisted of bride Mary Lou Abell, groom Joe Billy Aspley, and minister Henry Dickinson; other students played roles such as bridesmaids and flower girls. (Courtesy South Central Kentucky Cultural Center.)

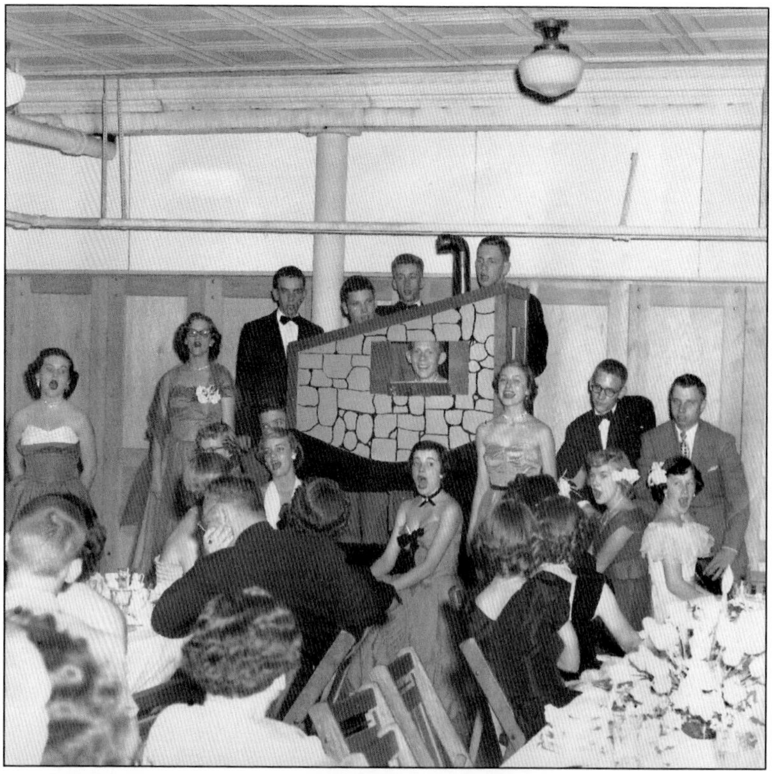

The Glasgow High School class of 1952 banquet included the musical number "Four and Twenty Blackbirds Baking in a Pie" with singers Martha York, Nancy Bertram, Bobby Wood, Bill Snyder, Carroll Redford Jr., Bruce Huntsman, Edythe Walbert, Judy Shaw, Anne Parker, Jane Smith, Hilbert Martin, Barbara Hester, June Meador, and Ray Dillingham. (Courtesy South Central Kentucky Cultural Center.)

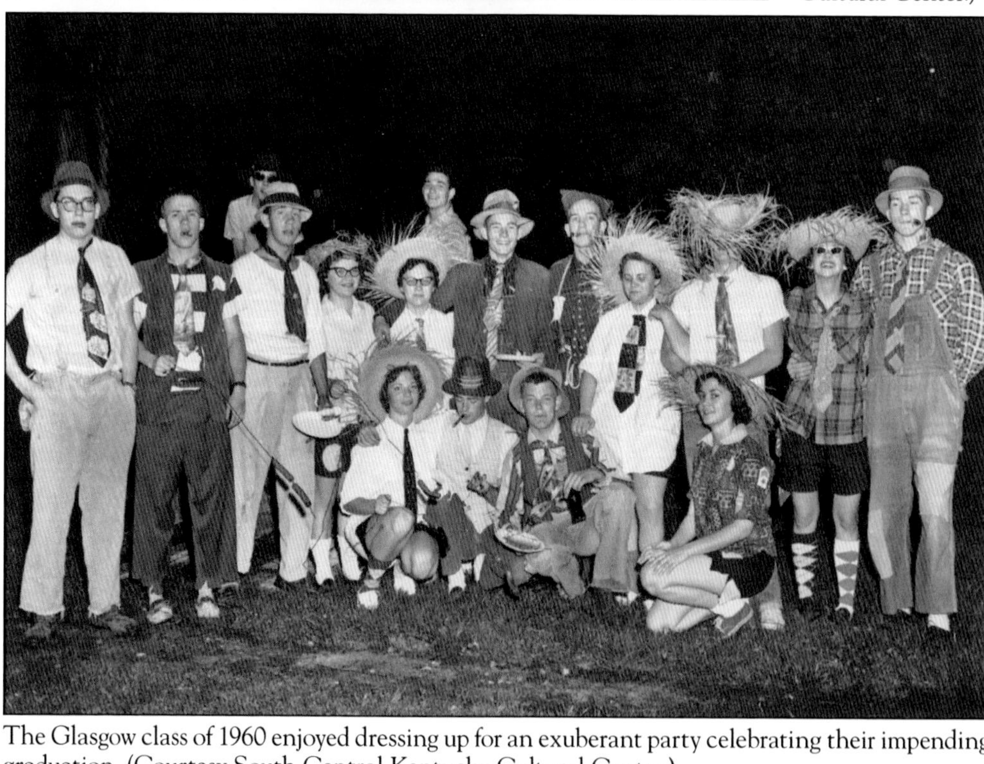

The Glasgow class of 1960 enjoyed dressing up for an exuberant party celebrating their impending graduation. (Courtesy South Central Kentucky Cultural Center.)

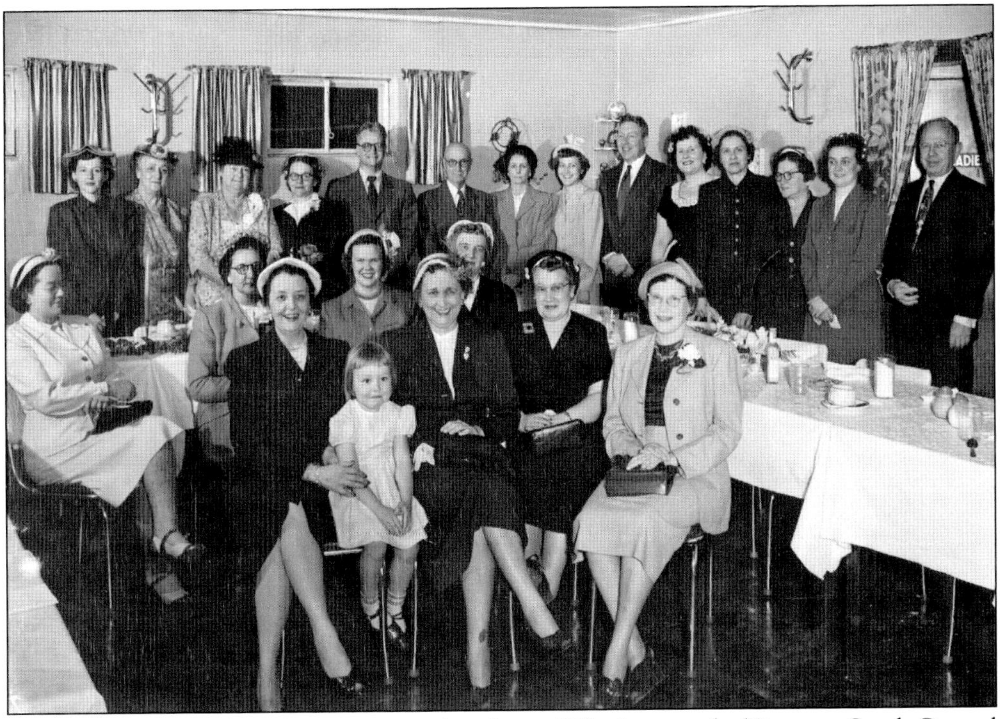

Glasgow High School faculty was captured in this *c.* 1951 photograph. (Courtesy South Central Kentucky Cultural Center.)

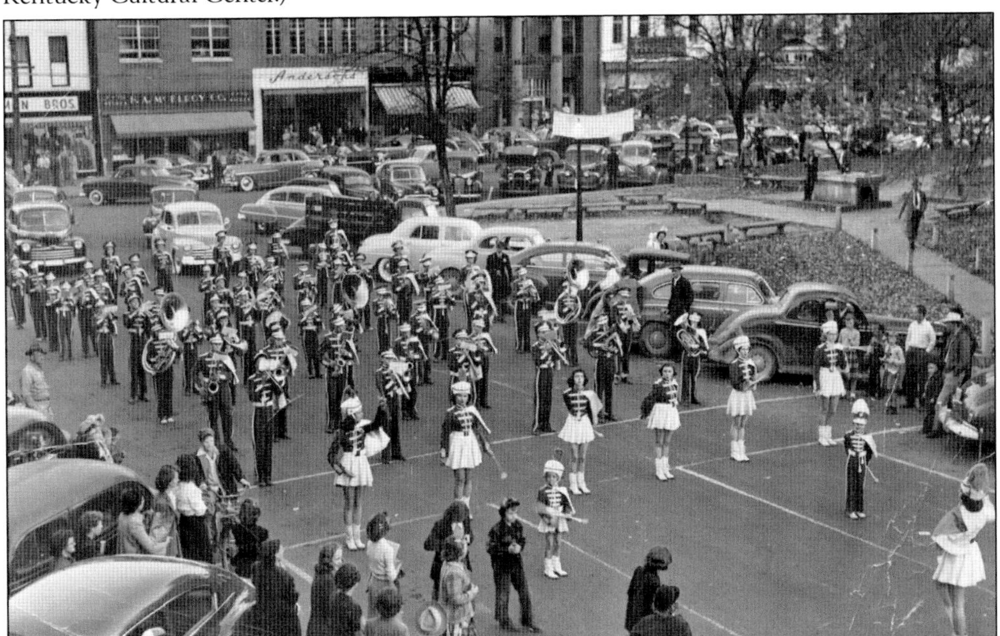

This early-1950s photograph captured the Glasgow Scottie Band performing on the downtown square. The drum majorettes are, from left to right, Barbara Smith, Mary Lou Abell, Eva Jean Geralds, Carol Dillingham, Lou Mae Davis, and Edythe Walbert. (Courtesy South Central Kentucky Cultural Center.)

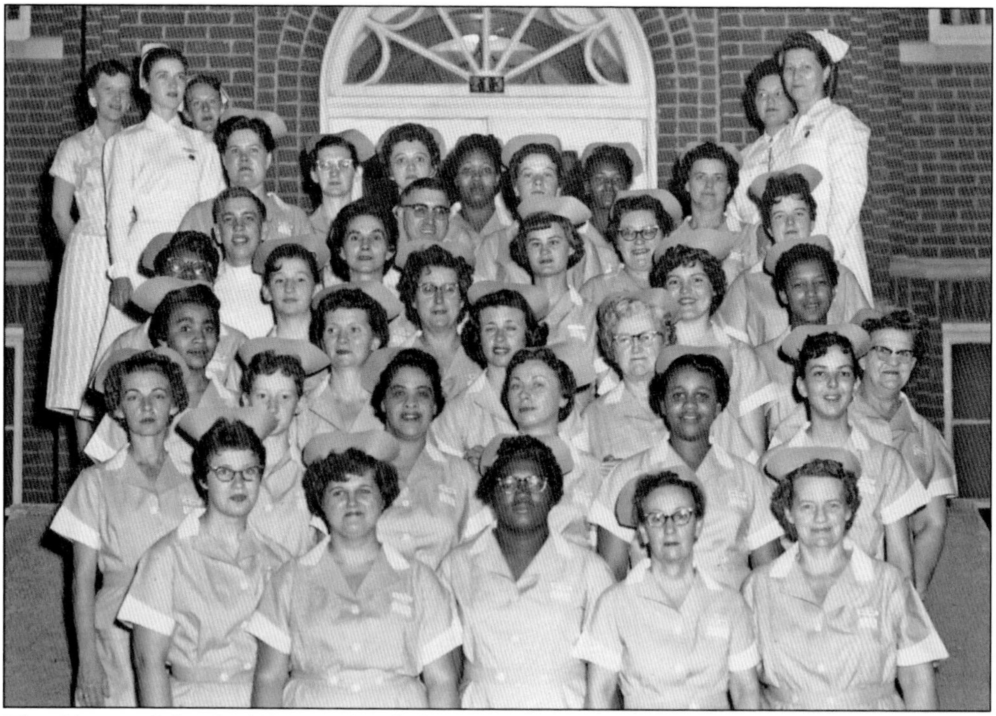

The Glasgow School of Nursing has helped many to achieve goals of working in the medical field. This group of graduates gathered on the steps of Glasgow High School for a photograph. Below, Ann Rodgers of the school and the local hospital speaks to the Glasgow Rotary Club about the importance of the work of the school of nursing. (Both, courtesy South Central Kentucky Cultural Center.)

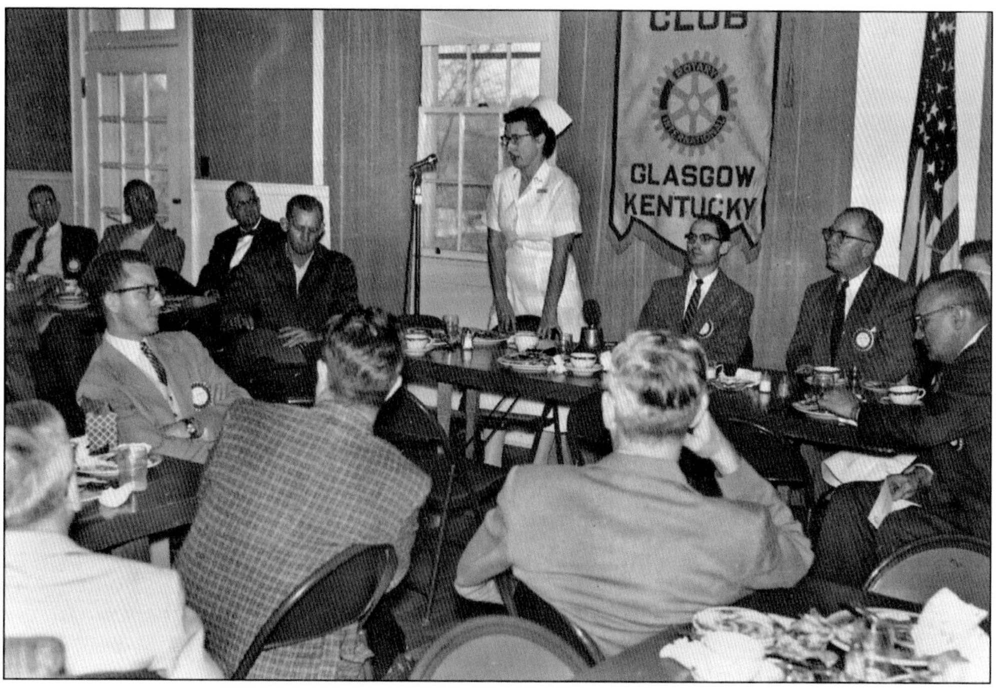

Six

At Play in Glasgow

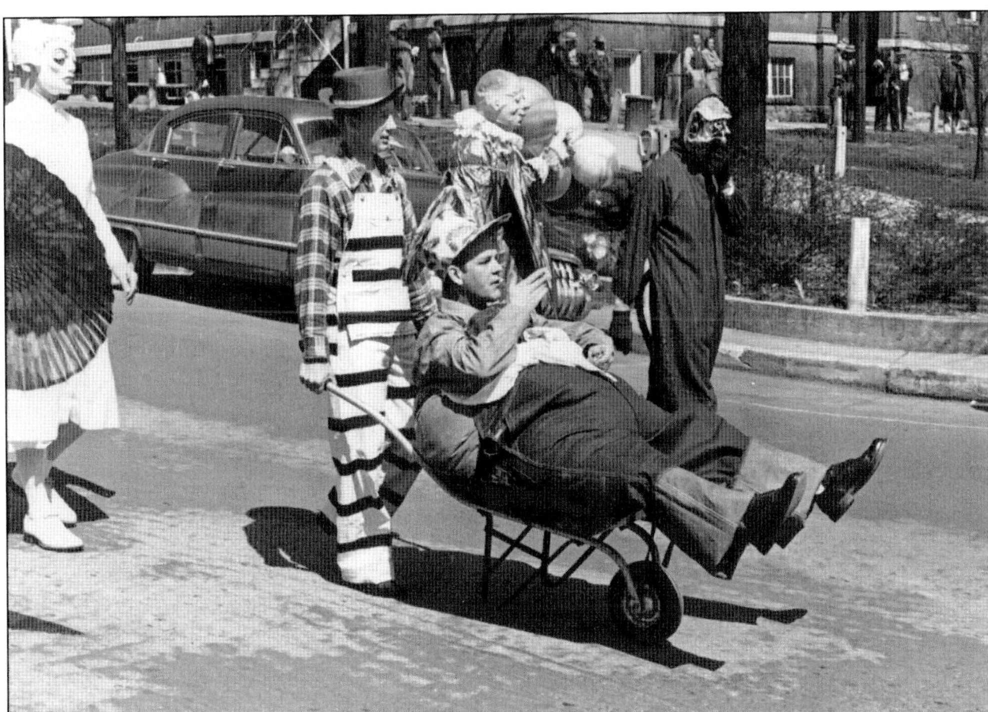

In addition to all the serious parts of life, Glasgow people love to be at play in a variety of ways, always with good-natured thoughts in mind. Such was the case when Rotary Club president Cornell Clark got a lift from the Lions Club president Jack Goodman as they settle a challenge about which group's attendance would be best. (Courtesy South Central Kentucky Cultural Center.)

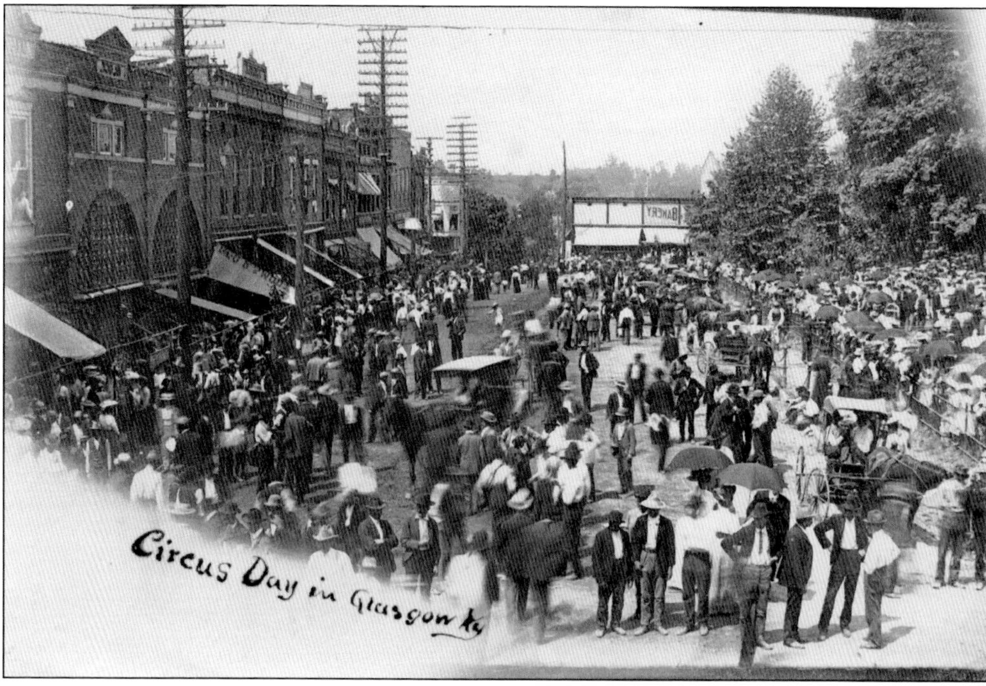

This image of Circus Day in Glasgow dates to around 1906. Don't let the image confuse you—the original photograph was printed backwards, which gives a different view of things on the square. (Courtesy South Central Kentucky Cultural Center.)

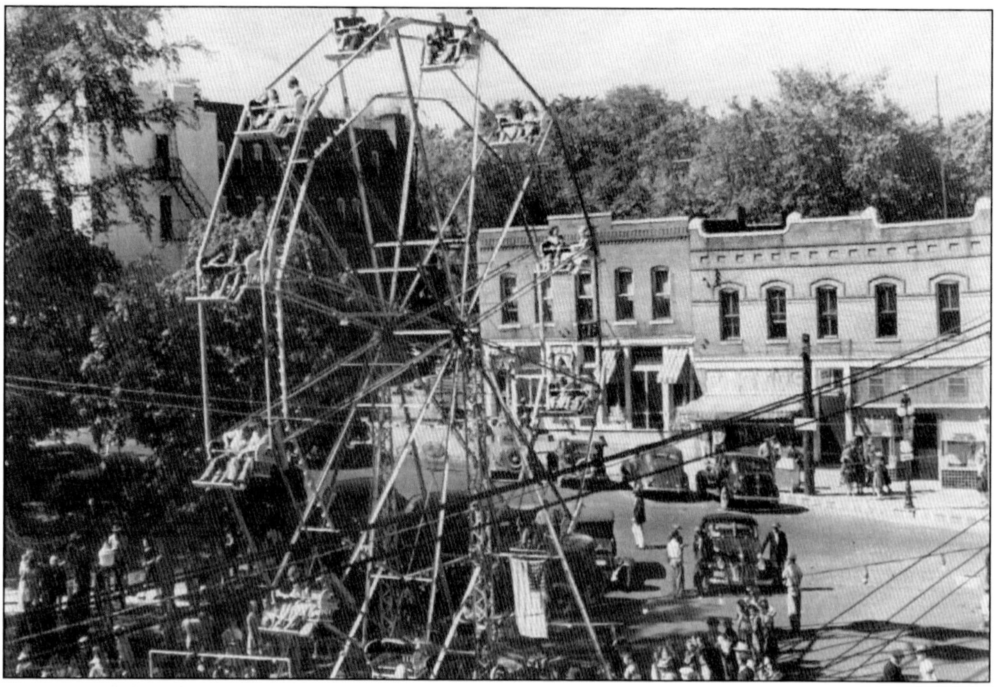

For several decades, Glasgow's downtown was the site of annual street fairs, some years more elaborate than others. In this instance, fairgoers were treated to a Ferris wheel on the North Public Square. (Courtesy author's collection.)

The Bohannon girls—Nell, Caroline, and Charlotte—enjoyed the ultimate fruit of summer—watermelon—in this 1880s photograph. (Courtesy South Central Kentucky Cultural Center.)

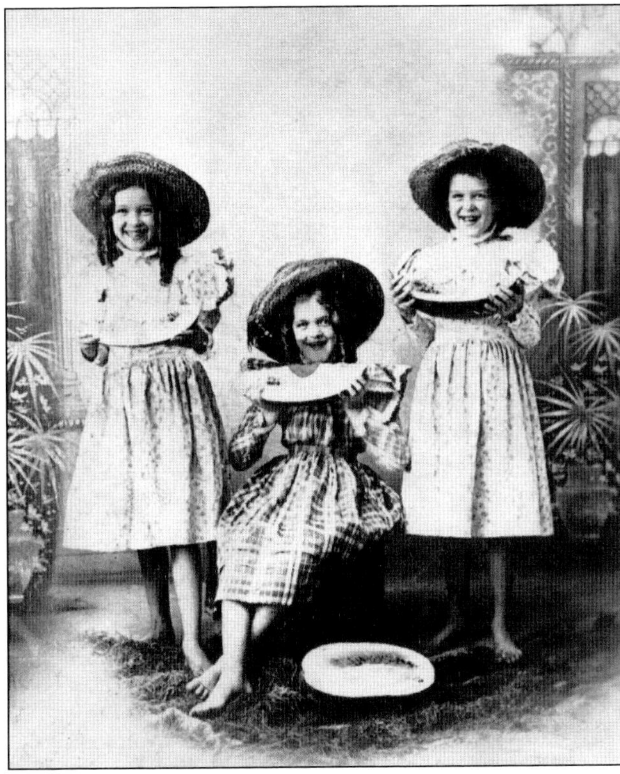

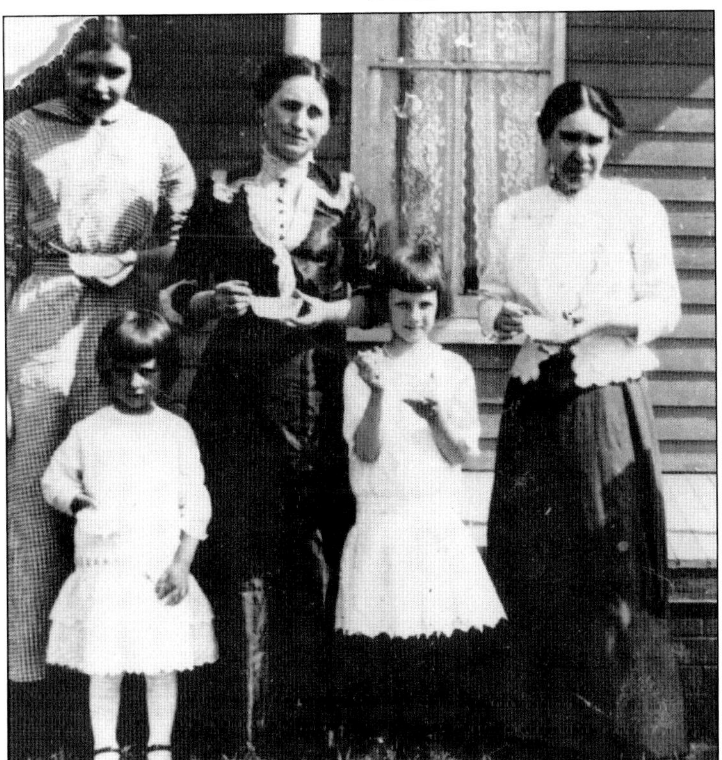

The Beals and Ford families enjoyed another summertime treat—homemade ice cream—in 1914. From left to right, Mary Beals, Christine Ford, Mrs. Joe Ford, Ruby Twyman Ford, and Callie Beals took a break from their repast for this photograph. (Courtesy South Central Kentucky Cultural Center.)

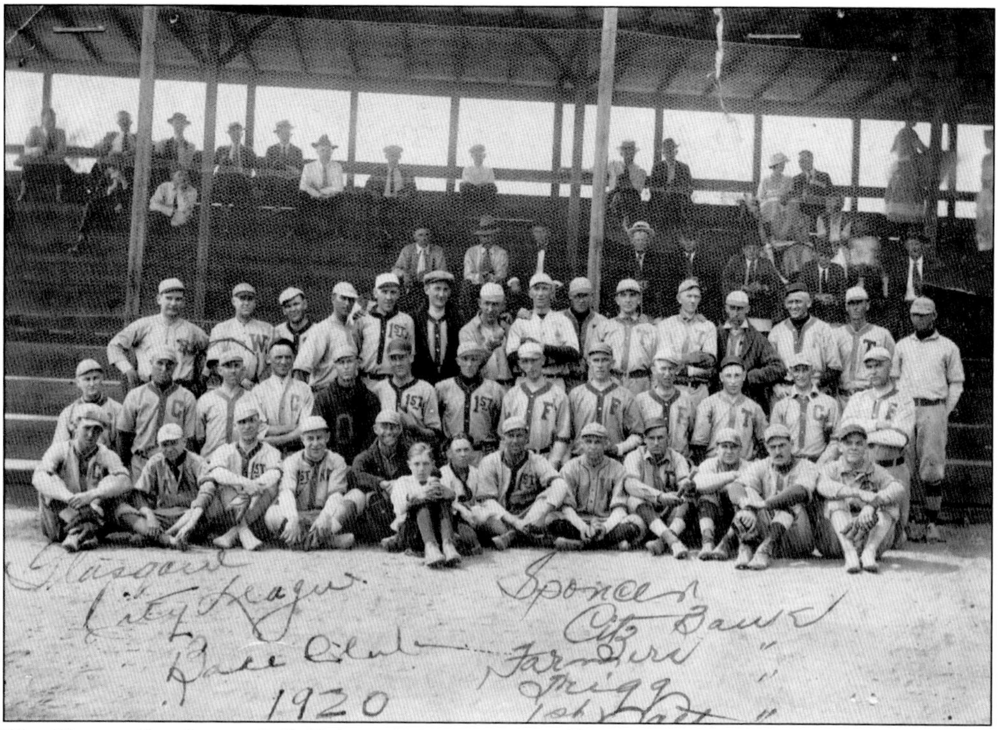

The Glasgow City League Ball Club in 1920 was sponsored by Citizen's National Bank, Farmer's Bank, Trigg Bank, and First National Bank. (Courtesy South Central Kentucky Cultural Center.)

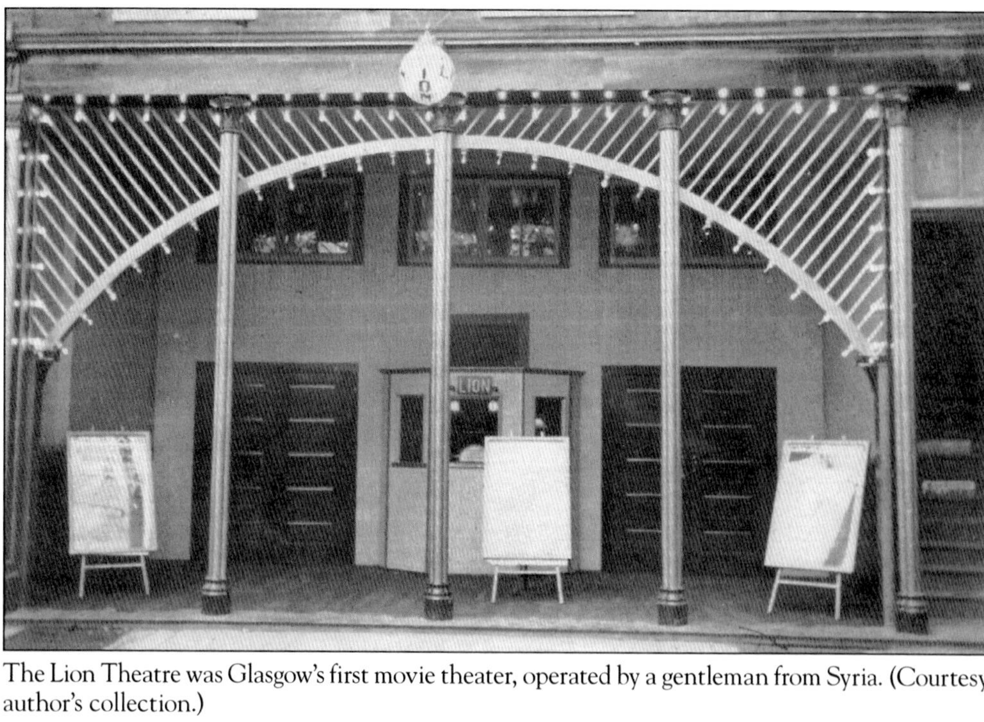

The Lion Theatre was Glasgow's first movie theater, operated by a gentleman from Syria. (Courtesy author's collection.)

The Trigg Theatre enthralled thousands of moviegoers with its live sound accompaniments provided by Durwood Haynes, organist for the theater. (Courtesy author's collection.)

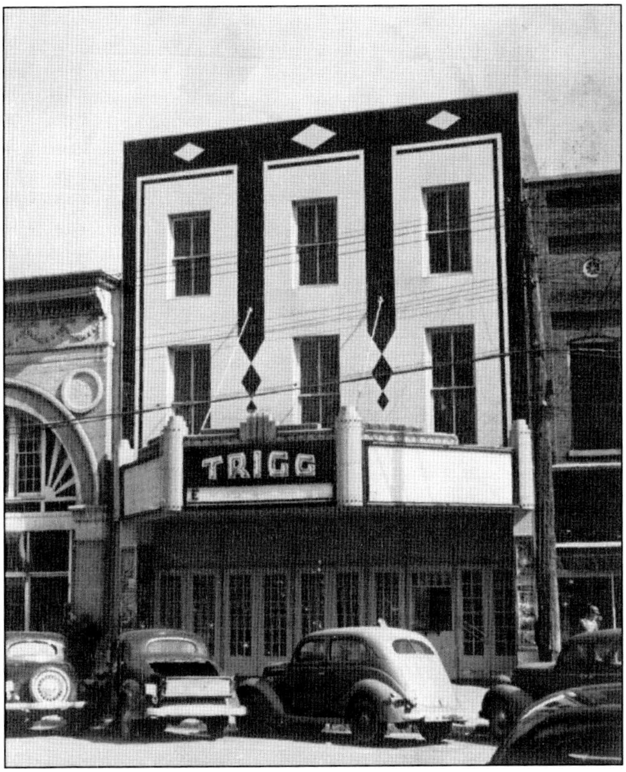

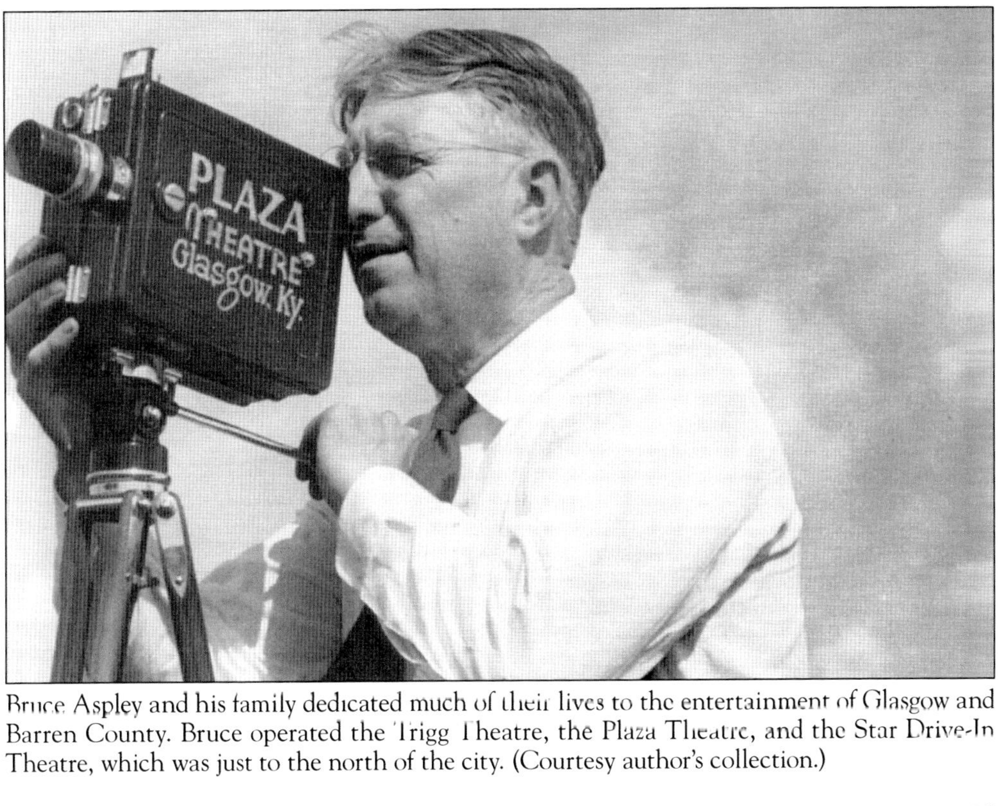

Bruce Aspley and his family dedicated much of their lives to the entertainment of Glasgow and Barren County. Bruce operated the Trigg Theatre, the Plaza Theatre, and the Star Drive-In Theatre, which was just to the north of the city. (Courtesy author's collection.)

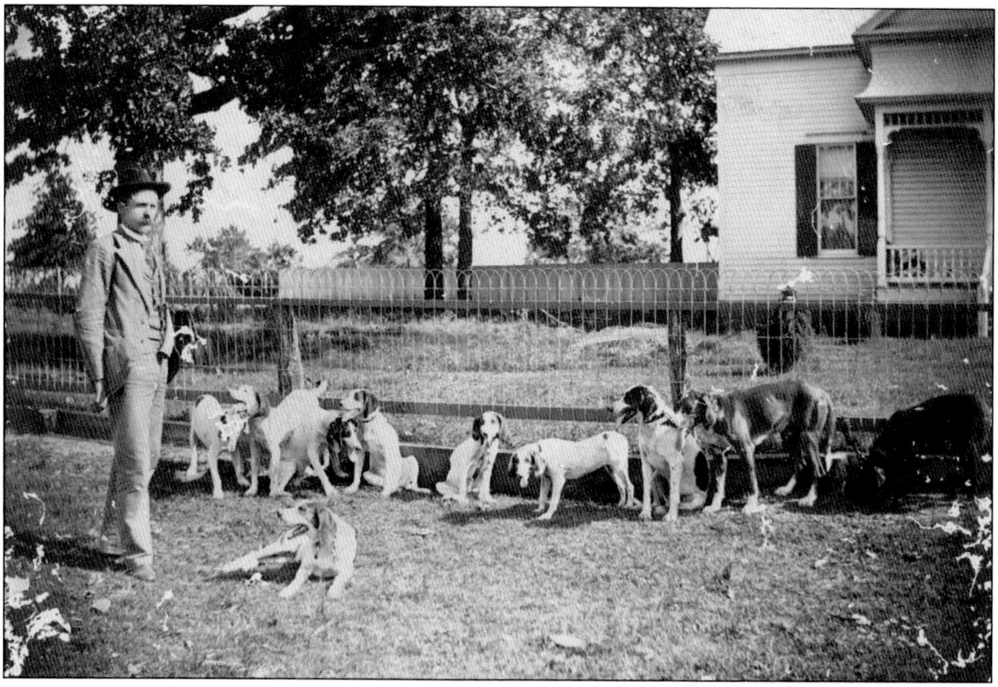

Glasgow and Barren County men have loved to play—and that includes with Trigg foxhounds. Here Morgan Brents shows off his hounds Ned, Chase, Trigg, Raiby, Bee, Baby, Whipowill, Mike, Dixie, and (in front) Racket. (Courtesy South Central Kentucky Cultural Center.)

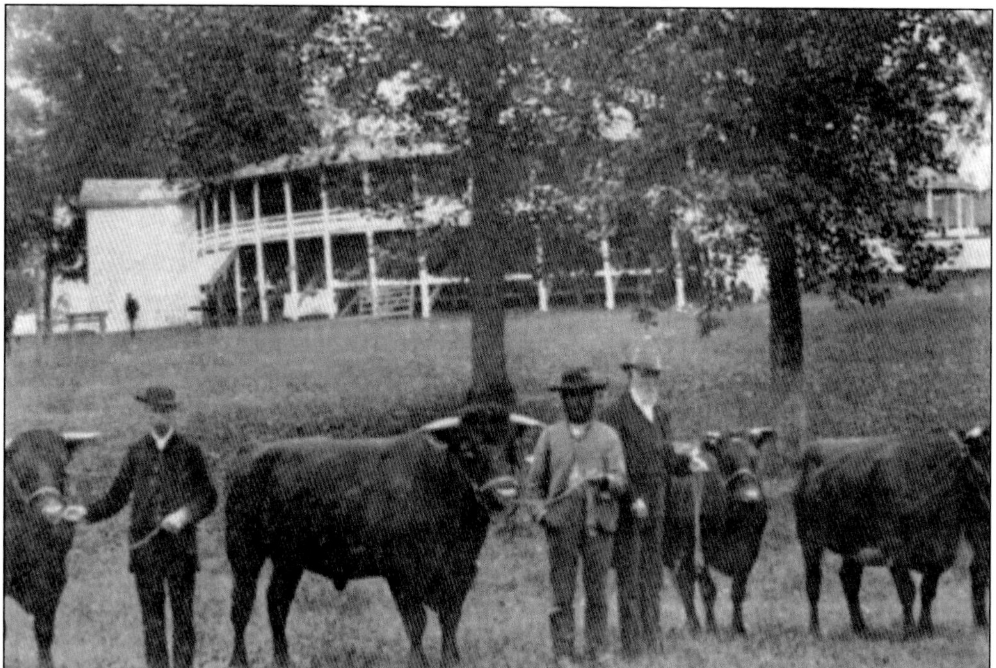

Another of Glasgow's favorite play areas was Gretna Green, the old fairgrounds, which hosted many local fairs and events. The gentlemen shown here appear to have great pride in their prized animals competing in a cattle show. (Courtesy South Central Kentucky Cultural Center.)

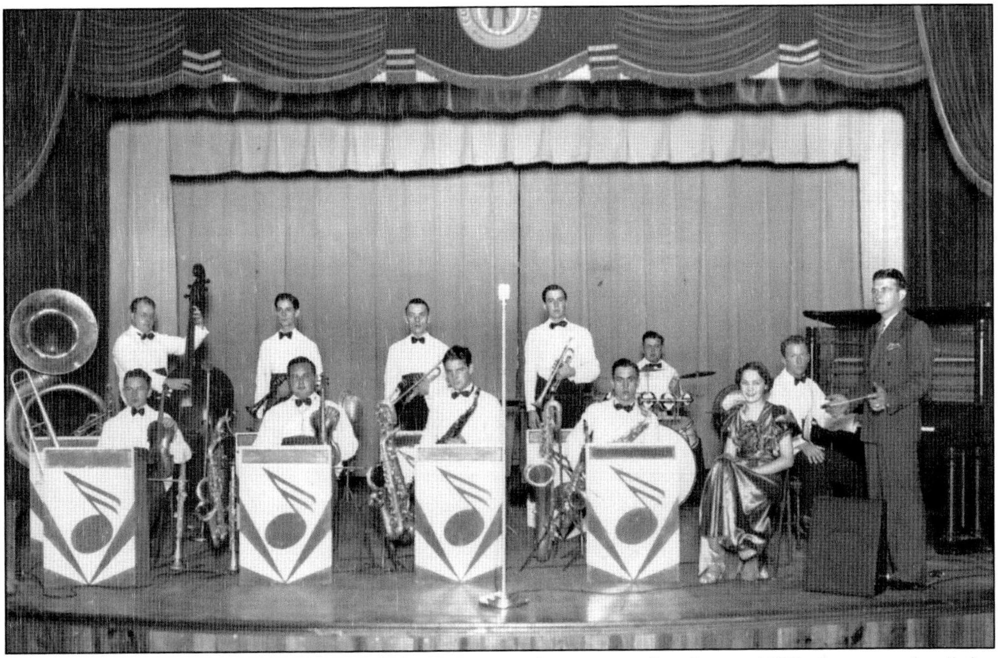

The Bowling Green National Guard Armory was the setting for this *c.* 1938 photograph of the classic big sound. From left to right are (first row) H. C. Biggers, William Gabbard Jr., James Pedigo, Jimmy Huffman, Beverly Hall, Billy Vaughn, and Roy Holmes; (second row) Tom Connors, David Highbaugh, Vic Showalter, Russell Daugherty, and Hall Potts. (Courtesy South Central Kentucky Cultural Center.)

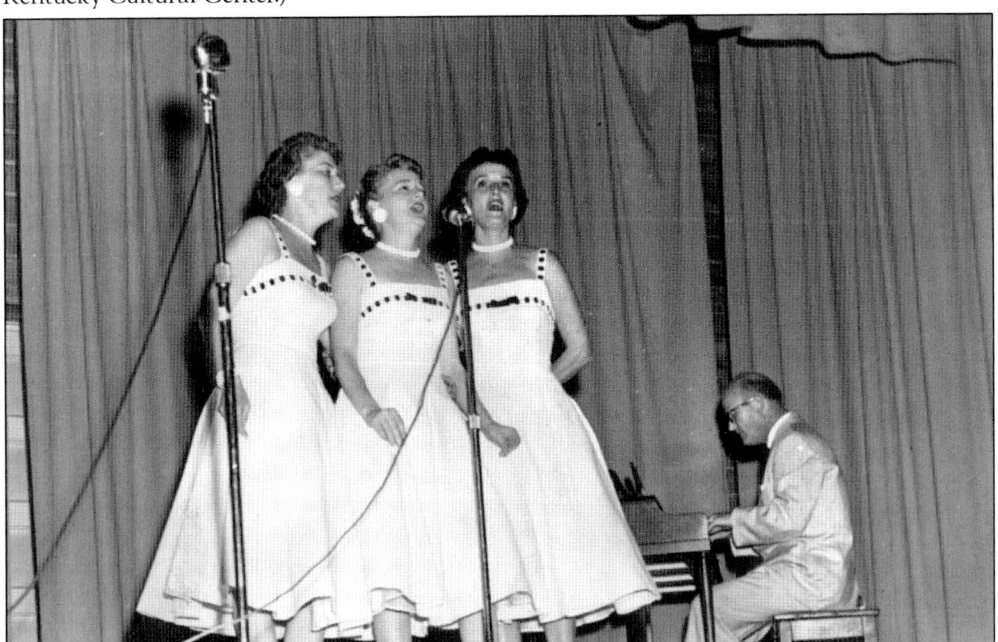

The Vaughn family provided immense musical entertainment over the years. This photograph captured, from left to right, sisters Grace, Charlotte, and Inez with their brother, Billy. (Courtesy South Central Kentucky Cultural Center.)

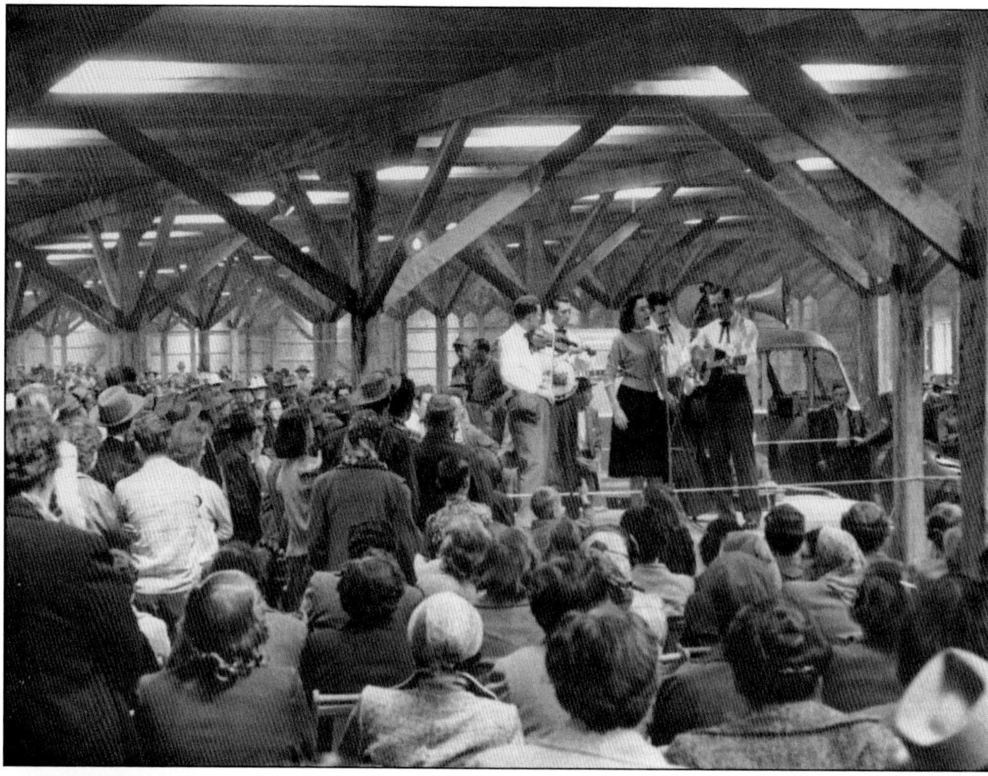

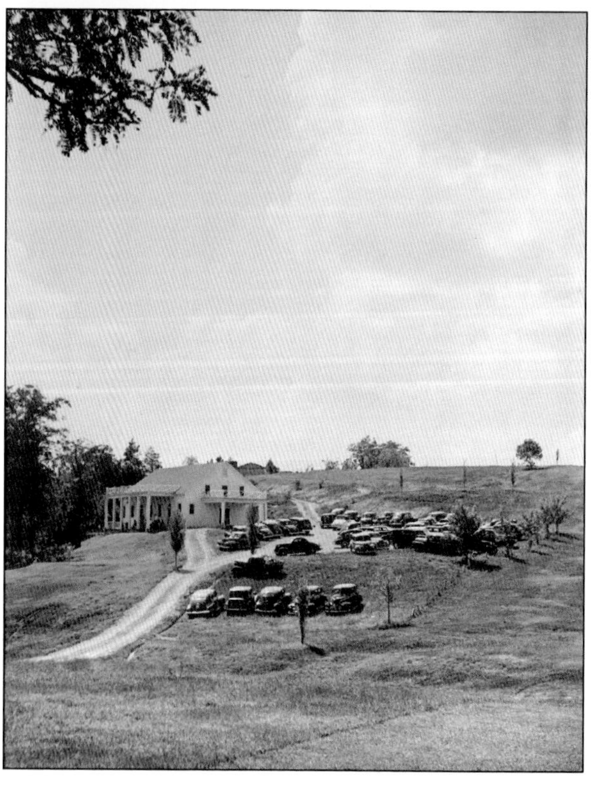

In off-seasons, Glasgow's tobacco warehouses served as sites for a variety of functions. Here a warehouse provides indoor space for musical entertainment. (Courtesy author's collection.)

After the old stone clubhouse of the Glasgow Country Club burned, the club erected a new modern clubhouse to accommodate 75 members at a cost of $8,500. The clubhouse was dedicated with a dance and reception. (Courtesy author's collection.)

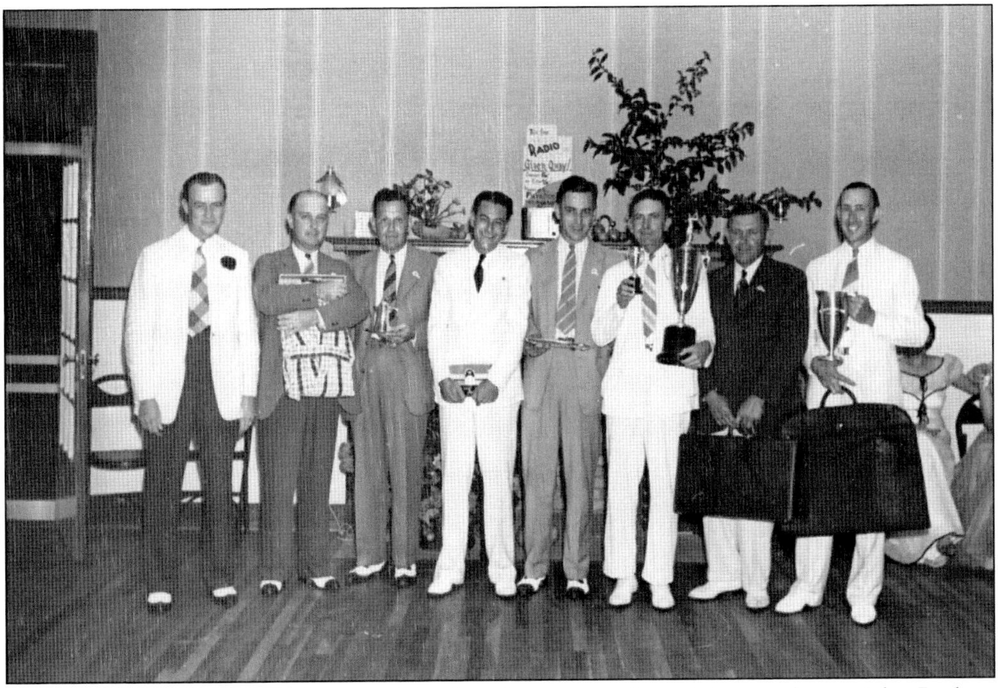

A group of country club golfers stood for this photograph. From left to right are John Richey, Sewell C. Harlin (president of the club), Glenn Ropp, Jack Ellis, Bobby Goodman, Charlie T. Renfro (club champion), Gordon Brown, and Dr. C. G. Follis. (Courtesy author's collection.)

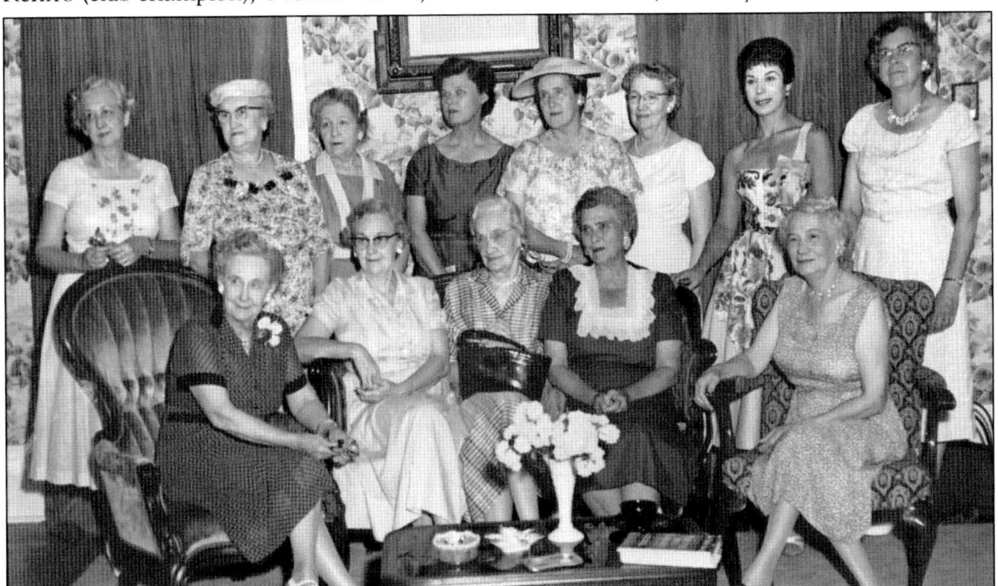

Glasgow ladies loved to play, too, in various ways. The June 1958 meeting of the Book Club at the home of Lois Ellis was captured on film. From left to right are (first row) Jennie Lee Mansfield, Gladys Baker, Haide Dean, Georgia Richards, and Lois Ellis; (second row) Shirley Giesecke, Hattie Lee Myers, Ruby Pedigo, Mary Wilson, Nelle Terry Ellis, Ida Pace, Nunie Ellis, and Frances Hatchett. Members not present were Indie Weldon, Ruth Leech, and Nell Rogers. (Courtesy South Central Kentucky Cultural Center.)

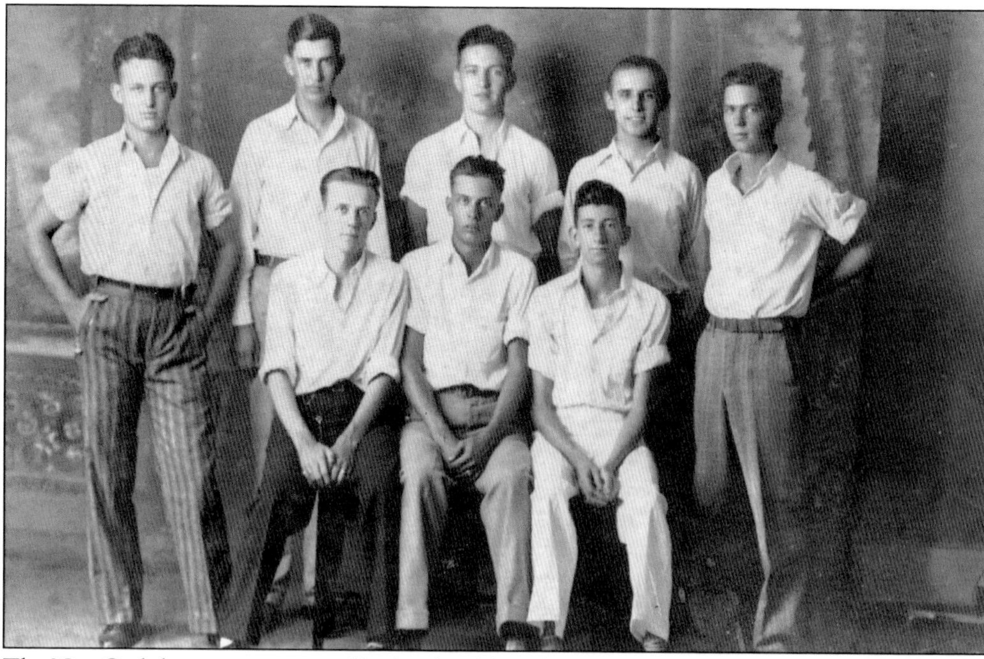

The Nite Owls began as a group of high school friends around 1928. The original members were, from left to right, (first row) Lathan Drane, Billy Sam Terry Jr., and Paul Holman Jr.; (second row) Francis Jackson, Addis Britt, Charlie Goodman Jr., Robert Vaughn, and Caldwell Rogers. (Courtesy author's collection.)

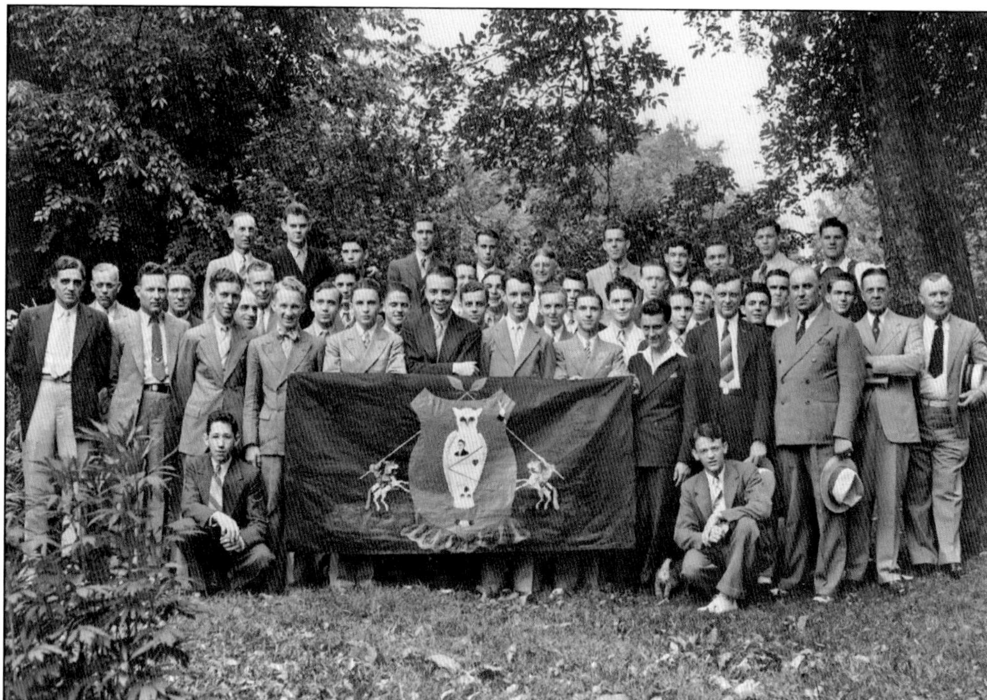

The Nite Owls managed to continue into the 1930s, as evidenced by this image of a much larger group of men. (Courtesy South Central Kentucky Cultural Center.)

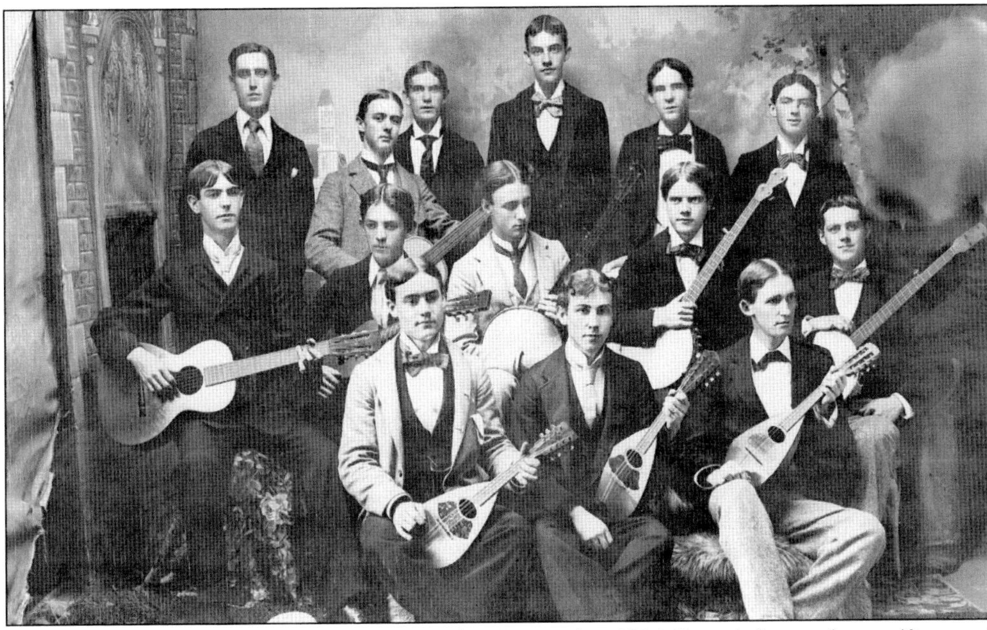

A group of distinguished musicians gathered in September 1894. From left to right are (first row) Al Baker, Perry Hawkins, and John M. Redding; (second row) Einar Breeding, Haiden Trigg, Edwin Porter, George Lewis, and Rice Ballard Trigg; (third row) Wilbur Moss, Robert H. Porter, Elvin Pedigo, Guy Dickinson, Jack Major, and Charlie Lewis. (Courtesy South Central Kentucky Cultural Center.)

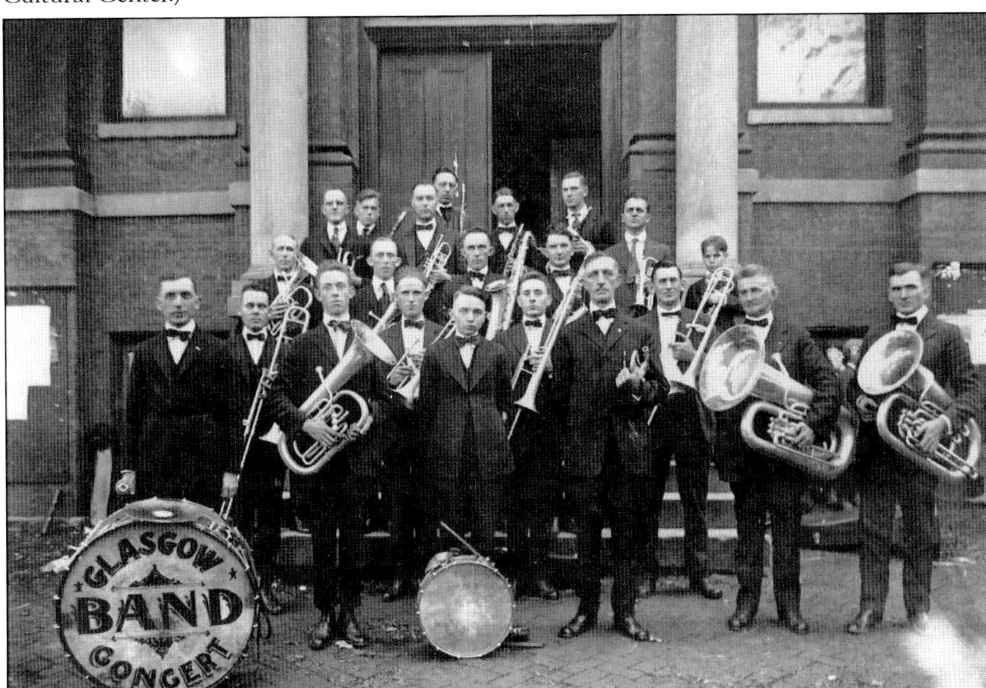

The Glasgow Concert Band is posed on the steps of the courthouse in this photograph. (Courtesy South Central Kentucky Cultural Center.)

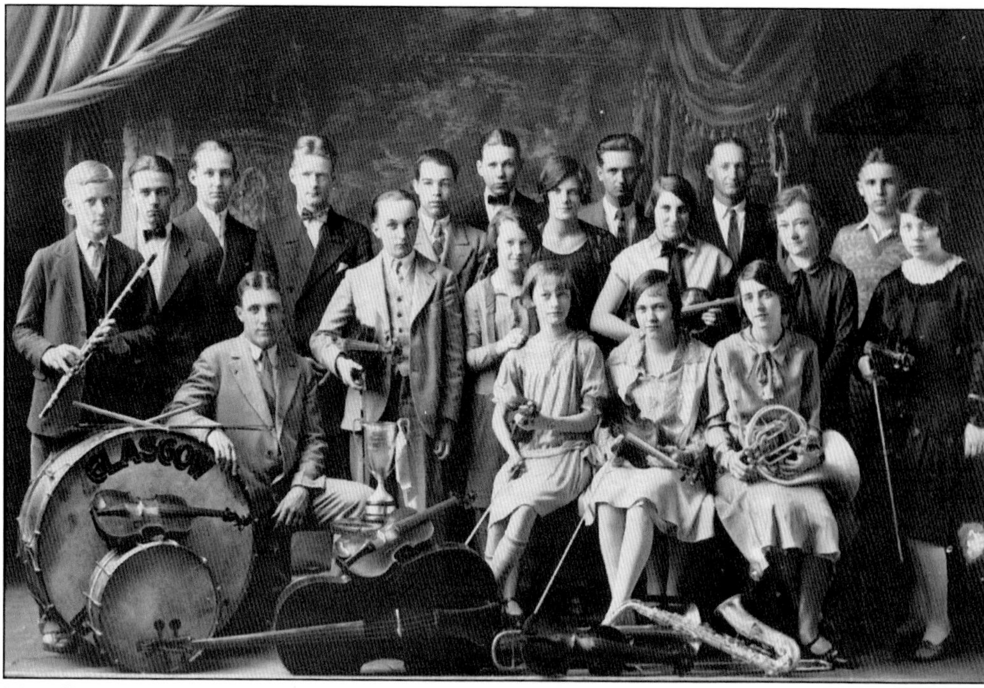

Mary Rapp was a music instructor for many years at Glasgow High School. Her school orchestra introduced many young people to the joys of music and music-making. (Courtesy South Central Kentucky Cultural Center.)

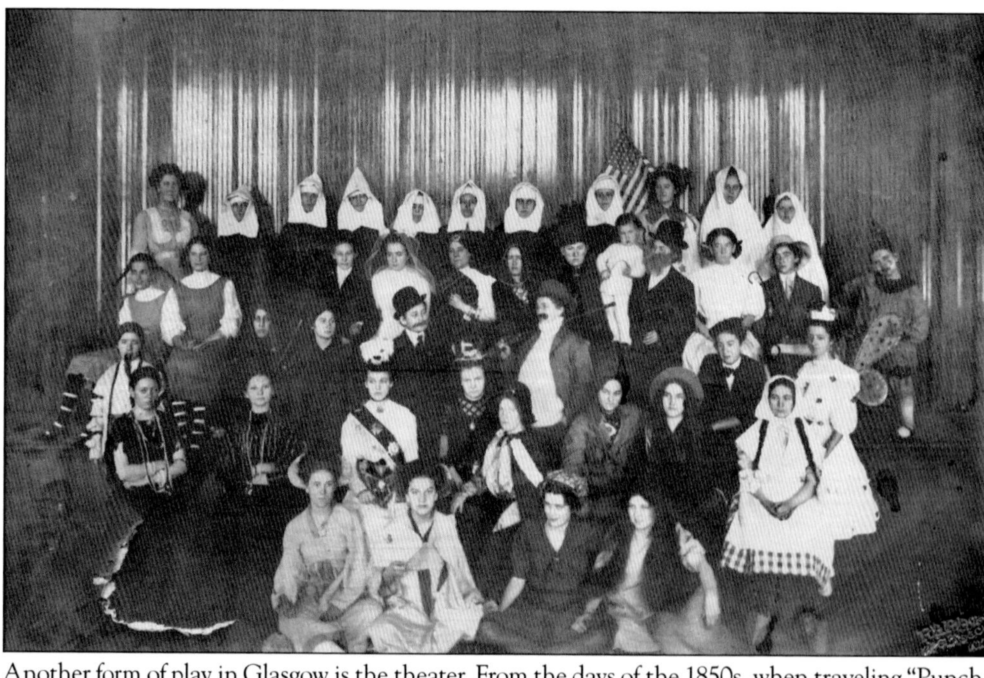

Another form of play in Glasgow is the theater. From the days of the 1850s, when traveling "Punch, Judy, and the Devil" shows came through town, to the present, Glasgow has had a great love affair with the theater. This cast photograph shows a large crew in costume for a performance. (Courtesy South Central Kentucky Cultural Center.)

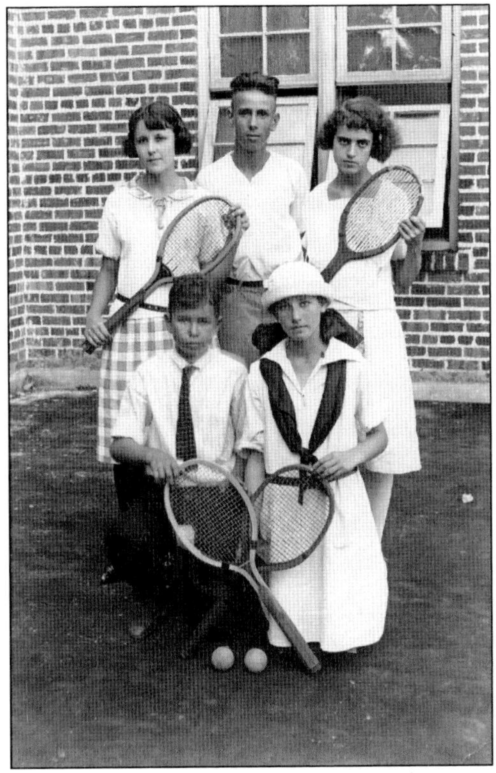

Glasgow has enjoyed lots of ways of playing, from the sophisticated to the ordinary. These images show unidentified young people and types of play they have enjoyed in the past, from tennis to snow sledding. (Both, courtesy South Central Kentucky Cultural Center.)

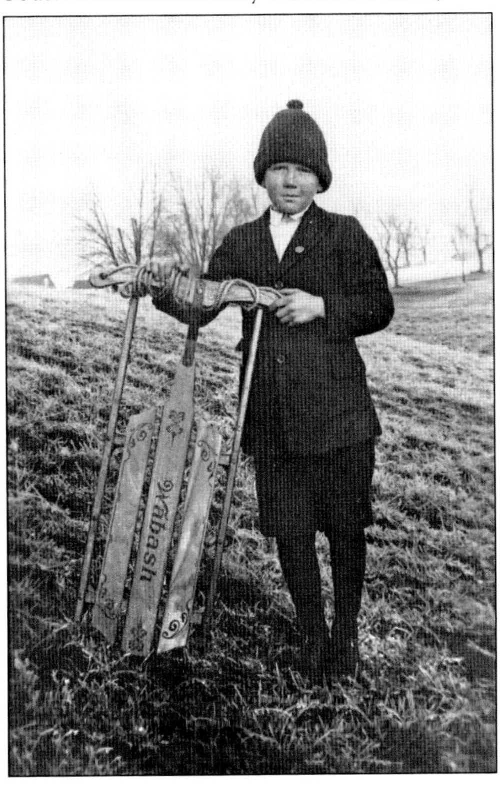

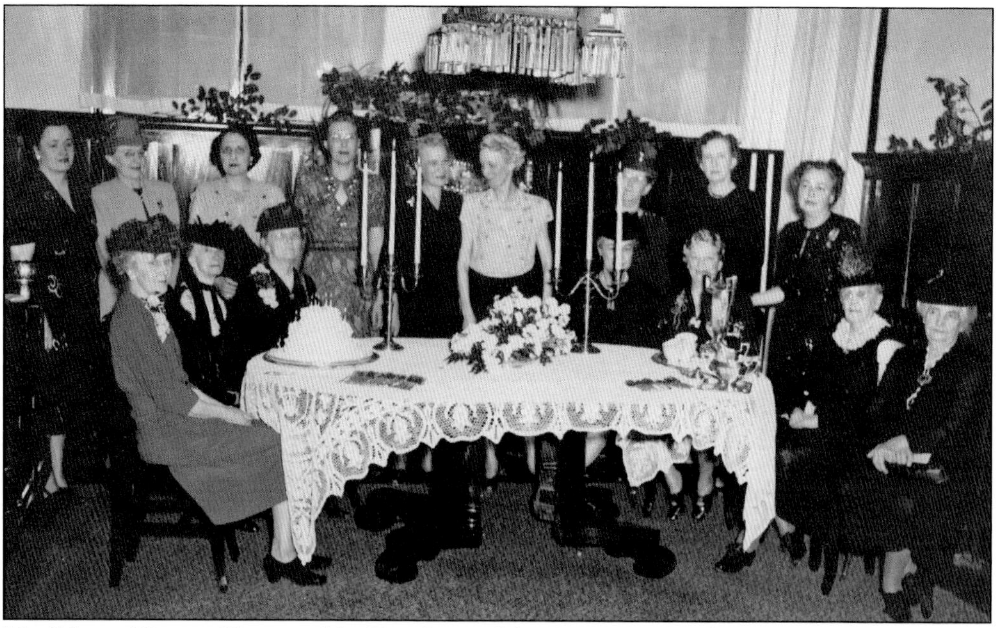

The Edmund Rogers Chapter of the Daughters of the American Revolution gathered at the home of Mrs. C. F. Terry to celebrate their 25th anniversary in December 1947. From left to right are (seated) Mrs. J. R. White, Mrs. E. T. Ellison, Mrs. Day Dickinson, Mrs. C. M. McGee, Mrs. C. F. Terry, Mrs. Catlett Thompson, and Mrs. J. M. Richardson; (standing) Mrs. Glenn Ropp, Mrs. William Gillenwater, Mrs. Charles T. Renfro, Mrs. Carl Walbert, Mrs. L. C. Ellis, Mrs. T. C. Delvaux, Bess Howard, Mrs. Wendell Honeycutt, and Mrs. W. R. Dickinson. (Courtesy South Central Kentucky Cultural Center.)

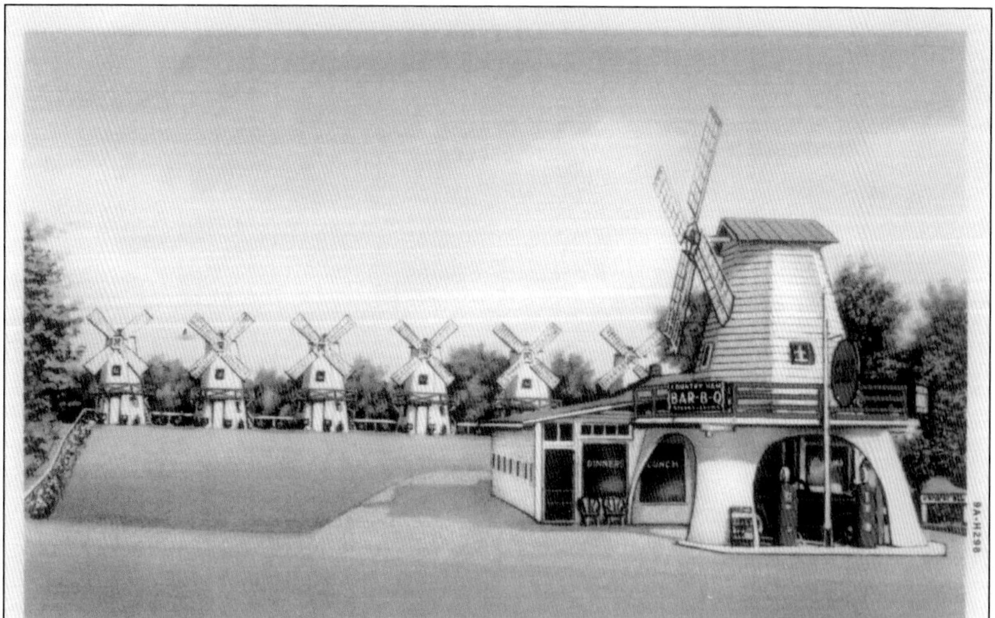

The Dutch Mill Village was another location for locals to play—in the form of dining and socializing at the popular hostelry. (Courtesy South Central Kentucky Cultural Center.)

Seven

All Dressed Up in Glasgow

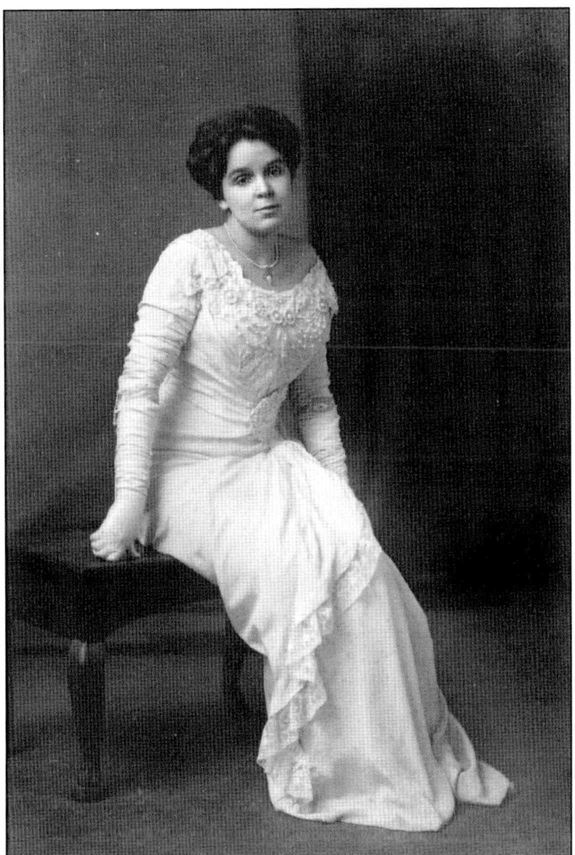

Charlotte Bohannon Knight was indeed all dressed up for a grand occasion when this image was captured on film. Dressing up takes on many forms: from formal occasions to just-for-fun occasions to no occasion at all. Come and take a look back at how Glasgow got dressed up. (Courtesy South Central Kentucky Cultural Center.)

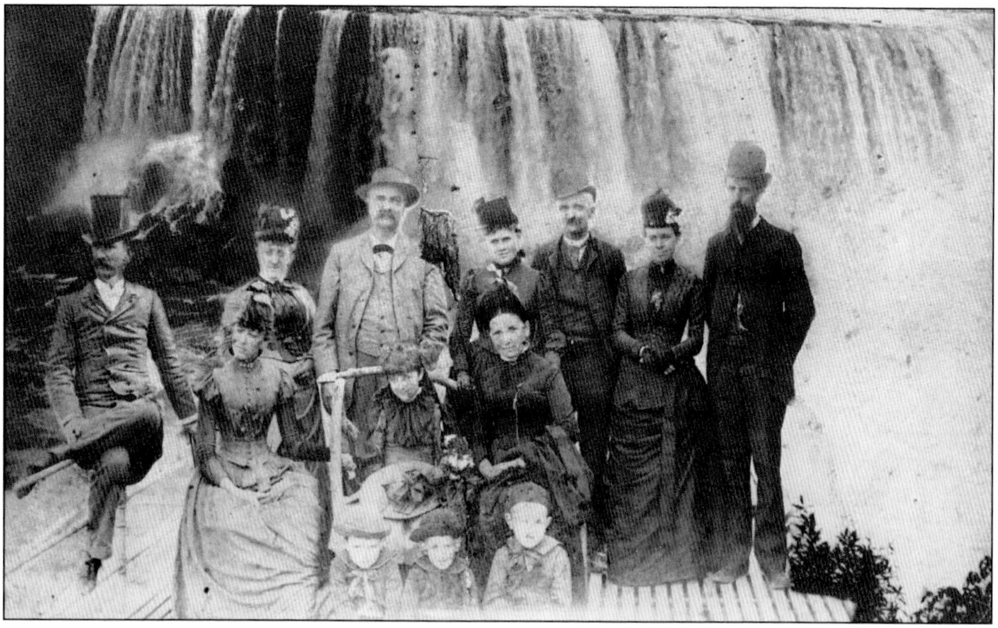

This group of Glasgow residents was dressed up on a visit to Niagara Falls, a popular destination in the years following the Civil War. Here Mr. and Mrs. Cherouse of New Orleans were joined by, from left to right, Mr. and Mrs. Henry Raubold, Mr. and Mrs. John A. Murray, and Mr. and Mrs. W. N. Locke. Included in the front are Gertie Raubold and Lease Locke, Guy Locke, Tom Locke, and Ted Raubold. (Courtesy South Central Kentucky Cultural Center.)

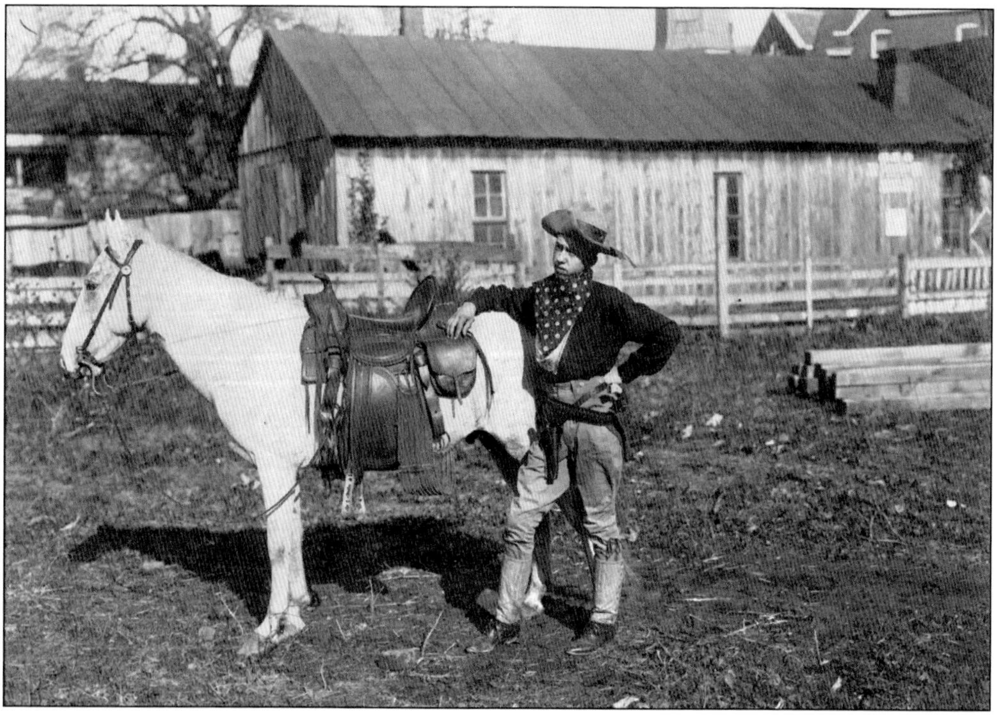

Clyde Breeding is all dressed up as a cowboy in this early-1900s image. (Courtesy South Central Kentucky Cultural Center.)

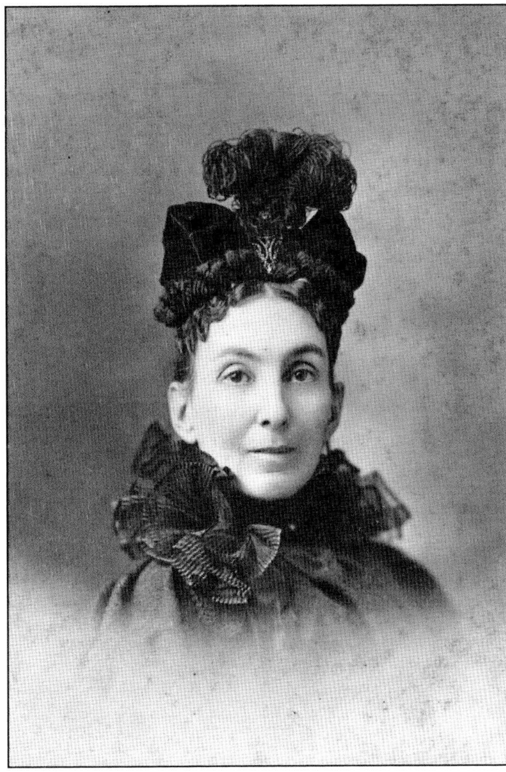

Sophie Dickinson Dickey and Prof. George C. Plemthard are dressed in stylish *c.* 1885 clothing in these images. (Both, courtesy South Central Kentucky Cultural Center.)

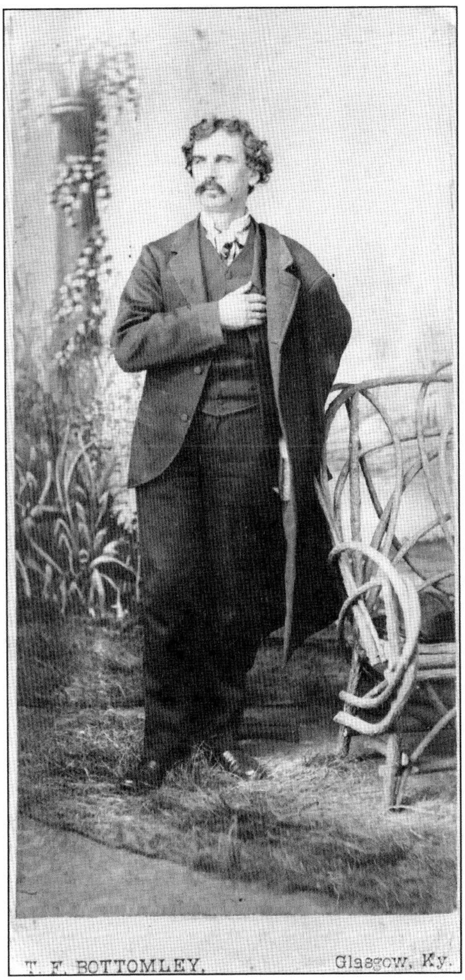

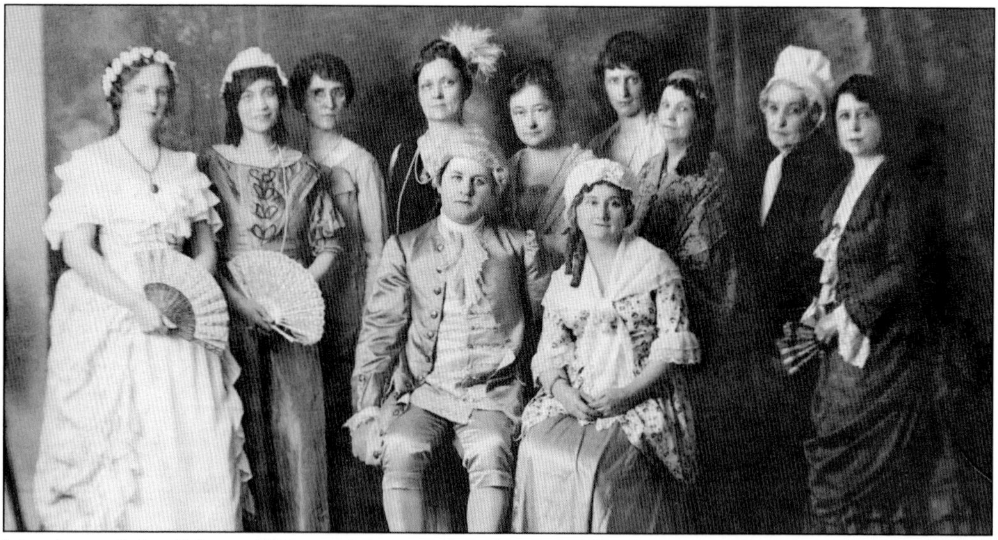

Members of the Edmund Rogers Chapter Daughters of the American Revolution were dressed up in honor of former presidents and first ladies when this image was captured. From left to right are (first row) Dr. George Pedigo as George Washington and Katherine S. Baird as Martha Washington; (second row) Mrs. D. B. Hodges as Mary Todd Lincoln, Mrs. Luther C. Ellis as Mrs. Martin van Buren, Mrs. Ed L. Kerley as Mrs. Calvin Coolidge, Mrs. Day Dickinson as Mrs. James Monroe, Mrs. Karl Rapp as Mrs. James Madison, Mrs. Tom Delvaux as Martha Randolph, Mrs. P. W. Holman as Mrs. John Adams, Mrs. Ella Dixon as Mrs. Anna F. Harrison, and Mrs. J. Hascal Mitchell as Mrs. Benjamin Harrison. (Courtesy South Central Kentucky Cultural Center.)

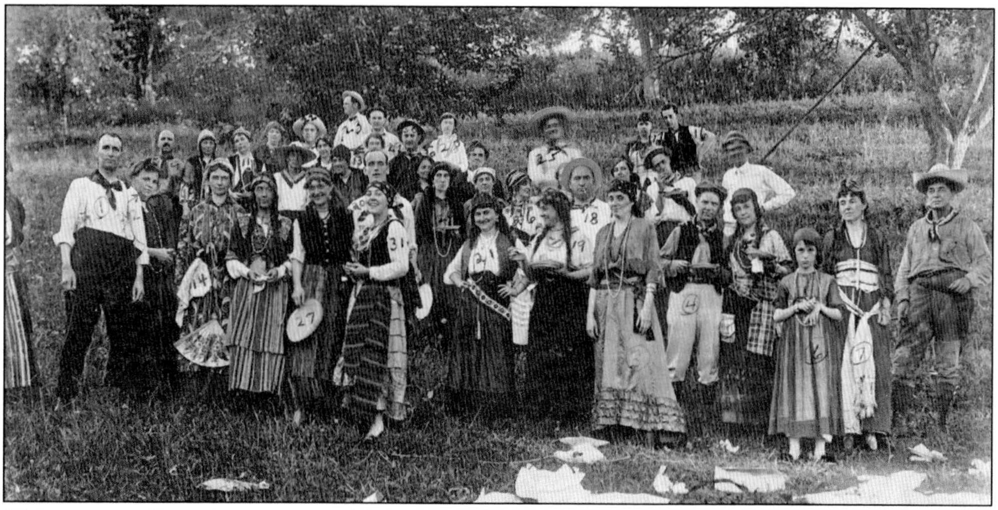

This costumed picnic group was likely dressed up using a "gypsy" or "hobo" theme popular in the early 1900s when this photograph was captured. Included (in no order) are P. W. and Annie Dickinson Holman, Jess Smith Porter, George R. and Helen Crenshaw Lewis, Eliza Trigg Caldwell, Edgar and Mary Moss Brents Caldwell, J. E. and Ella Shader Clayton, Annie Buford Williams, Maymie Porter Terry, Donna Ellison Smoot, Bess Green Mansfield, Annie Reid Bryan, Alanson Caldwell, Lucie Porter Terry, D. B. Strange and his wife, King Crenshaw, Virgil and Katherine Shirley Baird, Ballard Trigg, Mrs. Frank Richardson, Dave Bettison, Mary Pedigo Trigg, Mrs. Lizzie Pedigo Trigg, Karl and Mary Dixon Rapp, Jim Smoot, and Grace Fraim. (Courtesy South Central Kentucky Cultural Center.)

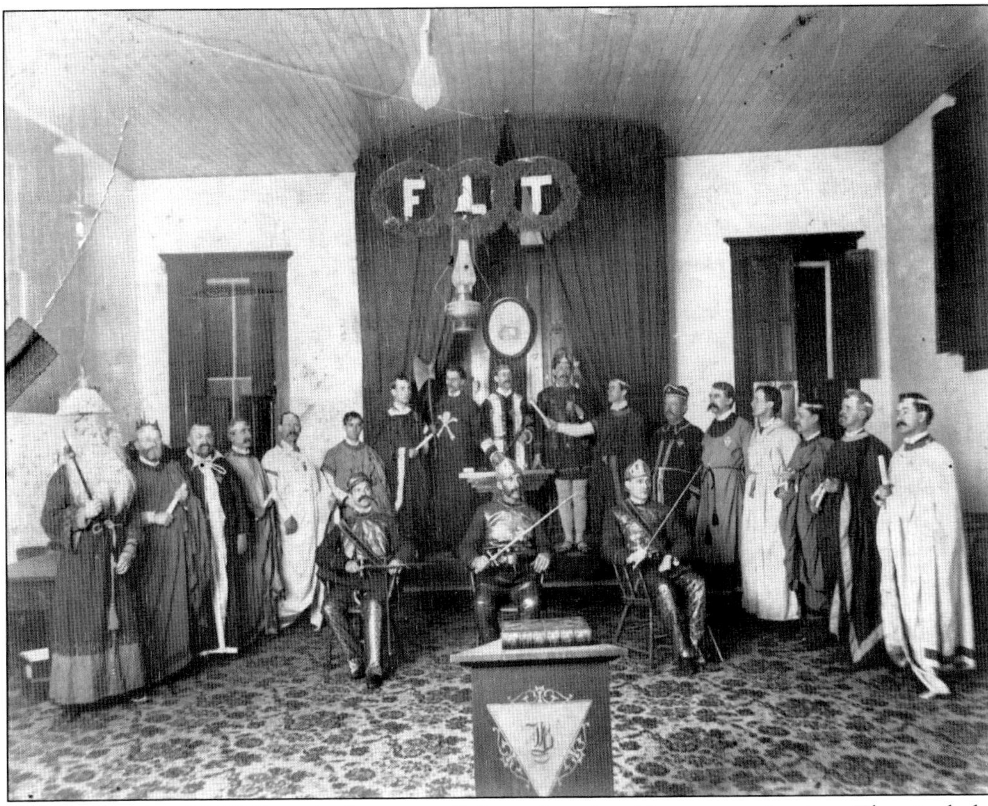

Members of the Odd Fellows Lodge were all dressed up for this moment in time. They include, from left to right, (seated) Clem Shobe and Will Pedigo; (standing) Capt. ? Crigler, R. L. Paull, Jim Davidson, Charlie Warder, Herman Morris, Charlie Powell (preacher), John Barrick, Judge ? Jones, Brents Dickinson, Chris Pare, John Murray, and Jim Frank Taylor. (Courtesy South Central Kentucky Cultural Center.)

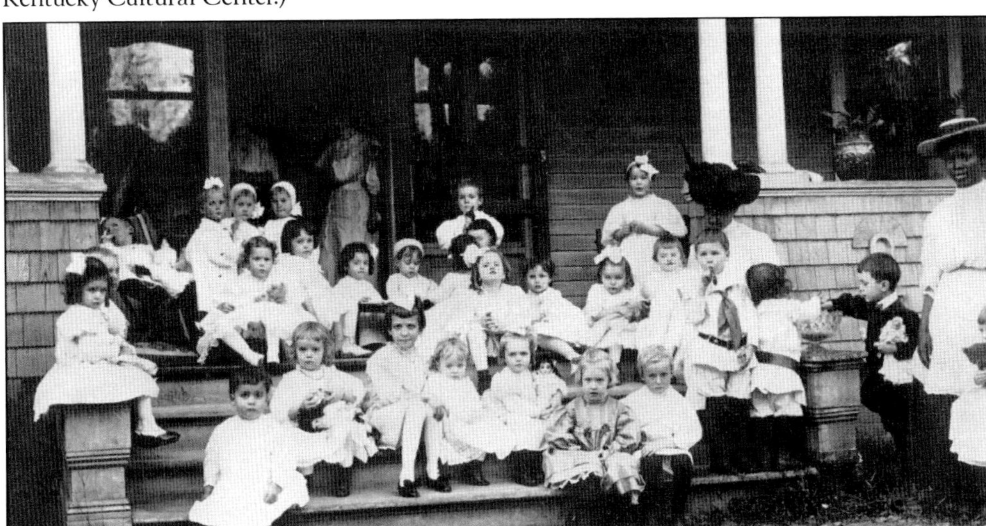

Eliza Trigg Caldwell was the hostess for this grand gathering of children at her home on South Green Street. All the dressed-up folks gathered for this c. 1909 event. (Courtesy author's collection.)

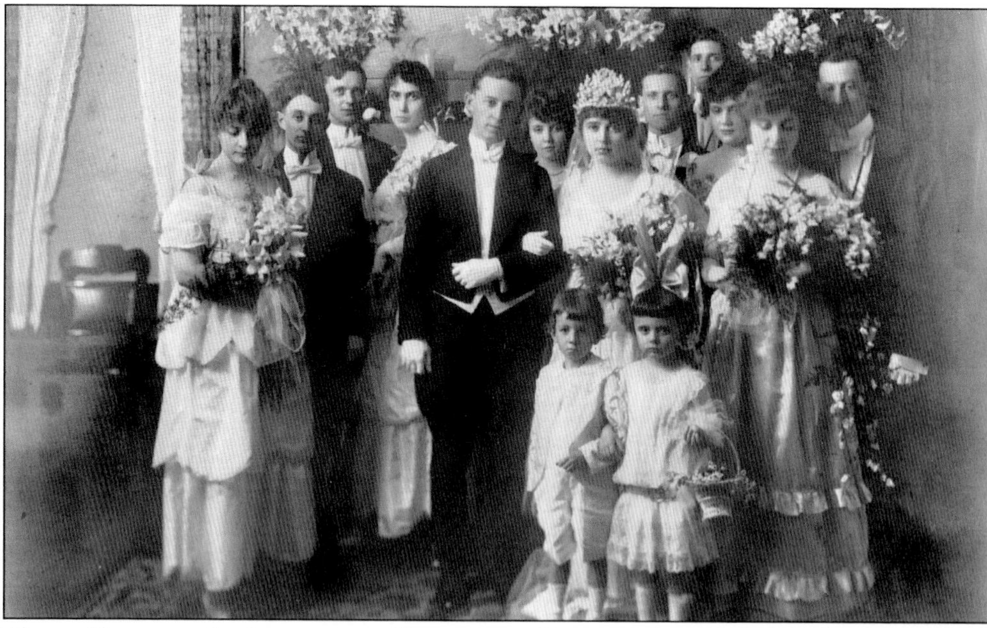

The wedding party for the marriage of Lucie Porter Terry and Alanson Caldwell included these dressed up folks: from left to right, Elizabeth Strange, Brents Caldwell, Winn Davis, Martha Dickinson, the groom, Mackie Davis, the bride, Cary Jewell, Thomas Dickinson, Rowe Combs, Grace Fraim, and William Reid Dickinson. The ring bearer was Paul W. Holman Jr., and the flower girl was Sarah Porter, later Goodman. (Courtesy South Central Kentucky Cultural Center.)

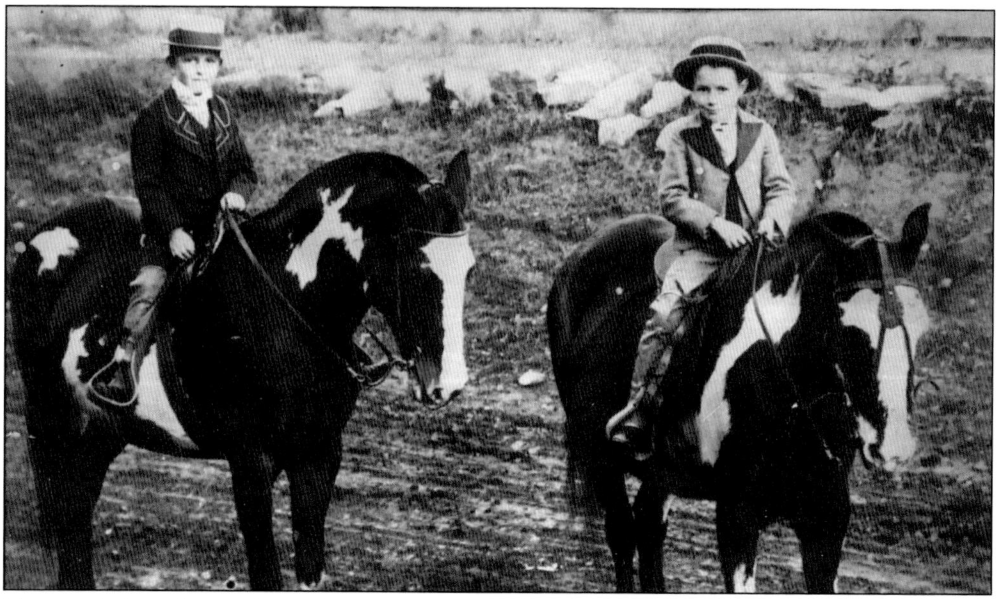

Mont and Guy Comer drove this pair of ponies, Punch (ridden by Hutchins Kemp) and Judy (ridden by Jim Tom Evans), from Gamaliel to Glasgow when the R. W. Comer family moved to Glasgow in 1900. The ponies pulled a sightseeing, no-top surrey, with seats back to back so that two people rode looking ahead and two looking back. The ponies were sold by R. W. Comer to Jim Tom's father, Tom Evans, in 1904. They were shown in the fairs at that time by Jim Tom's brother, Buford Evans. (Courtesy South Central Kentucky Cultural Center.)

Litie Shuster was all dressed up for a special occasion when this picture was taken. Note the small purse on her right hand; such devices were designed to hold calling cards and a small amount of money should the need arise. (Courtesy South Central Kentucky Cultural Center.)

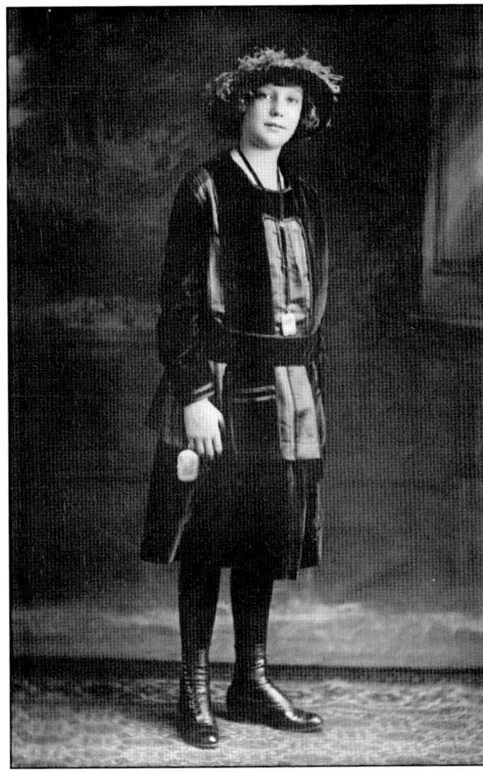

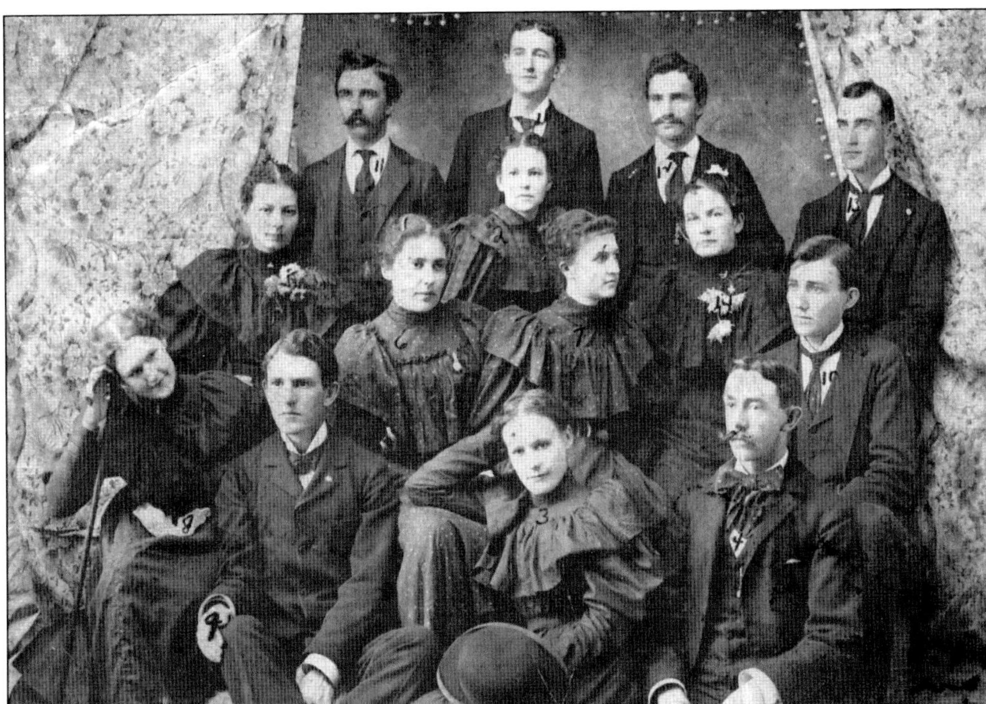

This 1890s group of well-dressed young adults included couples who later married. (Courtesy South Central Kentucky Cultural Center.)

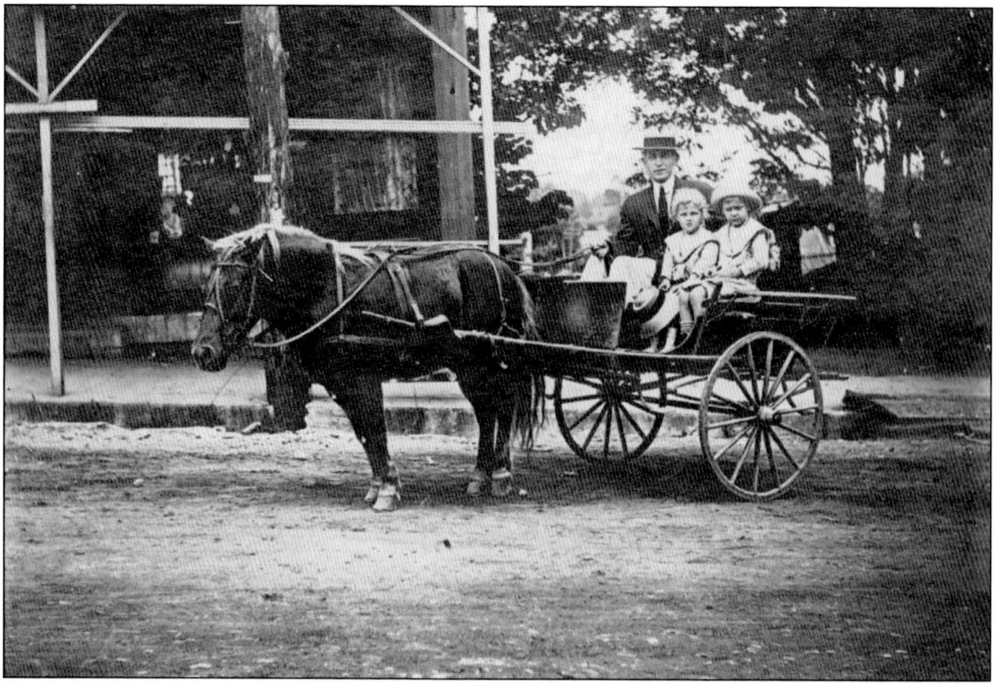

Howard B. Smith is pictured with his nephews, from left to right, Tom Parker Smith and Basil Huggins Smith, sons of Ed Smith. The beloved pony pulling the buggy was named Cupid. (Courtesy South Central Kentucky Cultural Center.)

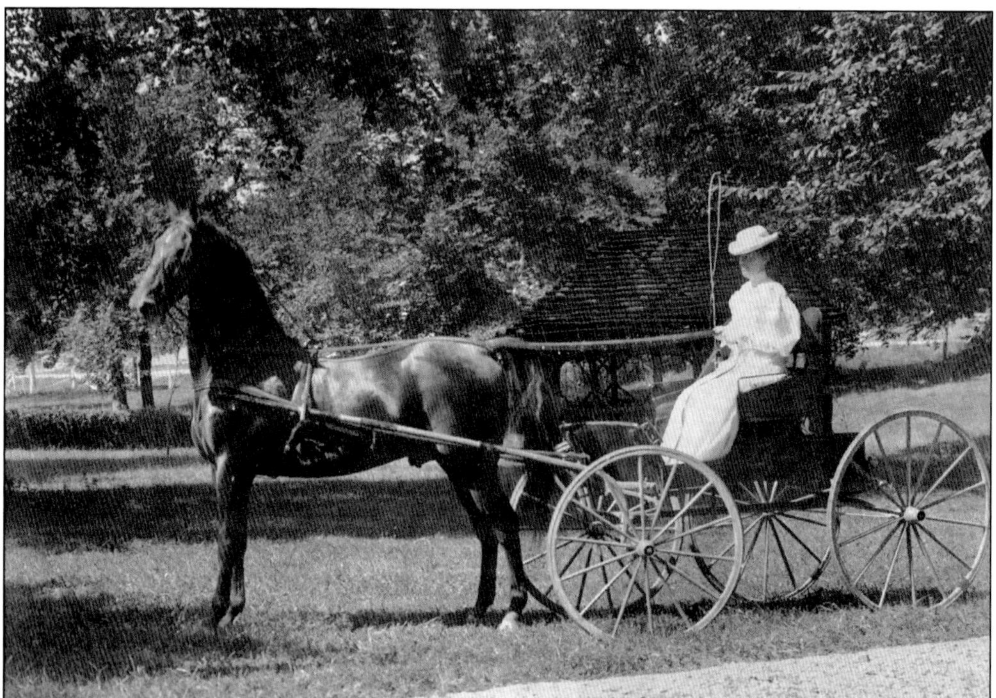

Frances Trigg is in a buggy pulled by Sensation, a well-known horse of the early 20th century. (Courtesy author's collection.)

Helen Mansfield and Jessie Wilkinson were dressed up for this photograph. (Courtesy South Central Kentucky Cultural Center.)

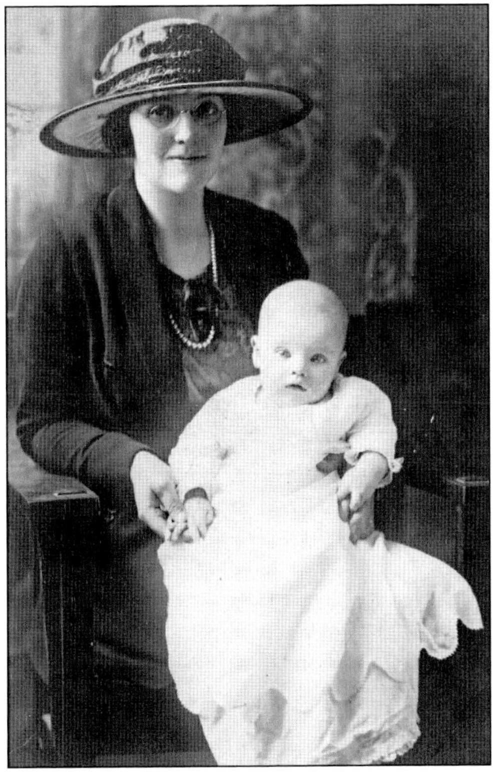

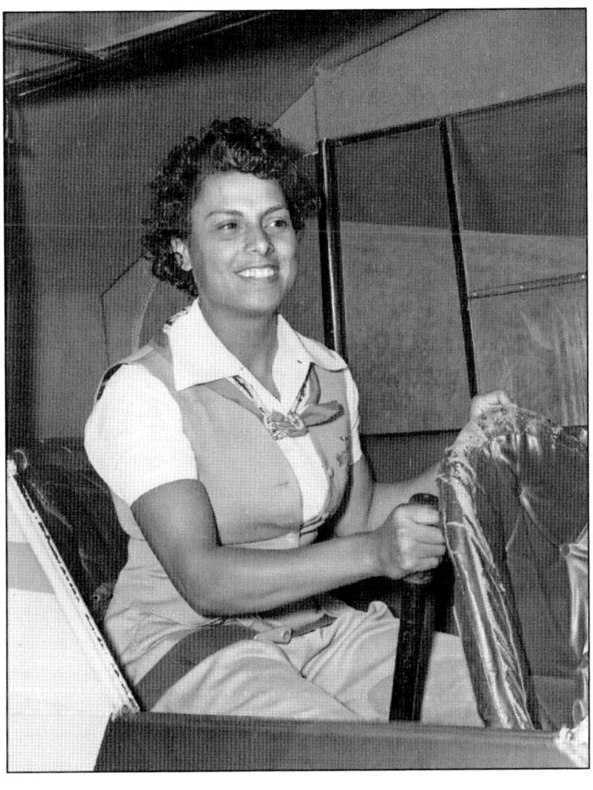

Willa B. Brown was a Glasgow native and the nation's first African American commercial pilot. She held a master's degree from Northwestern, and according to her admirers, she could "fly like an eagle." (Courtesy author's collection.)

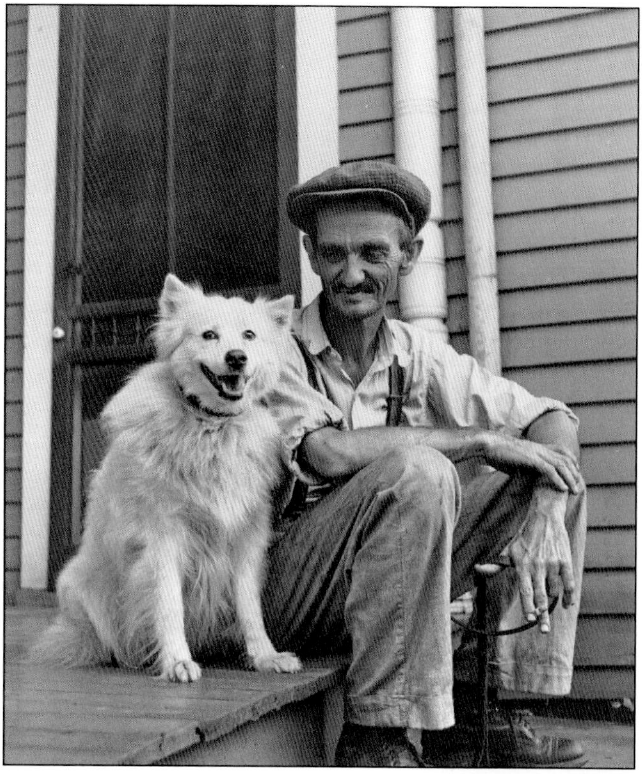

J. Mitchell Ellis captured both of these images of people dressed for no occasion or an occasion. Left, Roy Peden, a local sign painter, and his dog pose on a porch stoop. Below, an unidentified woman in a lace dress surely awaits an occasion of importance. (Both, courtesy author's collection.)

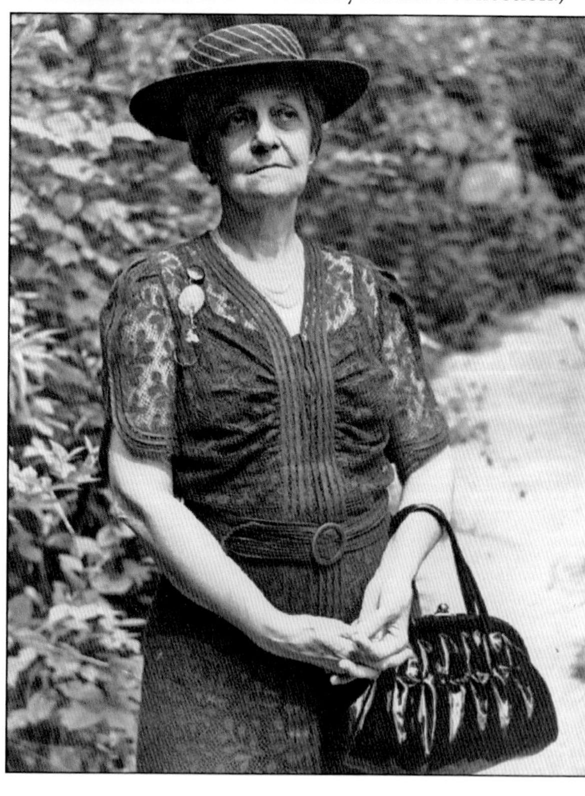

The 1948 Sesquicentennial Parade celebrating Barren County's 150th anniversary brought out a lot of people dressed in various ways. Right, an unidentified woman in the parade donned her old-fashioned clothes and a corncob pipe while riding in a covered wagon. Below, an unidentified African American woman appears to have a story to tell. (Both, courtesy South Central Kentucky Cultural Center.)

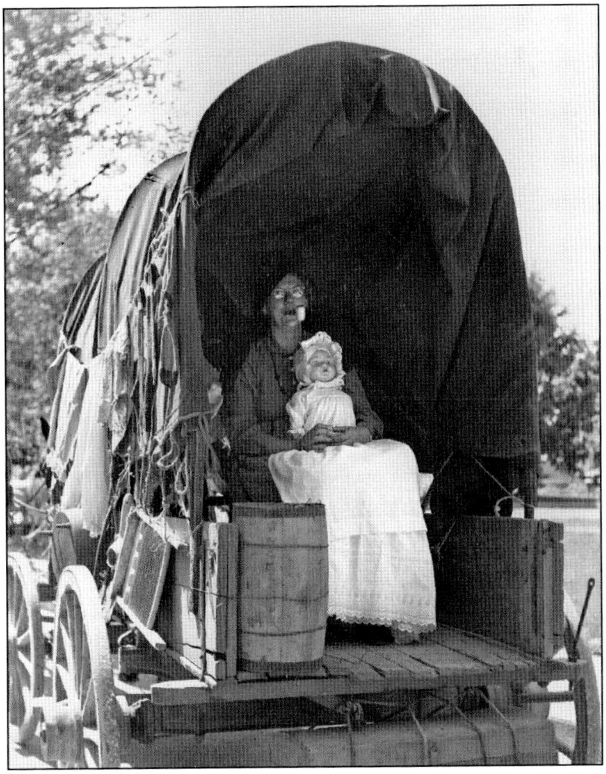

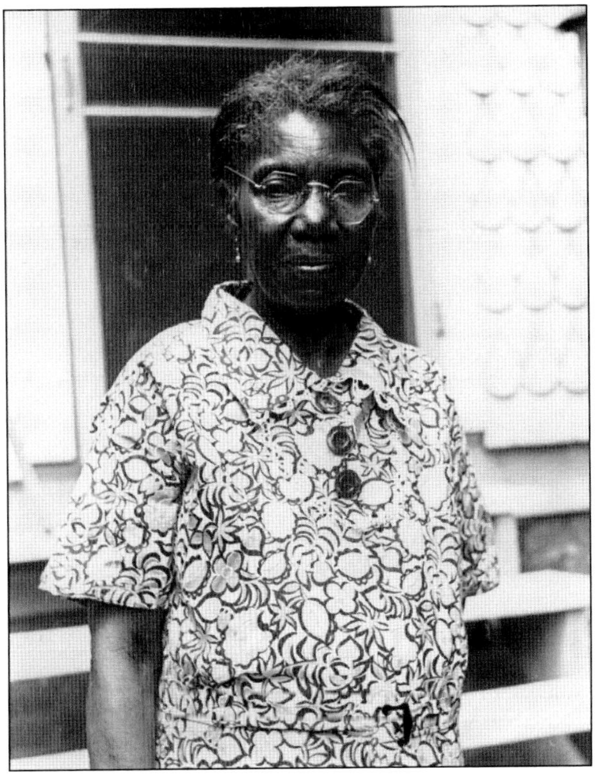

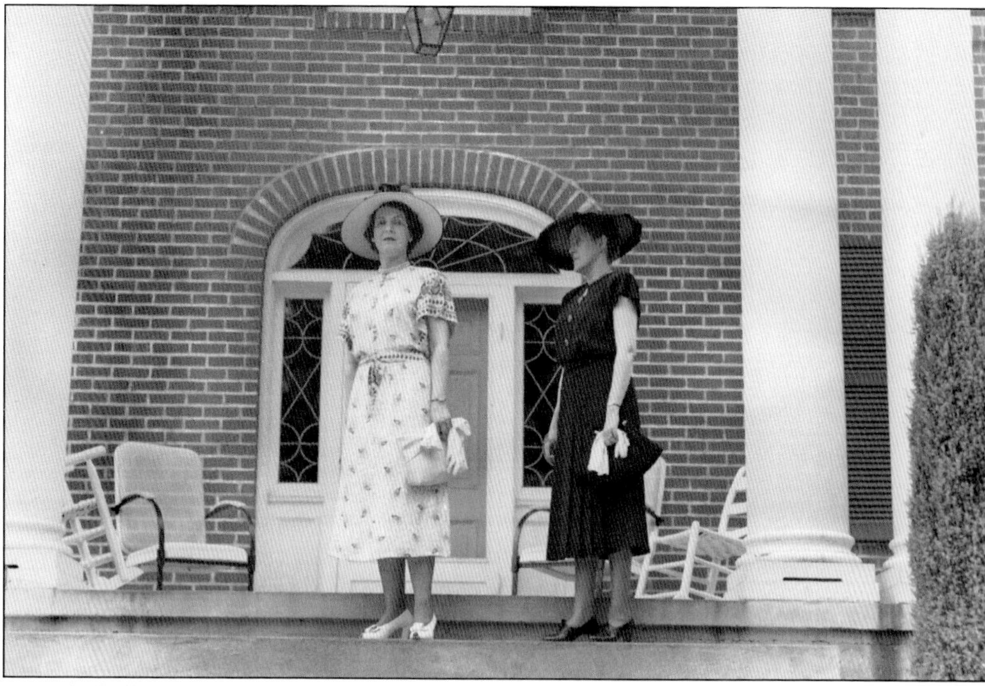

J. Mitchell Ellis captured this impromptu image of his wife, Nelle Terry Ellis, and her cousin, Dorothy Crossfield, on the front porch at their aunt Ruth T. Fant's home on Leslie Avenue. The ladies were dressed for the Sesquicentennial Celebration on the square. (Courtesy author's collection.)

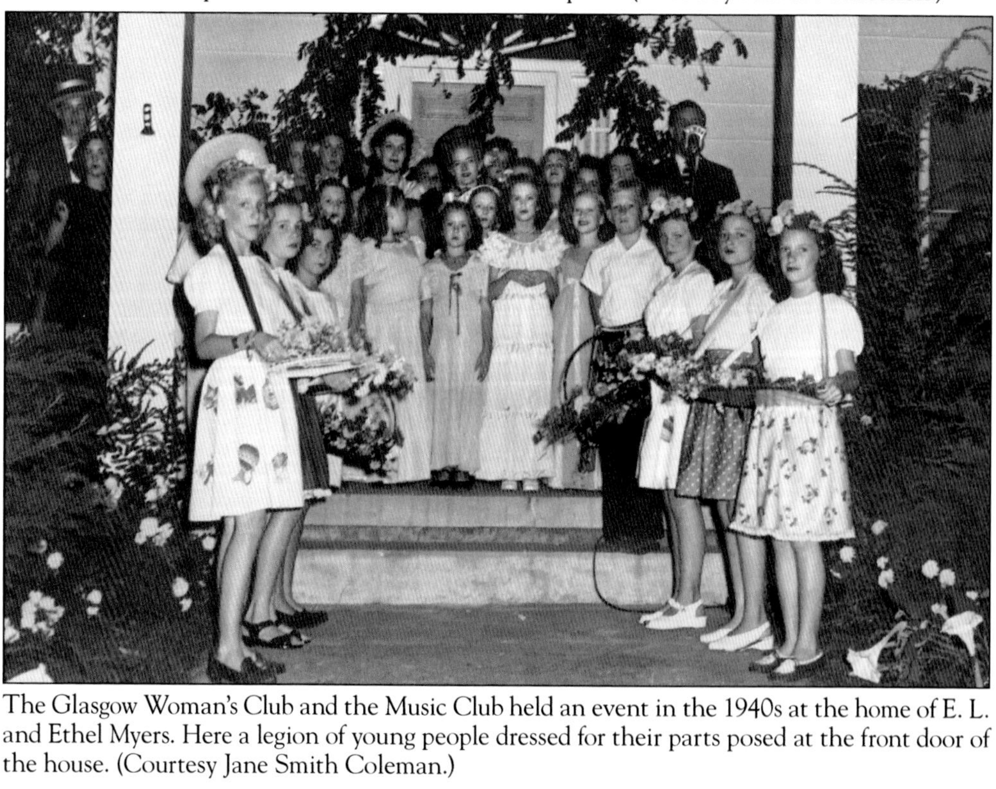

The Glasgow Woman's Club and the Music Club held an event in the 1940s at the home of E. L. and Ethel Myers. Here a legion of young people dressed for their parts posed at the front door of the house. (Courtesy Jane Smith Coleman.)

Beula and Gov. Louie B. Nunn were all smiles when they were dressed for the 1967 inaugural ball celebrating the new governor. (Courtesy South Central Kentucky Cultural Center.)

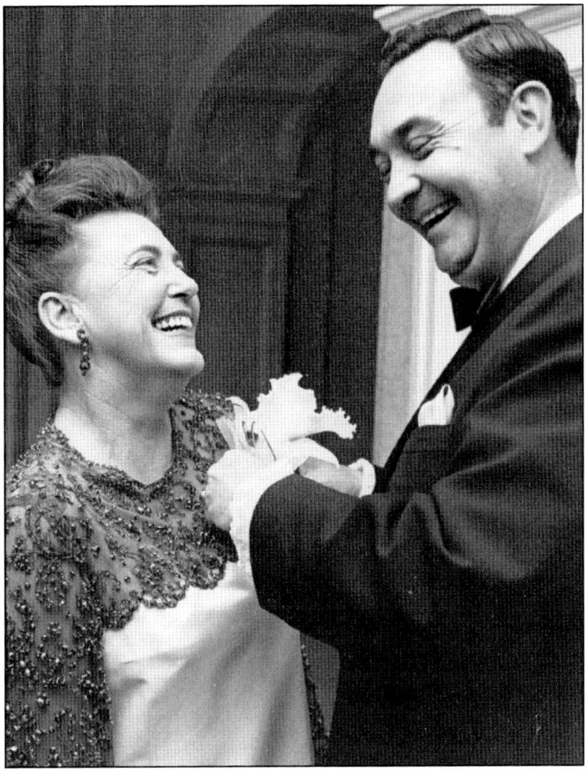

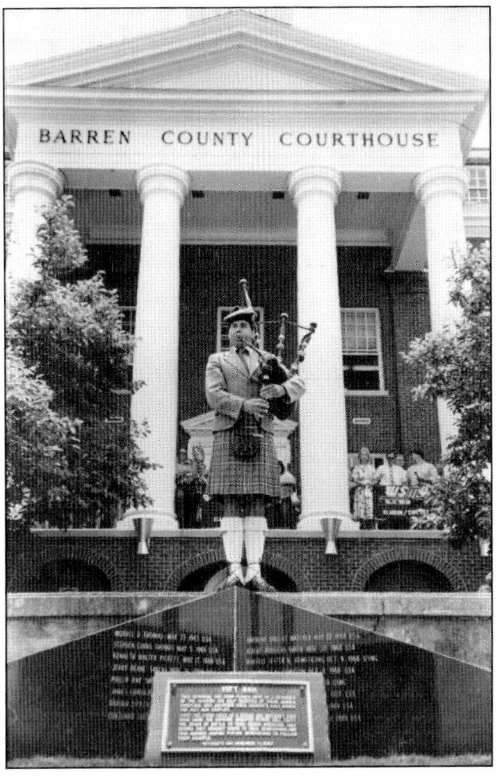

A kilted bagpiper opens the first Glasgow Highland Games. (Courtesy South Central Kentucky Cultural Center.)

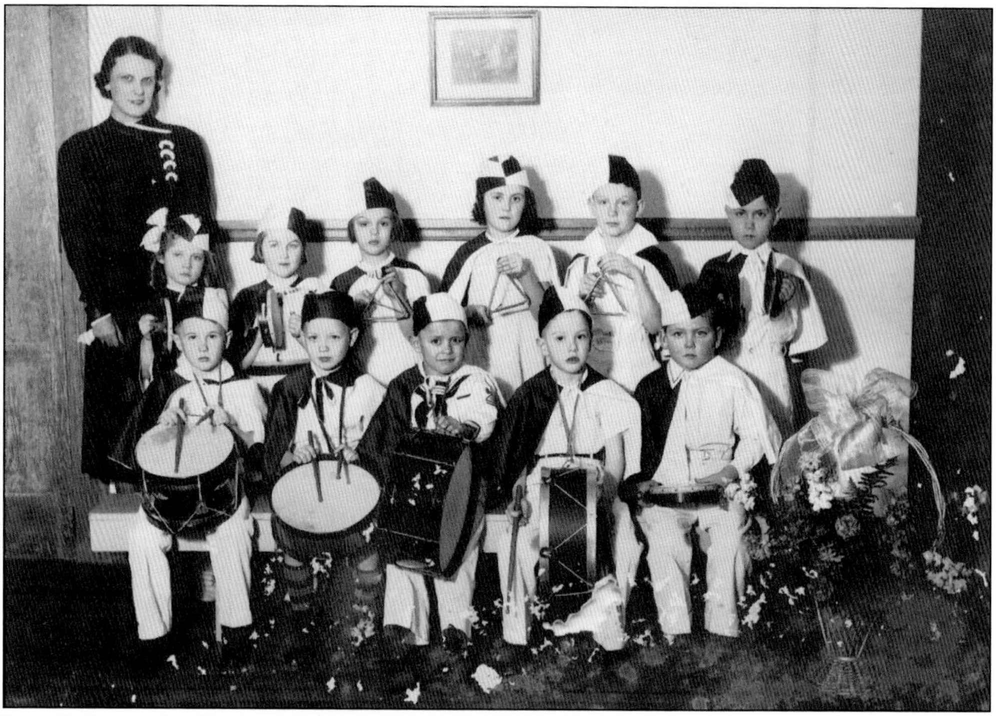

Jane Cady was the director of this children's band, dressed up and ready to play. (Courtesy South Central Kentucky Cultural Center.)

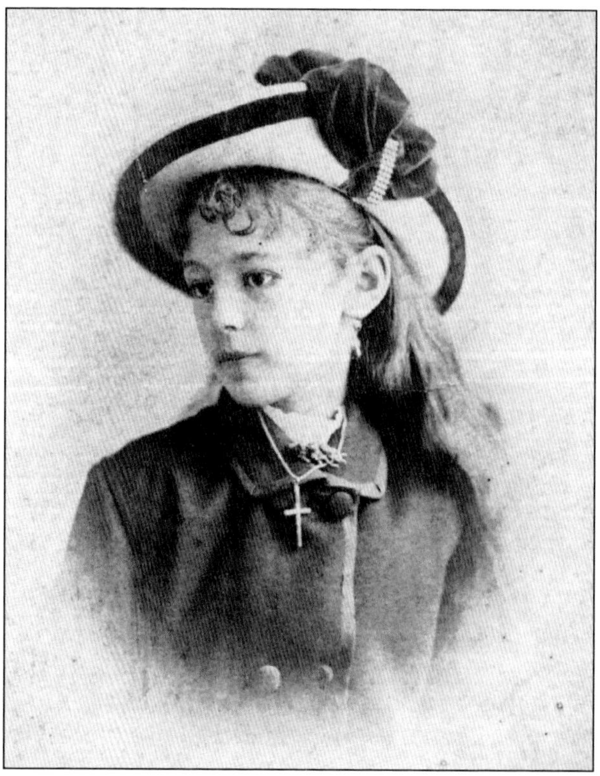

Mary Moss Brents was certainly dressed up in this 1870s photograph. As an adult, she was a noted artist, known for her paintings and hand-painted china. (Courtesy South Central Kentucky Cultural Center.)

Eight

Memorable Events in Glasgow

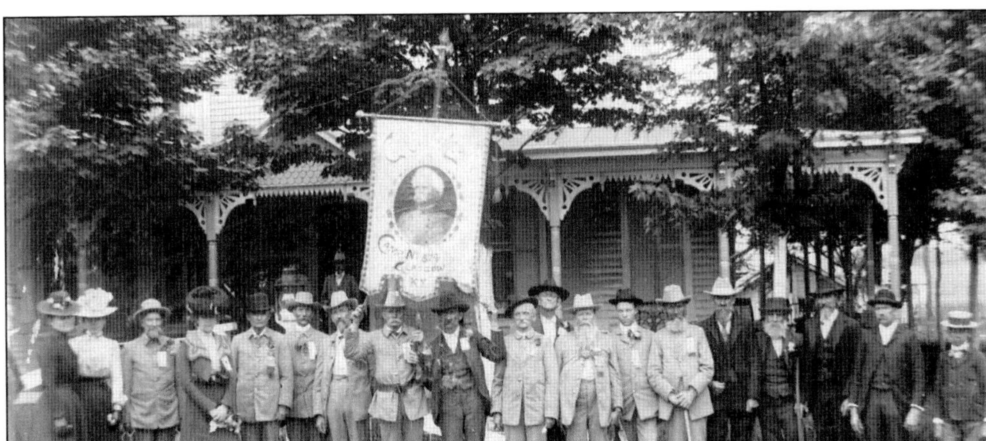

Memorable events tend to become lifetime memories, and Glasgow's are no different. In the late 19th and early 20th centuries, many residents welcomed Civil War reunions and organizations determined to recall various aspects of the war. Here the Gen. Joseph H. Lewis Camp No. 874 United Confederate Veterans (now known as Sons of Confederate Veterans) gathered for an occasion. (Courtesy South Central Kentucky Cultural Center.)

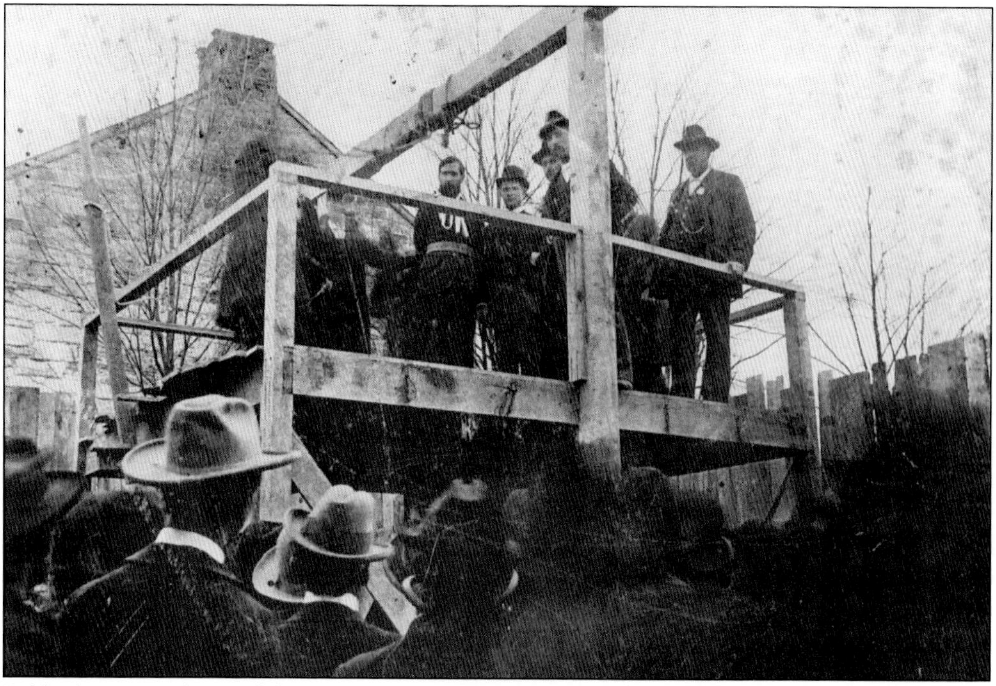

Public hanging, distasteful as it may be, would certainly be a memorable event in almost any mind. Glasgow's were no different, and the local sheriff even printed tickets for admission to the jail yard for the occasion. (Courtesy South Central Kentucky Cultural Center.)

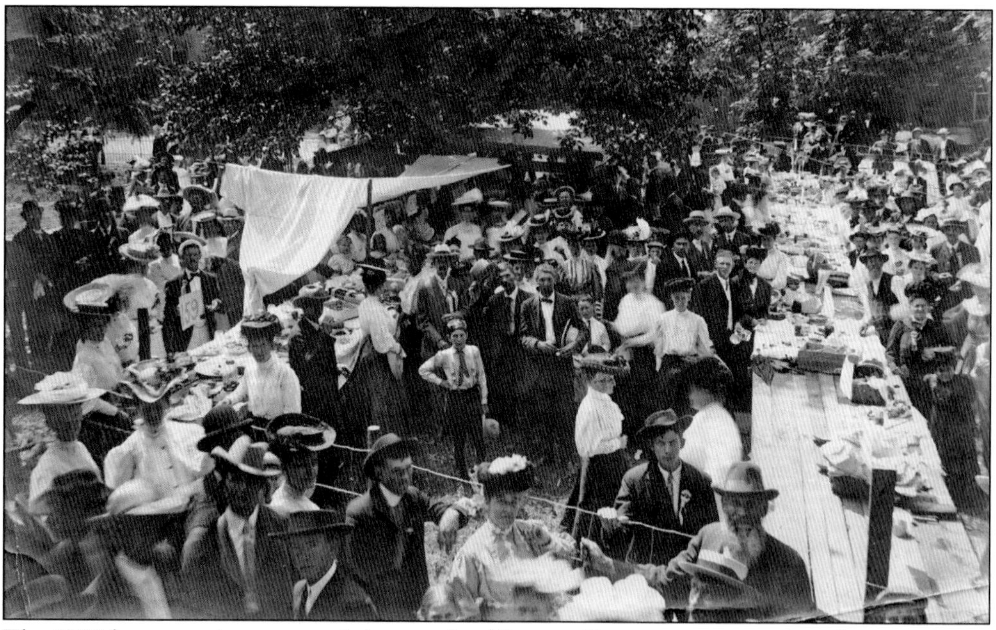

The 1906 homecoming attracted thousands of Barren County natives with a chance to visit, reacquaint themselves, and celebrate the local heritage. John A. Murray was chair of local arrangements and advertised for the construction of 752 feet of tables to be erected in the courthouse yard to accommodate the food for the basket lunch. (Courtesy South Central Kentucky Cultural Center.)

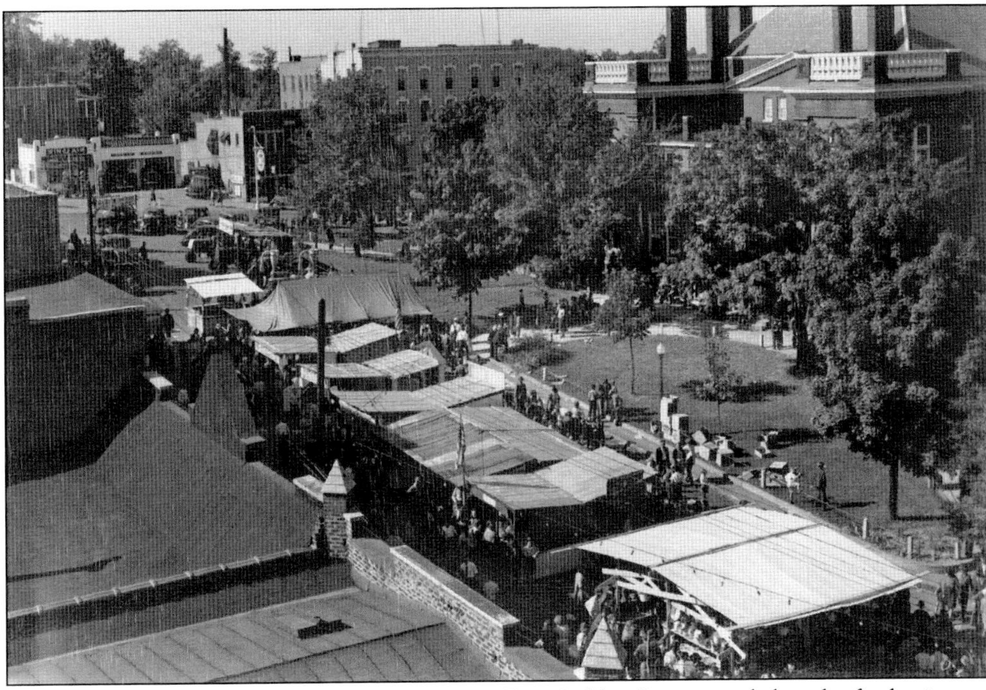

Glasgow street fairs generally filled the entire East Public Square with booths for businesses and organizations. One major part of the street fair was a spirited horse show. (Both, courtesy author's collection.)

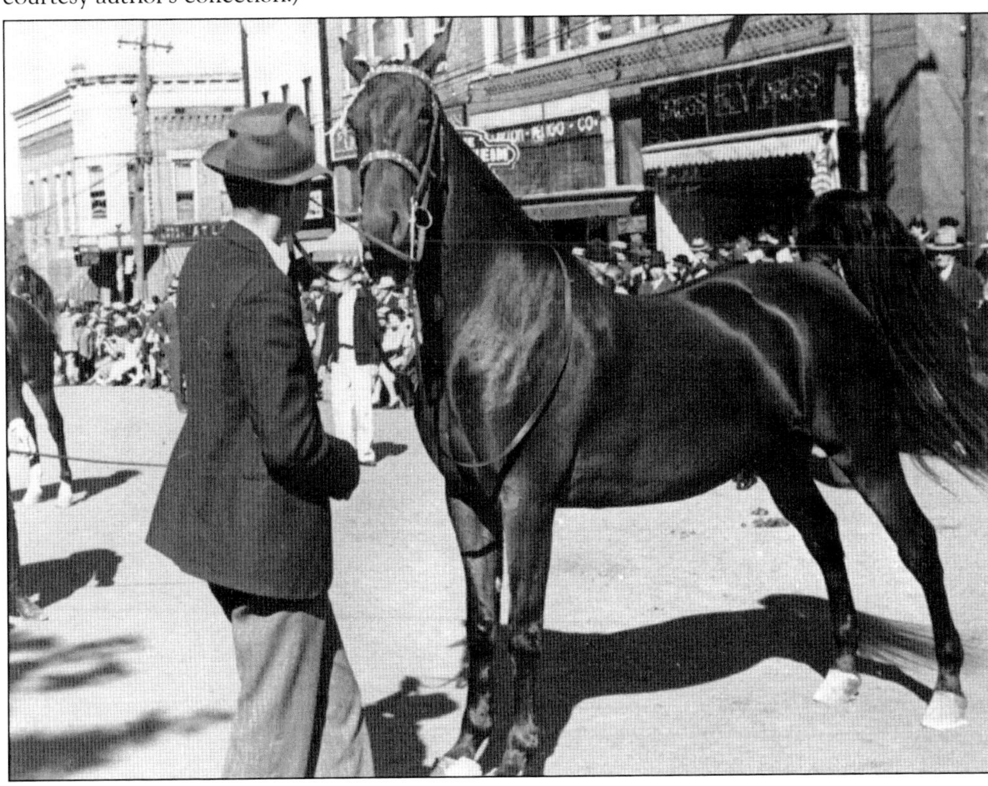

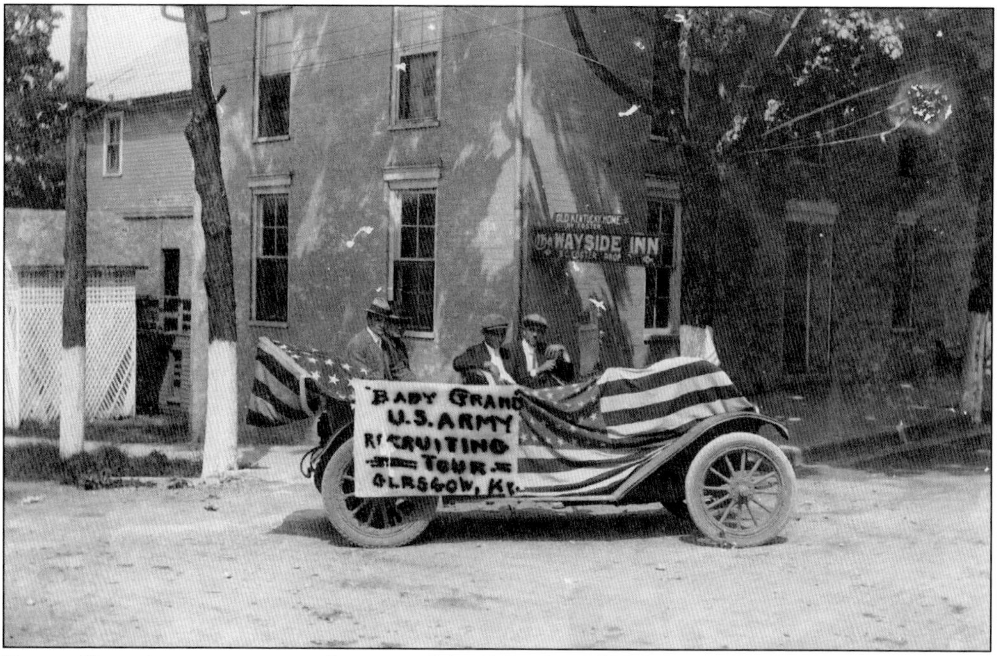

Barren Countians were recruited as part of the Baby Grand U.S. Army Recruiting Tour featuring locals James Billings, Samuel Quincy Adams, Ray Squires, and Milton Law. Only days later, this large group of men had been recruited for service in World War I. (Both, courtesy South Central Kentucky Cultural Center.)

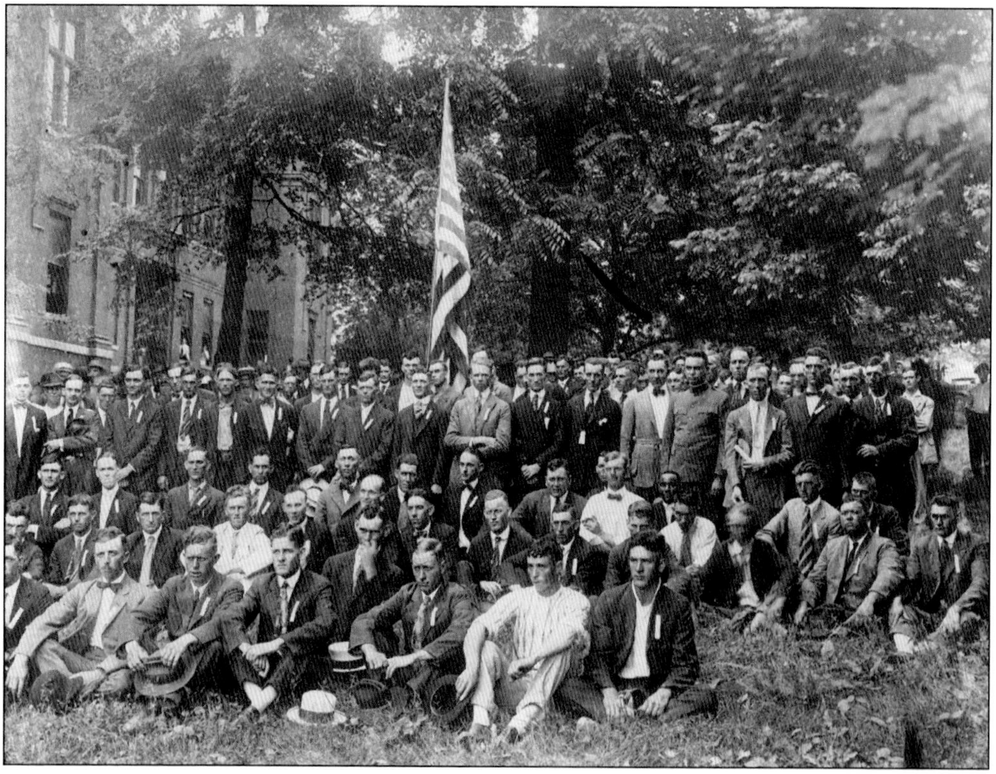

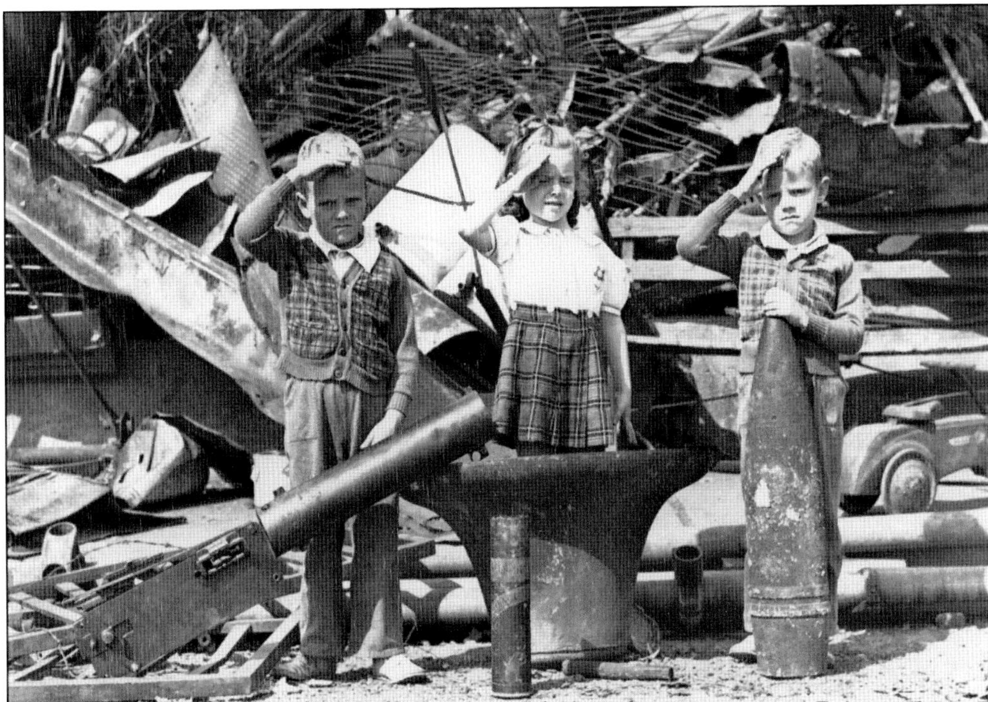

As part of Glasgow and Barren County's efforts to aid World War II, a scrap drive was held, with the cast-off metals being collected at the school campus. Here a trio of children salutes the effort while the school body poses with the scrap metal. (Both, courtesy author's collection.)

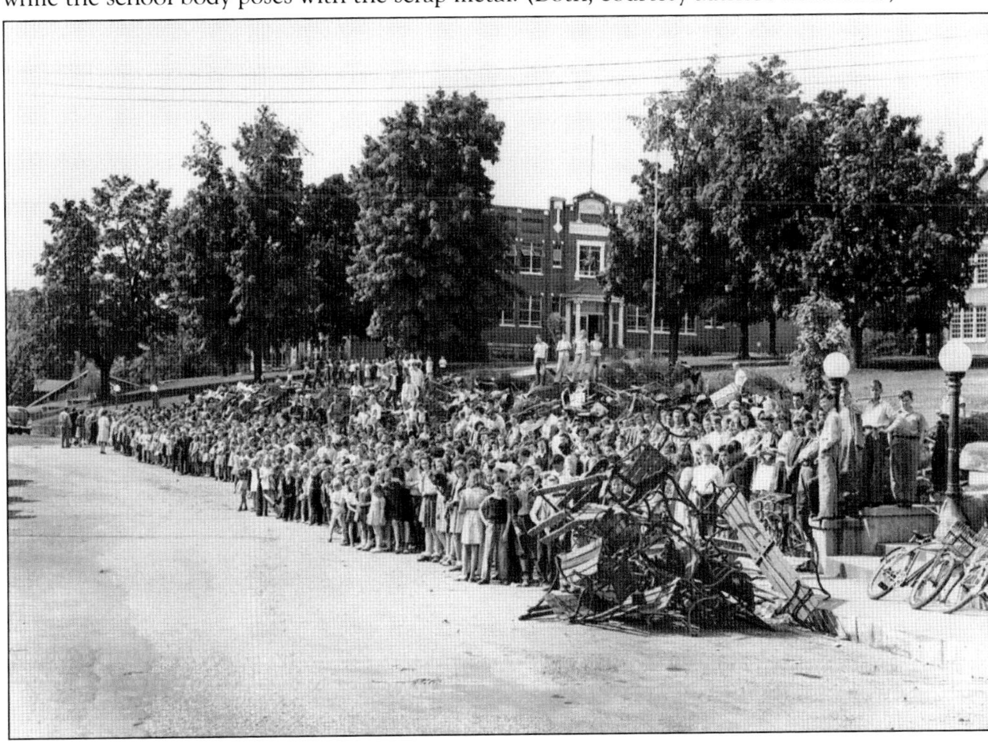

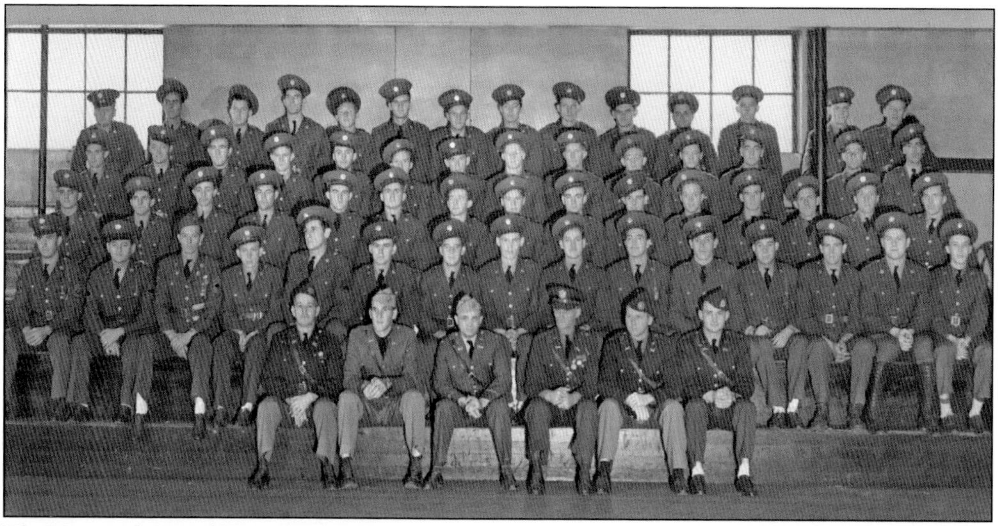

The National Guard Unit, Battery B, 106th Coast Artillery (Anti-Aircraft), prepares to leave for Camp Hulen, Texas, for a year's military training. (Courtesy author's collection.)

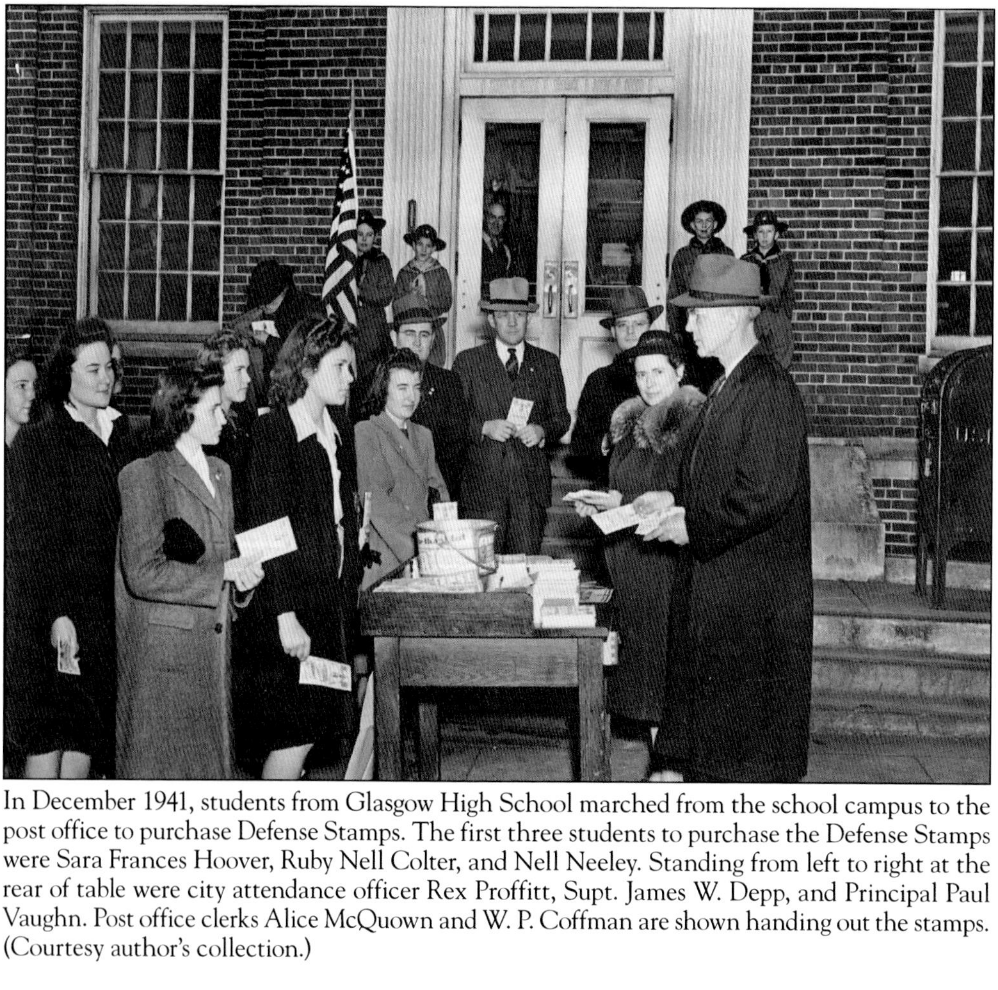

In December 1941, students from Glasgow High School marched from the school campus to the post office to purchase Defense Stamps. The first three students to purchase the Defense Stamps were Sara Frances Hoover, Ruby Nell Colter, and Nell Neeley. Standing from left to right at the rear of table were city attendance officer Rex Proffitt, Supt. James W. Depp, and Principal Paul Vaughn. Post office clerks Alice McQuown and W. P. Coffman are shown handing out the stamps. (Courtesy author's collection.)

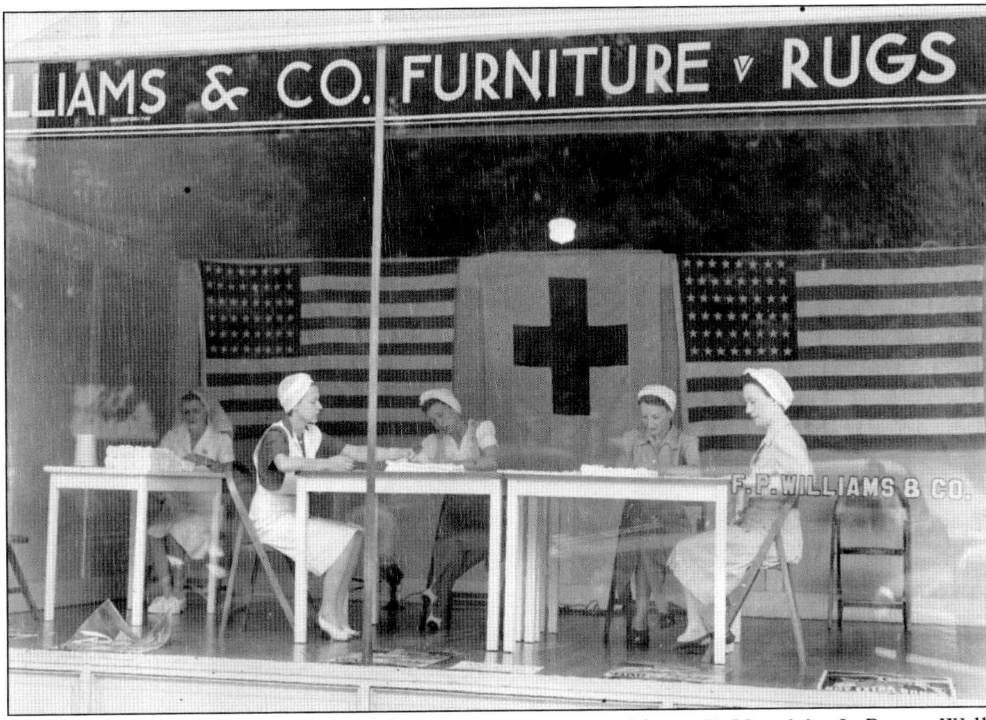

Glasgow's Red Cross Unit turned out to aid the effort in World War II. Here Mrs. L. Rogers Wells Sr. (left) and Mrs. Eugene Abell (right) set the pace for other volunteers in preparing bandages. (Courtesy South Central Kentucky Cultural Center.)

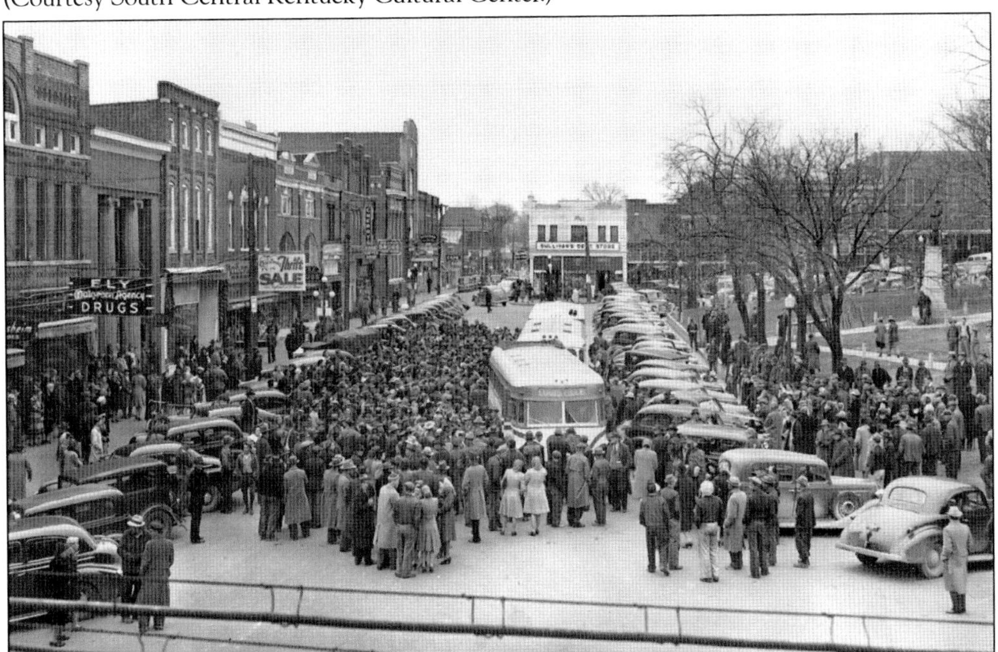

Whether the troops were departing or returning, Glasgow has always turned out in support of the military. Glasgow continues to hold one of Kentucky's finest Veteran's Day parades. (Courtesy author's collection.)

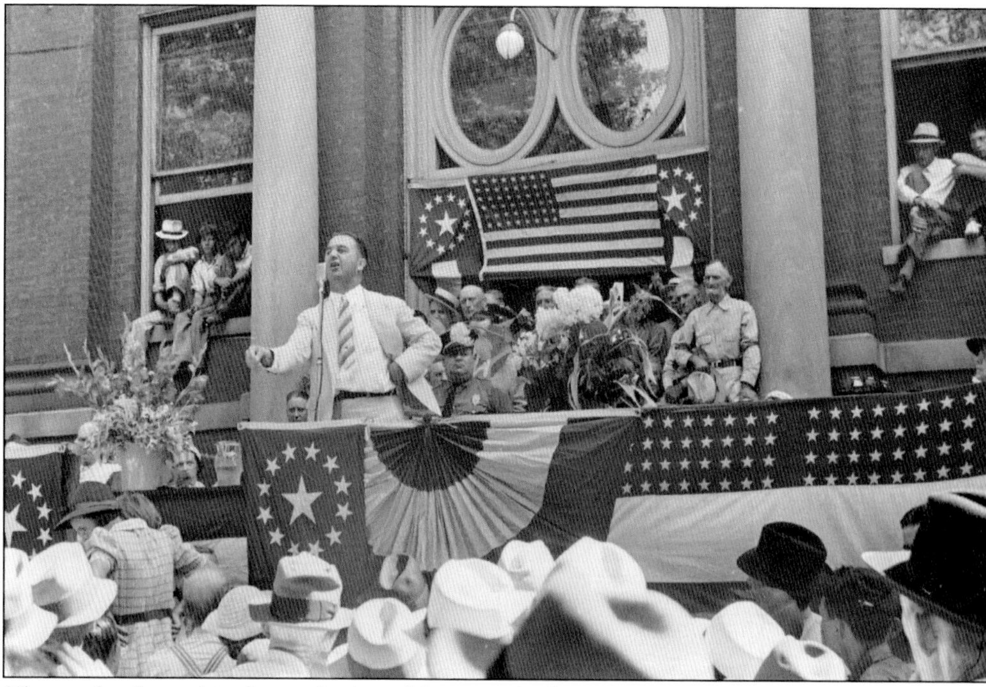

Glasgow has hosted its share of political figures, whether campaigning for office or in the throes of duty. Here A. B. "Happy" Chandler wows the crowd with a spirited campaign speech at the courthouse. (Courtesy author's collection.)

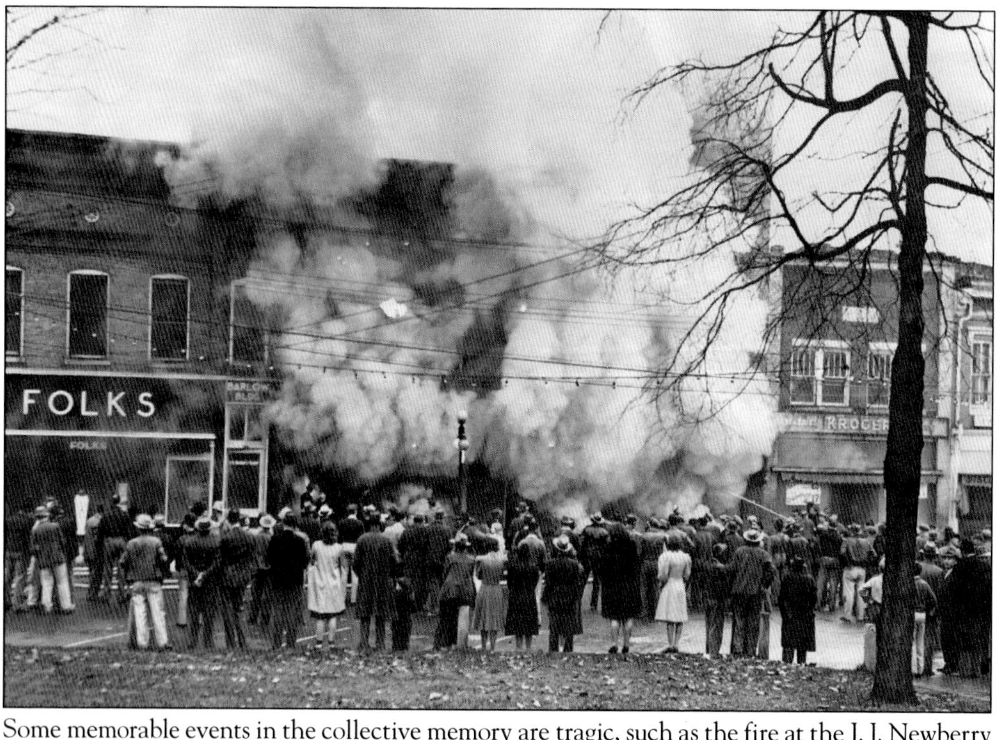

Some memorable events in the collective memory are tragic, such as the fire at the J. J. Newberry Five and Ten Cent Store on the North Public Square. (Courtesy author's collection.)

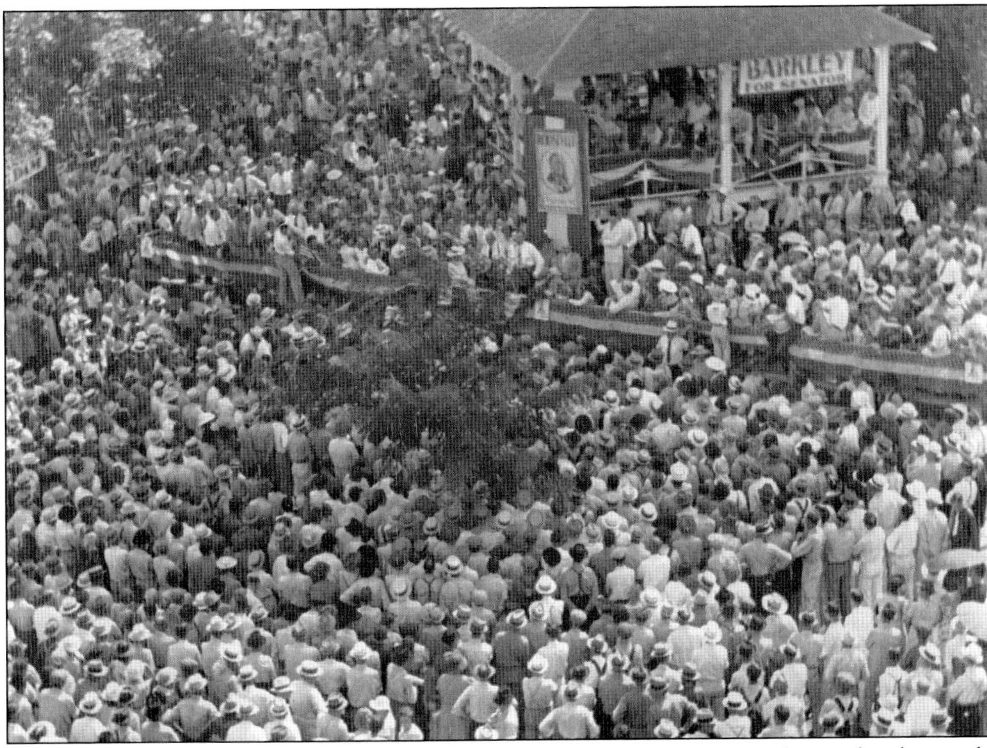

Alben W. Barkley came to Glasgow to campaign for the Senate, not realizing that he would eventually be elevated to the office of vice president of the United States. A Glasgow man, William Warder Vaughan, was one of Barkley's chief assistants during his term in office. (Both, courtesy author's collection.)

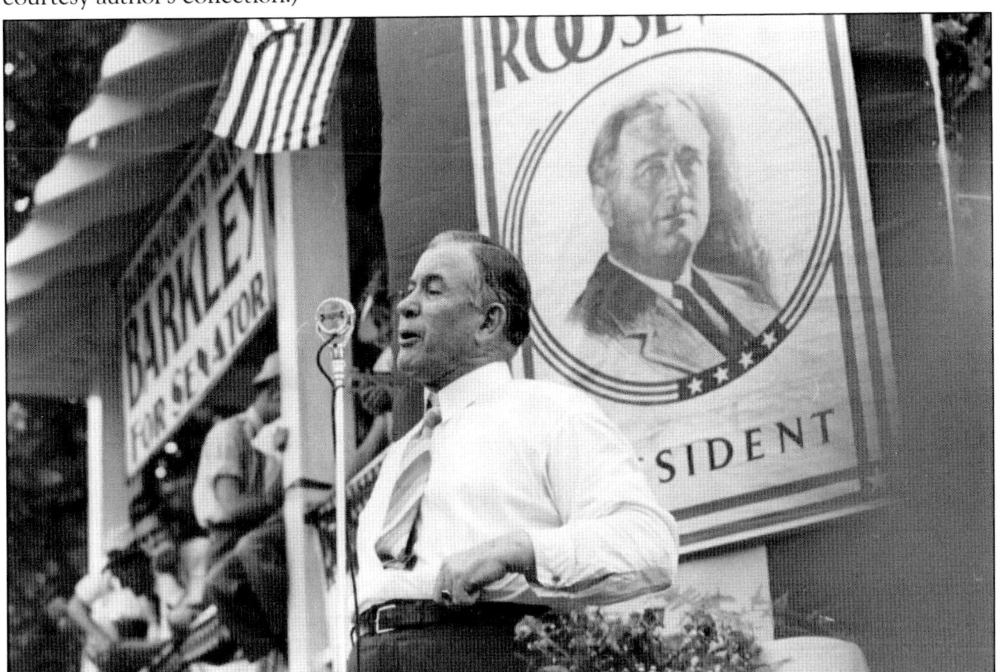

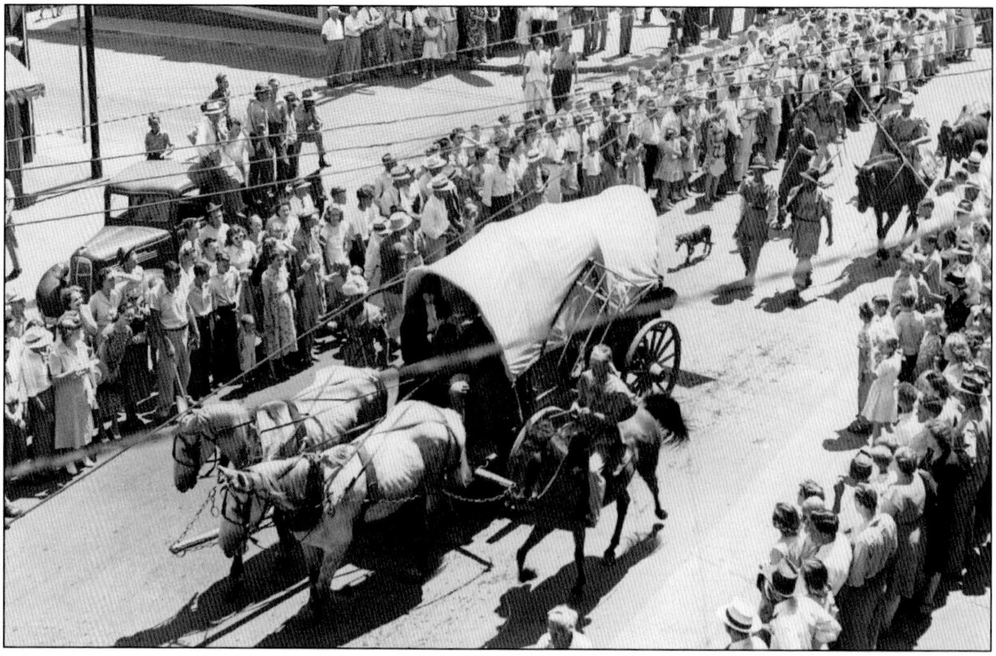

Thousands of people thronged the square for the 1948 Sesquicentennial Parade. Hundreds of entries celebrating every facet of Barren County history filled the streets, historical displays filled store windows, and the crowds were everywhere. Below, the Ladies Matinee Musicale float makes its way along the parade route. (Both, courtesy author's collection.)

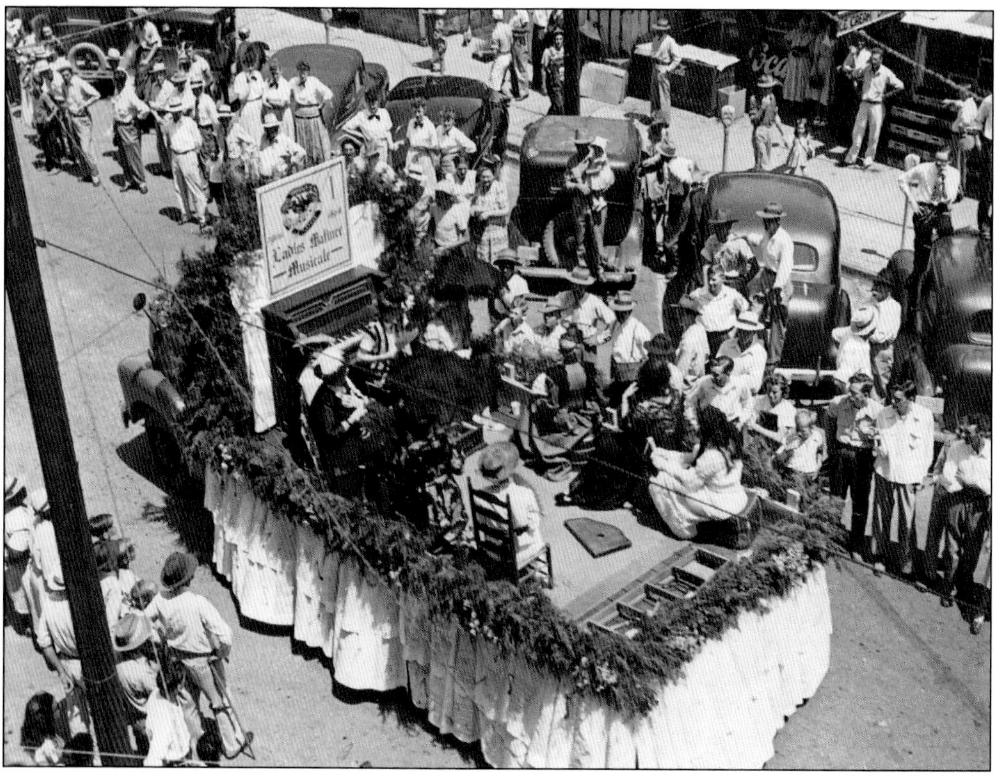

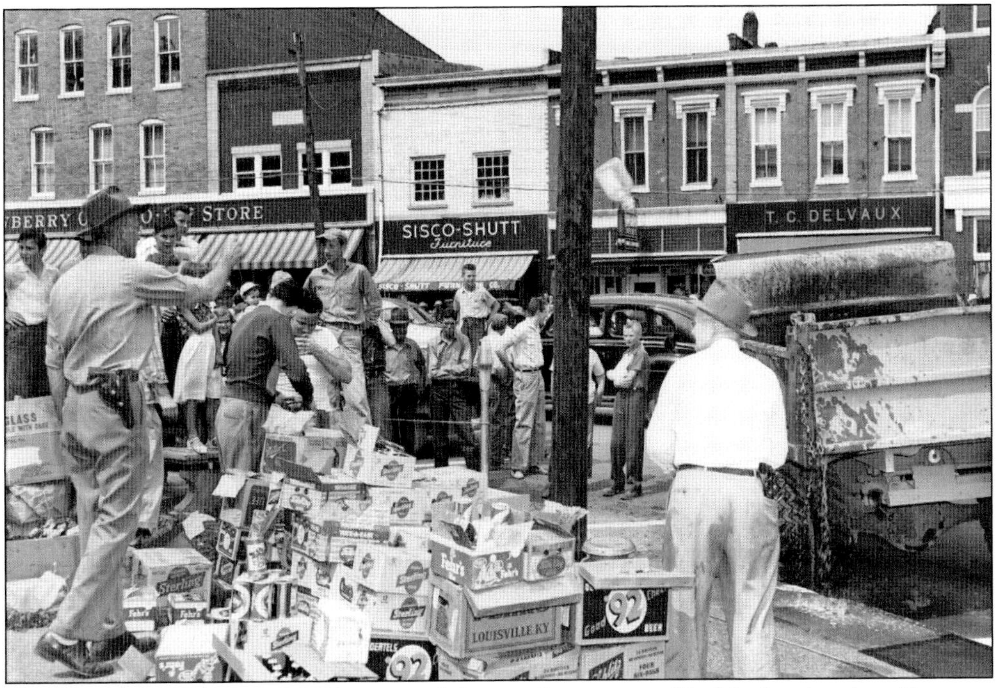

For most of the 20th century, Glasgow and Barren County were "dry" by local option. However, during those years, raids on bootleggers were not uncommon, and the disposal of the illegal alcohol occurred very much in public—right on the town square. (Courtesy author's collection.)

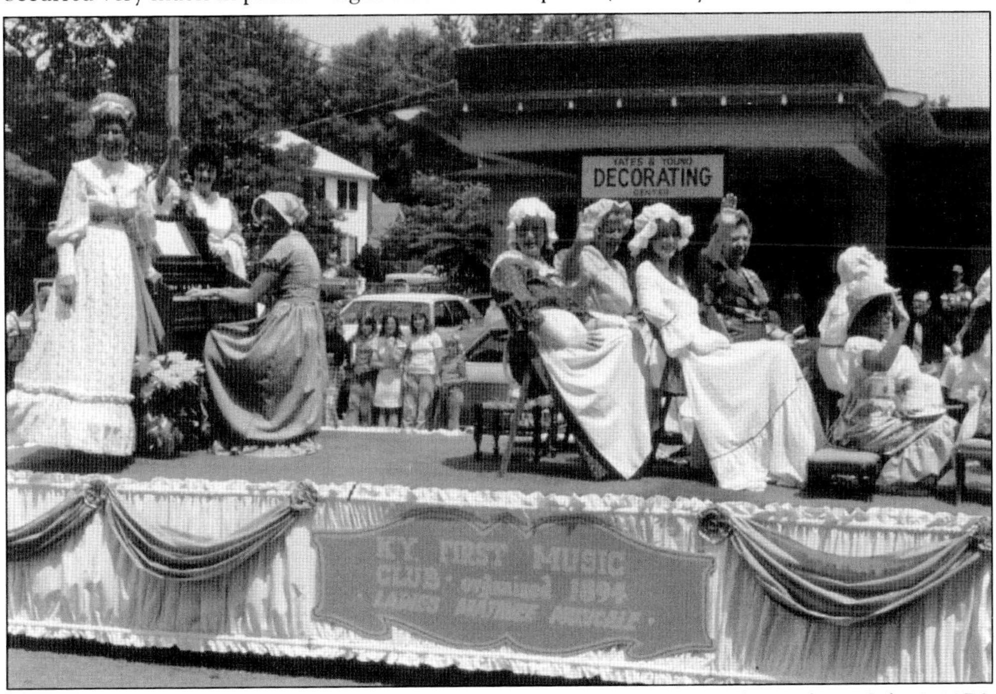

Glasgow celebrated America's 200th birthday with a gala Bicentennial Parade on July 4, 1976. The Ladies Matinee Musicale celebrated the occasion with a float. (Courtesy South Central Kentucky Cultural Center.)

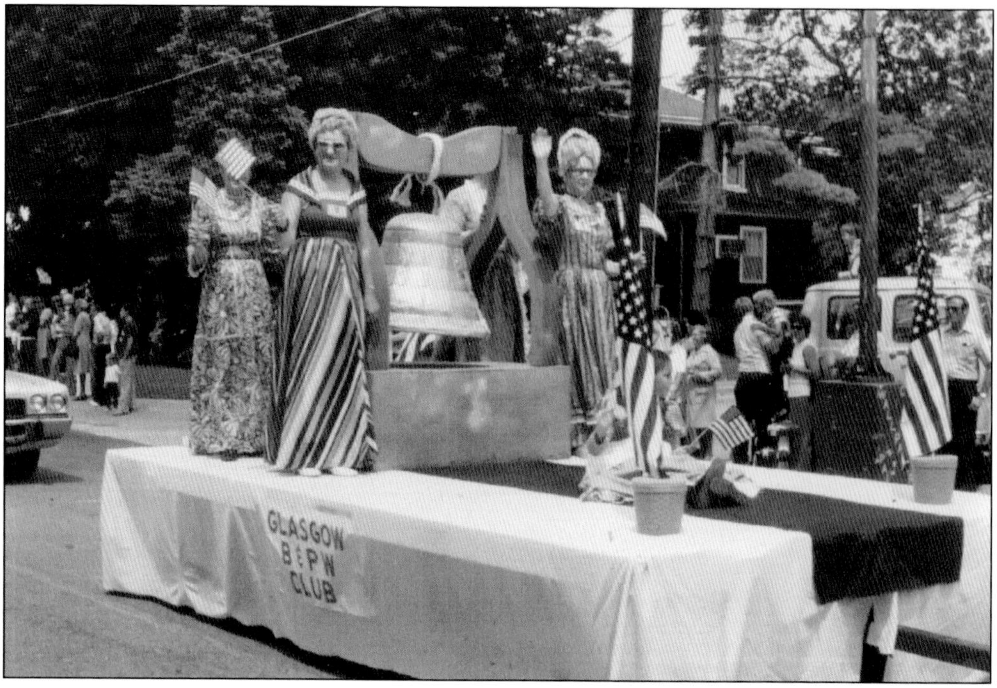

The Glasgow Business and Professional Women's Club entered this float in the 1976 Bicentennial Parade while the state senator Walter Baker family chose to ride in an open car. (Both, courtesy South Central Kentucky Cultural Center.)

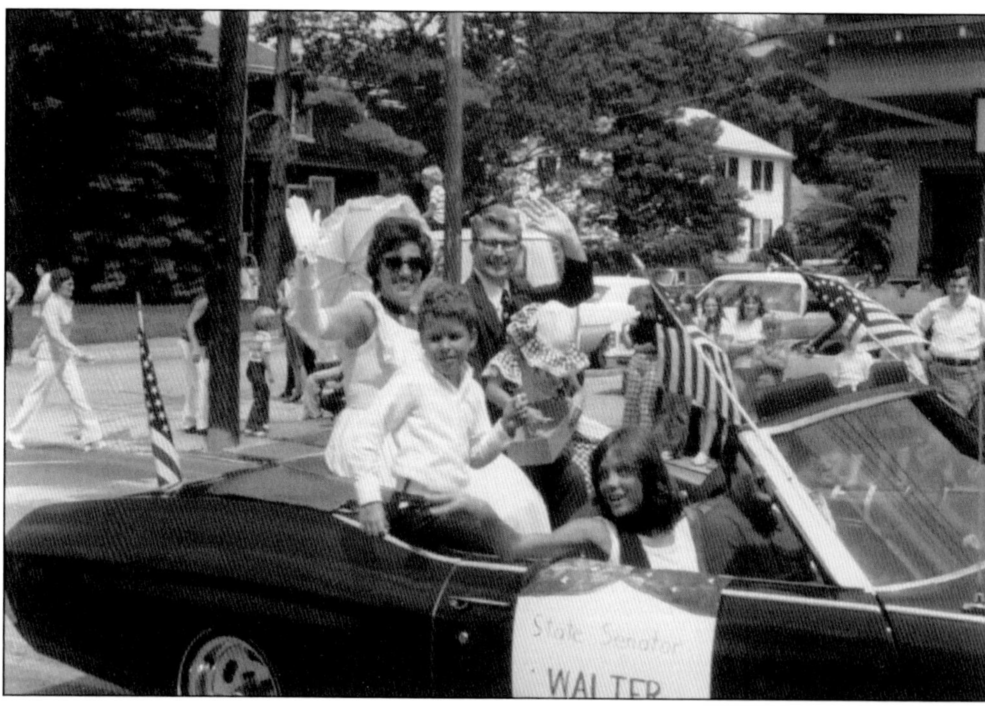

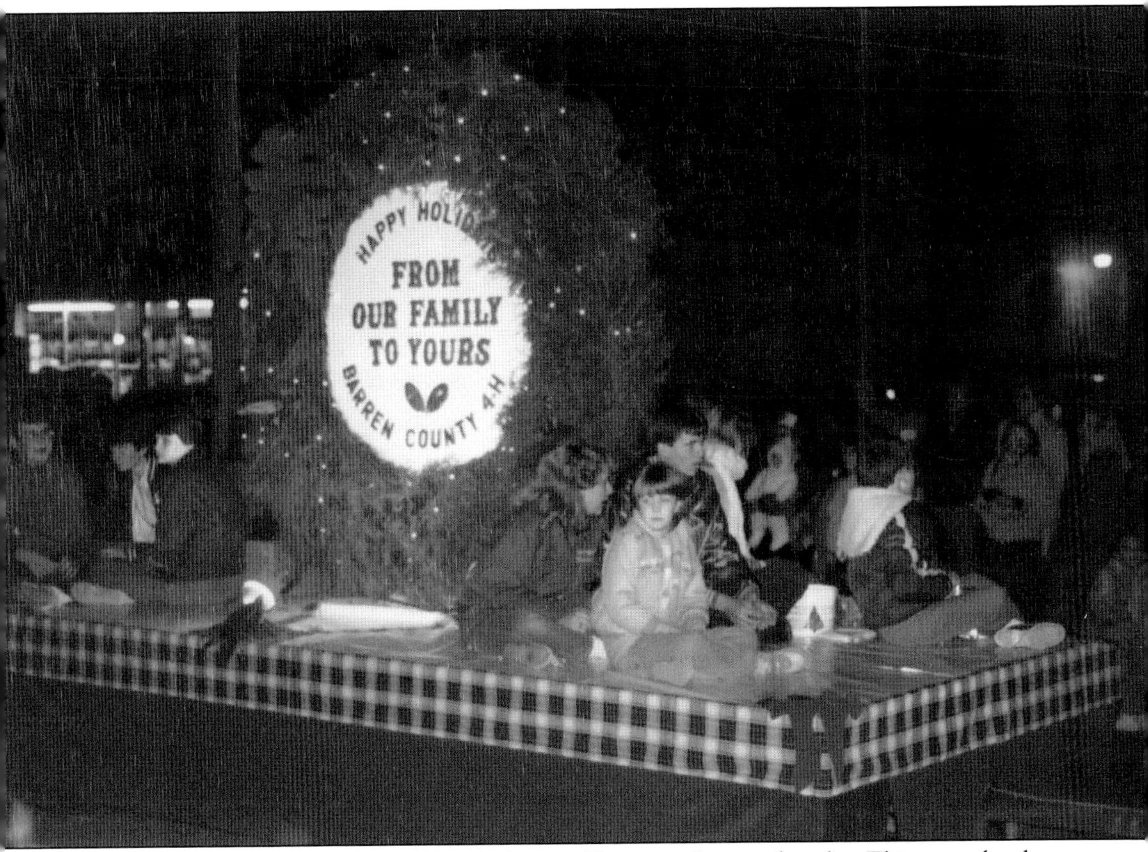

Glasgow's Christmas Parade has a long and storied history of many decades. This entry by the Barren County 4-H Council celebrated the work of 4-H clubs all over Barren County. (Courtesy South Central Kentucky Cultural Center.)

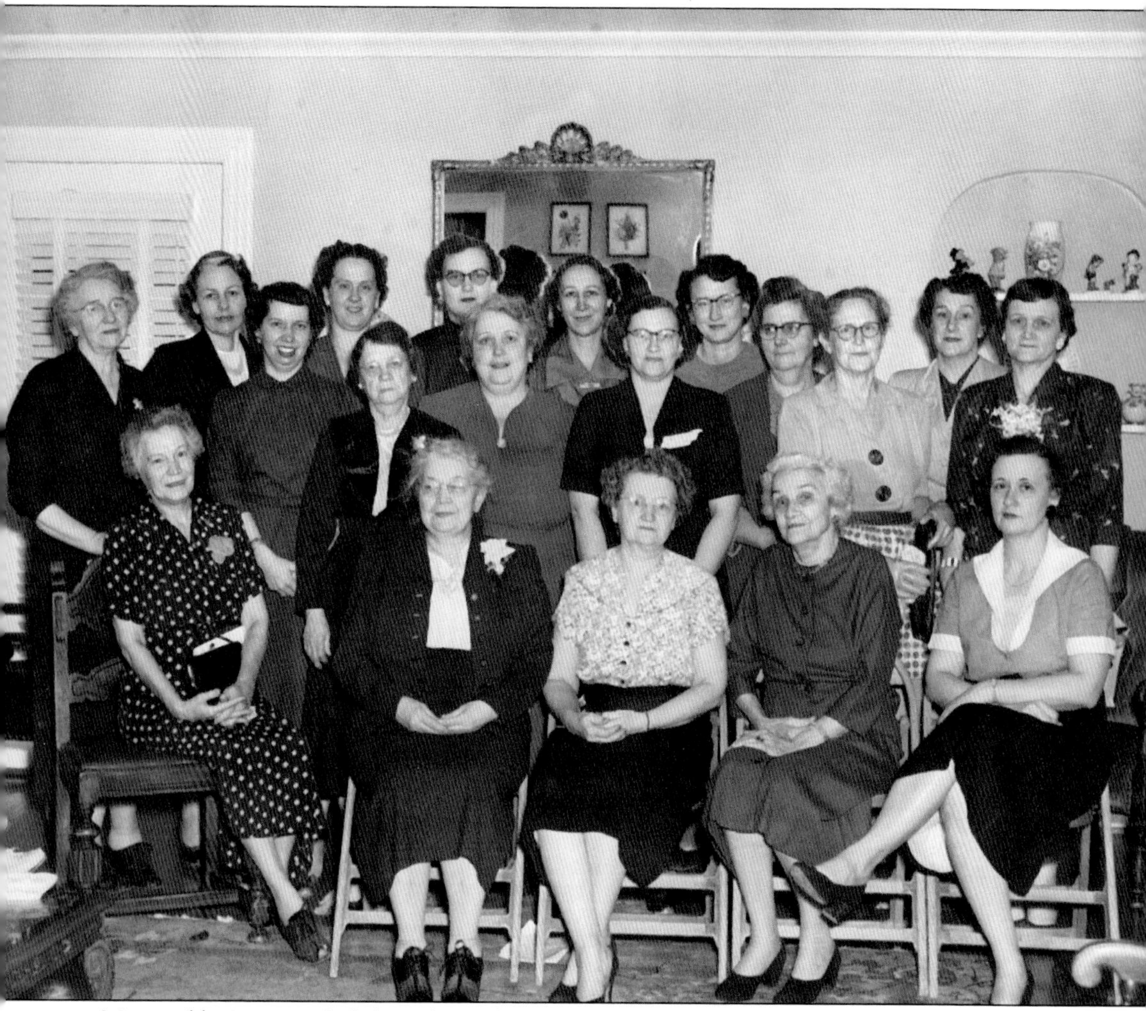

Memorable events included regular gatherings for club meetings and socials. Here one of Glasgow and Barren County's numerous Homemaker's Clubs posed for a group photograph. Such groups were important in bringing community members together to explore ways to have more fulfilling lives. (Courtesy South Central Kentucky Cultural Center.)

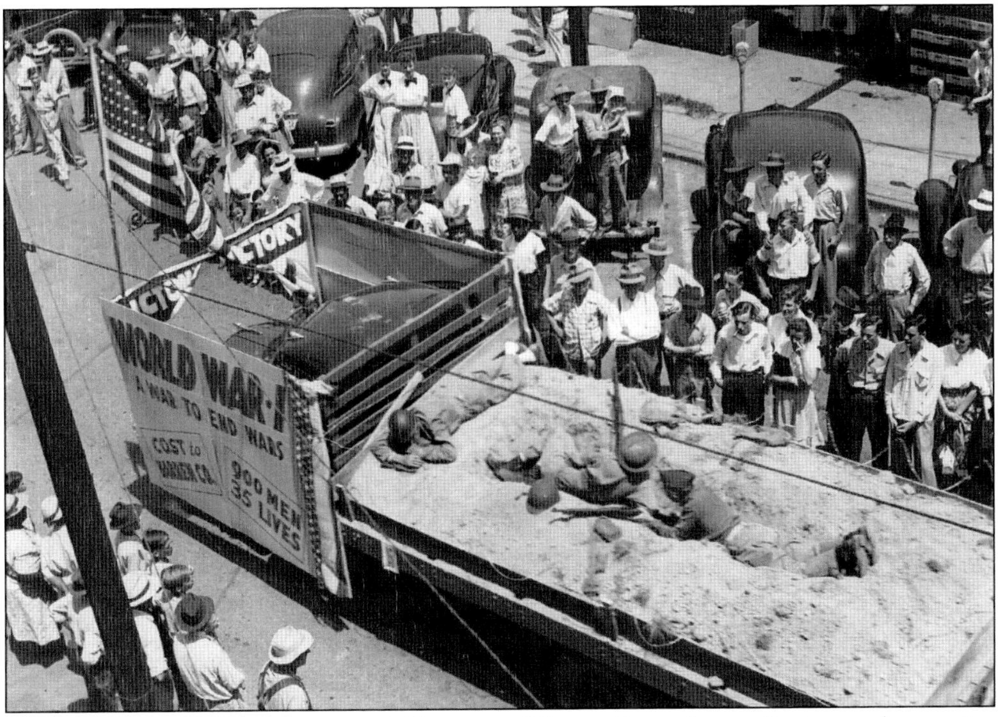

The Sesquicentennial Parade reviewed Glasgow and Barren County's contributions and memories. Above, World War I—a war to end wars—was commemorated with the reminder that Barren County sent 900 men; 35 lives were lost. Below, World War II was still fresh on the public's mind. Barren County supplied 2,900 soldiers, 79 of whom lost their lives. (Courtesy author's collection.)

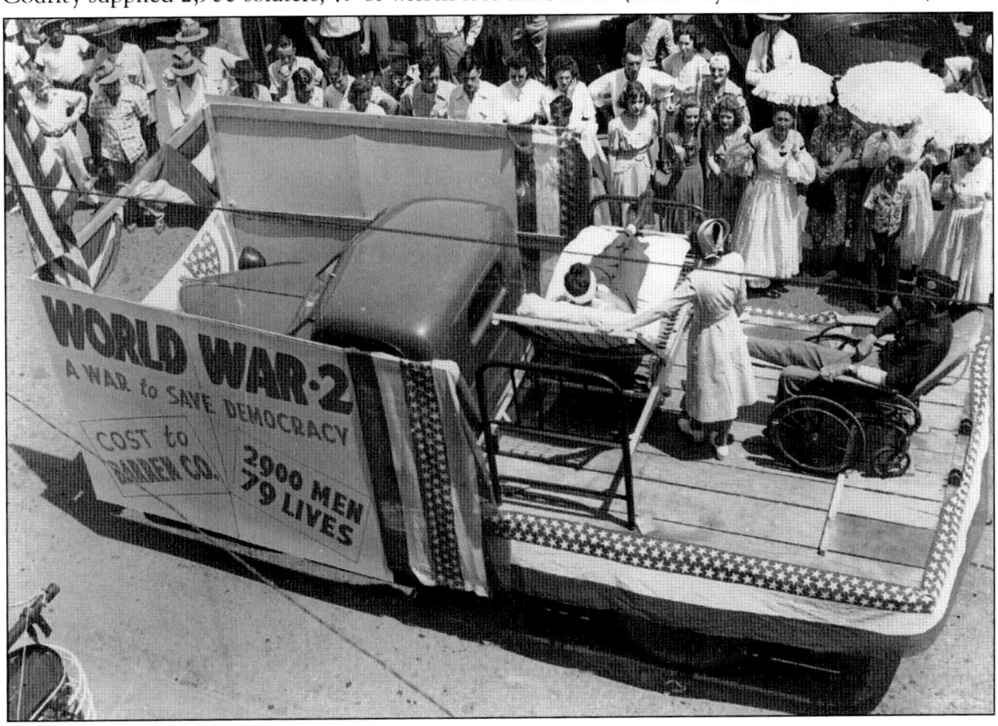